6/51

Spirited Women

I dedicate *Spirited Women* to three women who shared with me the mysteries of living, loving and letting go:

Kay Moechtar, who epitomised the spirit of generosity, love and courage in a woman truly alive

Sharne Weidland, whose life was full of passion for the preciousness of each delicate unfolding moment

and my grandmother,
Phyllis Myles-Phillips, whose heart knew no bounds and whose generosity of spirit gave me hope and inspiration

One a devoted Catholic, one a Buddhist, the other the most irreverent, yet deeply spiritual, woman I've ever known

these three

have given the world and me a deeper understanding of what it is to live, what it is to love and what it is to let go with grace and dignity.

Kay Moechtar

Sharne Weidland

Phyllis Myles-Phillips

Spirited Women

Journeys with Breast Cancer

Petrea King

RANDOM HOUSE AUSTRALIA

Random House Australia Pty Ltd
20 Alfred Street, Milsons Point, NSW 2061
http://www.randomhouse.com.au

Sydney   New York   Toronto
London   Auckland   Johannesburg

First published by Random House Australia in 1995
This edition first published in 2004

National Library of Australia
Cataloguing-in-Publication Entry

King, Petrea, 1951–.
  Spirited women: journeys with breast cancer.

  Includes index.
  ISBN 1 74051 334 7 (pbk.).

  1. Breast – Cancer. 2. Breast – Cancer – Psychological
  aspects. I. Title.

362.19699449

Cover image by Getty Images
Cover design by Nanette Backhouse, saso content & design pty ltd
Illustrations by Skye Rogers
Photography by Jill White
Typeset by Midland Typesetters, Maryborough, Victoria
Printed and bound by Griffin Press, Netley, South Australia

10 9 8 7 6 5 4 3 2 1

Contents

Acknowledgments

M Y DEEP THANKS TO WENDIE BATHO WHO ASSISTED ME IN every phase of writing this book. Wendie interviewed all the spirited women who contributed their stories and wrote the chapter, 'Women Who Love Women'. Wendie has been my sounding board, my support, my critic and my dear friend throughout the process of writing.

To say 'thank you' to the many hundreds of women who've contributed to this book is an insignificant tribute to their enormous courage and insight. However, I thank you all for your willingness to share your stories with the readers of this book. Thanks also to the women who allowed us to photograph them.

The renowned photographer, Jill White, has done a remarkable job in capturing the beauty of women touched by breast cancer. She herself carries the wounds of this disease.

Thanks go also to the following people:

Anita Levy, who helped while I was writing the book, and whose presence is always loving, cheerful and positive; she is a friend indeed.

Dorothy Rooney, who facilitated groups, and Neville Bailey who taught the meditation groups while I was writing the book.

Carol Carr, who participated in interviews and then spent countless hours transcribing both group and individual taped interviews—truly a labour of love—thank you. Thanks also to June Curtis who helped with the transcriptions.

Susan Benson, who encouraged me and gave valuable advice along the way.

Dr David Pennington, who read and commented on the manuscript.

My children, Kate and Simon, for their patience with my preoccupation with writing. Special thanks to my mother, Rae, for her comments, feedback and encouragement and for the contribution of her experience of her mother's journey with breast cancer.

Margaret Sullivan from Random House, for her support, advice and encouragement and to Julia Cain for her editorial assistance and expertise.

Preface

THE IDEAS AND INFORMATION IN THIS BOOK HAVE BEEN gleaned from working since 1984 with many thousands of women with breast cancer.

This book isn't intended in any way to give advice about the treatment of breast cancer. It is not intended to be a substitute for the discussions you're encouraged to have with your doctors.

The book has been written with the intention of giving women practical information and support for their emotions and psychological reactions to the diagnosis, treatment and the 'living with' that's essential once you've been diagnosed with breast cancer. It provides information, suggestions, skills and techniques whereby women can regain a sense of control over their lives and actively participate in their healing.

The quotations throughout the book have been contributed by women from diverse backgrounds, from around Australia, who've been willing to share their stories. Where requested, names have been changed to protect the identity of the individual.

Throughout the book I've acknowledged the fact that women are in relationships with other women as well as with men, hence the inclusion of Chapter 9, 'Women Who Love Women'.

Foreword

*H*OW OFTEN DURING OUR JOURNEY THROUGH LIFE DO WE meet someone who, for one reason or another, has a powerful effect on us—maybe it's something they did or said, or maybe it's just their presence. For me, Petrea King was such a person. Little did I know when we first met that, within a year, I too would become one of her *Spirited Women* and begin my own journey with breast cancer. As a medical scientist in women's health I found I knew a lot of medical facts but I needed to know so much more about coping with the illness, the treatments and the battle of emotions.

The journey with breast cancer is filled with so many emotions and questions right from the moment of discovery of a lump or change in the breast. These emotions are vividly described by the women themselves in the quotes throughout *Spirited Women*. The many spoken and unspoken questions are answered as Petrea describes the stages of the journey and it provides a resource handbook for living with breast cancer.

In *Spirited Women*, Petrea has allowed women to tell their own stories. She has conveyed the thoughts, hopes, feelings, joys and frustrations of many women who have had breast cancer and who have sought her counsel, either personally or in groups. The quotes from these women not only reveal their shock and grief but, more importantly, tell of their growth and the wonderful spirit that has emerged from their encounter with breast cancer.

They illustrate vividly the journey from diagnosis to surgery, treatment, recovery, recurrence or dealing with death. As told by the women, it is not an easy journey and we need so much more information and help to meet our psychological, physical, emotional and spiritual needs than is generally forthcoming from our medical advisors. This book fills the gaps in communicating with doctors, dealing with treatments, pain, diet, sexuality and, importantly, methods to find an inner peace and harmony through relaxation and meditation.

From her own journey with cancer, Petrea has found a unique way to help others find within themselves an inner strength of spirit which can bring about healing—an inner peace, harmony and joy which has the potential to boost the immune system and work in concert with medical treatments such as chemotherapy and radiotherapy. Much of what is written in these pages is a summary of Petrea's counselling or group sessions to help women live with breast cancer. The incredible joy and zest for living that I experienced in the groups is conveyed in the quotes shared.

I hope in reading *Spirited Women* that you too will experience the strong, positive messages of love and healing that Petrea conveys through her sharing of the stories of others or through her own words, and that in this way you will share the extraordinary experience of growth through a life-threatening illness.

Barbara A Gross
B Pharm MSc PhD

Introduction

ONE OF THE CONTRIBUTORS TO THIS BOOK WROTE TO ME SAYING, 'There's no real information on *living* with breast cancer. The information consists either of simplistic booklets which tell you it's not a problem, treatment is easy, not to worry about it and get on with your life, or medical textbooks which leave you thinking you're going to die the next day. Something in between these two extremes would be great'!

In 1983 I was diagnosed with leukaemia and was told I had weeks to live. At that time I'd been studying health and healing for some fifteen years. I'd embarked upon nursing, had qualified as a herbalist, naturopath, massage therapist and yoga and meditation teacher. I believed I knew about health so to be diagnosed with cancer was an embarrassment! Since my recovery I've had the privilege of working with tens of thousands of people on a one-to-one basis and have facilitated thousands of support groups for people with life-threatening illnesses. I have learnt more about life, health and healing from these people and my own experiences than in all my studies.

Many of these people have been women with breast cancer. My role with them has been one of friend, counsellor, nurse, meditation teacher, support group facilitator and naturopath. My function has been to minimise their emotional, spiritual, psychological and physical distress and to provide information and guidance about how to regain a sense of control in their lives and how to actively participate in their healing process.

It is my belief that the crisis of breast cancer, or any life-threatening illness, can precipitate us into a journey of self-discovery, self-healing and self-accomplishment. In this way, regardless of the outcome of the illness, the destination can become deep and profound peace. To achieve this peace is a victory beyond words.

Breast cancer is the most common form of cancer diagnosed in women. Internationally, the incidence is highest in the white population of North America, where it's five times more common than in women from Asian cultures. It can appear at any time in a woman's life and, as yet, understanding all the factors involved in its cause is still unclear. The women who've contributed to this book range in age between fifteen and seventy years at the time of their diagnosis.

The best way to face breast cancer is with good emotional support and information. You need information to de-mystify the strange and fearful world you've entered. Once informed, and with faith restored in yourself, you can proceed with a sense of calmness. *Spirited Women* provides a guide to dealing with your emotions and the many questions, choices and decisions which lie ahead.

Spirited Women is not intended to be a medical explanation of the cause, diagnosis or treatment of the disease. Indeed, you're actively encouraged to discuss all aspects of breast cancer with your team of doctors. The suggestions within this book are not offered as an *alternative* to medical treatment but are *complementary* to it. You're encouraged to discuss any aspect of this book with your doctor or to use it as a stimulus for discussion at home.

This book is brimful of ideas and extracts from women's stories to help you not only live effectively with breast cancer but to gain greatly from your experience. Having cancer is not an entirely negative experience. In fact, most women will say they're grateful for what they've learnt from having the disease. They invariably qualify that statement with one that says, 'I'd like the cancer to go away now but I wouldn't want to lose what I've learnt from *having* it'.

To be diagnosed with breast cancer turns your world upside

down. A thousand questions demand your attention and you're required to make all kinds of decisions at a time when both your psychological and emotional equilibrium are upset. Women may react very differently. Some will choose not to tell anybody, others will reach out for support and understanding immediately. Some feel that breast cancer is a mammoth blow to their femininity whilst others are grateful that it has happened in a part of their body which is easily accessible for surgery. There's no right way to respond to breast cancer.

The many avenues which you can explore to regain a sense of control over your life and participate in a healing program are detailed within these pages. Some of the suggestions will sit comfortably with you and others may have less appeal. Most of the suggestions come from women who've travelled the journey upon which you have embarked. Take from this collected wisdom that which seems to suit you, your philosophies, beliefs, attitudes and lifestyle.

I encourage you to commit yourself to finding peace of mind. When you have peace you also create the very best of environments for healing within your body. If you can only have peace if you overcome cancer then your *quality of life* could be dictated by your disease rather than yourself. It is possible to find peace, even in the midst of active disease.

Peace is not a wishy-washy attitude of passive acceptance. It is a dynamic state of being which requires an openness to life and a deep willingness to participate in your own healing. Peace of mind is the best foundation on which to build health and bring about healing.

Spirited Women is about how to find, refine and maintain the qualities that lead to peace. In the following pages you'll meet hundreds of women whose experience of breast cancer dates back many years as well as those new to the journey. They're everyday women who are the heroines of our times and of this book. Their stories often start like this:

Never did I think I'd be diagnosed with cancer! I was a healthy, happy, married, mother of four beautiful children aged eleven, nine, seven and six years. My life was well-ordered and organised. I worked three days a week, did volunteer work one day a week and had lots of life plans.

Well, in one day it was blown to pieces!

JUDY, AGE 38
aged 36 at diagnosis

These spirited women are the true authors of this book. I know you'll feel you're amongst friends as you delve into its pages.

1

From Fear to Fact

I dashed out of the office saying I'd be back in two hours.

I'd been to the Breast Care Clinic before, disliked the procedure, fought against the apprehension and breathed a huge sigh of relief when it was over. This trip was different. It was to mean a long time away from work and finally, for me, the realisation that my life was changed and from now on I'd live it in a very different way.

The tests took many hours. When a small elderly lady appeared as my volunteer, smiling and pressing my hand, I knew I had a problem. The doctors and nurses were kind but detached and impersonal, intent on tracking the disease. They told me nothing of what had been found. The moment when they said they had arranged for a surgeon to make a special visit

1

to see me, now, *my heart sank. I was more afraid than I had ever been before. At the end of the day I was shaking so hard it was impossible for me to control—they sent me home in a cab to tell my family. On the way it was only by pressing my hand into my mouth I could stop from screaming, 'Cancer, I have cancer . . .'.*

JOAN, AGE 54
aged 51 at diagnosis

On my way to the doctor's to get my results I saw a pretty sundress on sale and bought it, arriving in the doctor's office with a bargain in a brightly coloured plastic bag. I only wore that dress once, on my way to hospital to have a mastectomy. That simple, somewhat frivolous, act of picking up a pretty bargain came to symbolise for me a way of life that ended that day.

JULIET, AGE 61
aged 46 at diagnosis

I went along and they did the test and I got dressed and they said, "Oh, it wasn't good". Would I come back in again. So I got undressed and they did it again and then they said, "Oh, just wait here", and I got dressed again. They came back and said, "Would you get undressed again" and, I said, "Have you found something?" and they said, "Yes", straight away.

SUE, AGE 54
aged 50 at diagnosis

Prior to the operation, I was gripped with fear. I couldn't stop crying, and felt bereft of resources to cope with the situation. Maybe some good drugs (joke) or at least an aromatherapy massage would have helped. I think I cried solidly for two hours, as I waited and worried. I remember blinking and saying to the surgeon as he stood beside my bed, "When are you going to do the operation?" and he said. "We've already done it. And I'm sorry to say it is cancer".

2

So there it was. One moment I was a normal human being and the next I had cancer.

What a bummer.

FIONA, AGE 34
aged 33 at diagnosis

Over the space of three days my right breast changed shape and collapsed. After a mammogram, I was referred that same afternoon to a specialist who informed me that I had breast cancer. Next day, bone scan and blood tests, the following day admitted to hospital and surgery the day after that. It was all so sudden, unexpected, terrifying, with no time to think or feel. I became like a robot, numb in an effort to get through.

JUDY, AGE 38
aged 36 at diagnosis

When we came home from our holidays, Christmas 1992, there was a niggle at the back of my mind—the tissue in my right breast felt "different", so after a talk with my local doctor we made an earlier-than-usual appointment with the Breast Clinic. (I'd lost my seventy-year-old mother five years before with breast cancer, so I had been having a precautionary mammogram each year.)

There was "cause for concern", they told me on a Friday. Following the mammogram they did an ultrasound and a needle biopsy, then told me to ring on Monday for the pathology results! I felt total shock, then went numb . . . how could this be happening to me? How was I going to tell my lovely family? How could I get through the next few dreadful days?

My visit to the surgeon confirmed a small cancer and all arrangements were made for hospital. I still felt detached and unbelieving, yet when I came to, after the operation, I felt a huge sense of relief that "it", the lumpectomy, was over and the cancer had been removed. I had great confidence in my surgeon, who did an excellent job removing glands and all, and looked after me very well through the following weeks when I had bad drainage and fluid problems.

LYNNE, AGE 55
aged 52 at diagnosis

I'd had the lump there for quite a while. I was aware of it before I left my husband. I was ambivalent about it. I almost thought of it as my little friend. Somewhere in the back of my mind I must have thought it's possible that this is cancer and I don't know if I want to do anything about it. For as long as I can remember, ever since I was a child, I'd wanted to die.

DEB, AGE 40
aged 38 at diagnosis

On my check-up after I had the baby, I had a large lump and the doctor looked at it and said, "Oh dear". I think that first night was the worst, the sudden realisation that this lump that for twelve months I had thought was just lumpiness in my breast, might be nasty. I went to the surgeon the next day and he said, "No, I don't think that's cancer—just have a needle biopsy". And then, because I was breast-feeding, they couldn't get a definite result from the biopsy. The mammogram and ultrasound didn't show up any cancerous features and it didn't feel cancerous to touch. It was Easter so he couldn't biopsy it for ten days. My obstetrician tried to get someone else but they were all going away for Easter, so I was just stuck there waiting. It had been such a strain feeding the baby anyway but I didn't want to stop if it was all right. How could I keep functioning as if there was nothing wrong? They seemed to have no comprehension of what that felt like; to be left with the uncertainty.

LISA, AGE 33
aged 32 at diagnosis

I was relaxing in a bath after work and decided it was as good a time as any to check myself out. I found a lump to the side of my breast and in a panic I kept checking the other side, hoping to find the same thing so that I could be assured that this was normal and both breasts were the same.

When I couldn't find anything I decided, "OK, there is a lump there". So I sat in the bath saying "Shit" for a while and my German Shepherd, who was the only one awake in the house besides me, came into the bathroom and I found myself talking to him. When I realised what I was doing I burst out laughing. I toyed with the idea of waking my husband but decided there was no point in all of us not sleeping.

Next day (Saturday) I told my husband about the lump. The same morning we went to the doctor only to find my fears more or less confirmed. Monday saw the mammogram and ultrasound, also confirming my fears. Tuesday I saw the surgeon and things were definitely confirmed then. I think I was in shock for those days.

LIZ, AGE 49
aged 47 at diagnosis

My story starts one night while I was lying in bed reading a book. I ran my hand along the top of my right breast and, to my horror, I found a lump. A week went past and I told myself that this "thing" will go away and I kept saying to myself, "It's just not there, just ignore it". Another week went by and it was still there, so I started worrying about it and therefore lost my appetite and also lost weight. I thought to myself I have to tell someone, I can't go on like this. The next day I went to my local doctor and she arranged a referral to a surgeon.

My surgeon took a specimen from the lump and arranged a mammogram and an ultrasound. At this point, I thought cancer could be a possibility, but I was thinking more along the lines of a cyst. I was only thirty-two years old and I felt it couldn't possibly be malignant.

I will not forget this day—Thursday, 17th May 1984—when I was told very coldly that the X-ray and ultrasound showed a suspicious lump. Because it was Thursday, I had to wait until

Monday for my surgeon to see me. No one said to me after they told me the news, "Will you be OK, is there anything I can do to make the next couple of days easier for you"? If not for my family and friends, I think I'd have gone mad. The X-rays lay on my bed unopened for three days. The following Monday I returned to the surgeon. To my horror he told me he'd have to perform a mastectomy, and how did I feel about that! I thought my whole world was at an end. I was going to die!

GERALDINE, AGE 42
aged 32 at diagnosis

It was just before Easter and I was working furiously, putting in twelve to fourteen hour days. I'd noticed the lump in my left breast, and had filed it in the "important things to do, when I get a chance to draw breath". People often ask me "How did you find the lump"? I found it when I was putting my bra on one day. It would have been there for probably two weeks, in my consciousness, but I am sure that we got it early, as they say.

I went off straight after Easter and presented myself to face the music. My GP was sympathetic, but basically unconcerned. "You're far too young at thirty-three to have breast cancer, Fiona. Nonetheless (and thank God he considers himself to be almost verging on paranoia), George insisted on doing a needle biopsy. He also gave me a referral to have an ultrasound and a mammogram. As I was terribly busy, and there seemed no urgency in the procedure, I was surprised to receive a letter from him asking me to make an appointment. I still believed that there was very little chance that I had anything wrong with me.

At this stage I hadn't had the mammogram or ultrasound, however the tests had come back and indicated some a-typical cells. It all sounded inconclusive, but George decided to refer me to a leading breast cancer expert, who he believed would want to remove the lump.

The lump was beginning to feel "strange". It was hard to define what I meant by this, but I knew that there was something cooking down there. It hurt, it didn't feel normal, and it felt like it was growing.

I had to wait three weeks to see the surgeon and this perturbed me. I now wish that I'd insisted on seeing him earlier. That's a thing I'd urge women to become—pushy!

FIONA, AGE 34
aged 33 at diagnosis

My name is Maree and I'm forty-six. I had breast cancer ten months ago which resulted in a radical mastectomy. My story is somewhat different as I didn't have a lump in my breast or any indication something was wrong. I decided to have a mammogram after a friend of mine died from breast cancer. I was over forty and thought I should have one just to be on the safe side.

As I am a school teacher, I left it till my holidays along with a haircut, eye test and dental check-up, etc. I wasn't told anything at the mammography centre—which seemed to take ages although my friends had told me it would take only five minutes or so. I was told I had a lumpy left breast but it was nothing to worry about. My doctor had also ordered an ultrasound and I was booked in after a short trip away to Singapore. I arrived home four days later at 5.45 a.m. and was due to have my ultrasound at 9.15 a.m. and then report back to my doctor. An agonising four days for myself, husband and two daughters as we didn't tell anybody. We were all hoping for the best.

Then he broke the news! I had calcification spots—not just a few but groups of six or more—which is an indication that something sinister is happening. He booked me into a surgeon that same day. The surgeon tried to explain everything but I was just in a state of shock. I'm so glad my husband was there to ask questions and remember everything. I had my mastectomy the following Monday which was four days after I'd learnt the news.

MAREE, AGE 46
aged 45 at diagnosis

7

I often got sore breasts and they got a bit lumpy before a period. I was very sore and I touched myself and there was a big lump and I thought it was pre-menstrual. I thought I'd wait until the next period came and see if it was still there. My partner and I had booked a holiday to China for two weeks which we'd been longing for, so I decided that I would not do anything about it until we returned.

When we got back I went to my GP and she immediately arranged for me to have a mammogram and an ultrasound. She wanted me to come back for the results the following day and they indicated it was a suspicious malignancy and I should have a biopsy.

Two days later was the earliest she could get me into a breast surgeon and he did the biopsy on the spot, in my first consultation with him, without any anaesthetic or anything. It was a full cut biopsy which was very painful because the lump was very painful and then he said he'd get the results two days later. I went to see him then and he told me it was cancer. I didn't believe him, I was very shocked and . . . I wanted to ask him had the results got mixed up in the lab. I had in my head: this can't be true, this is a mistake, I was in a state of shock.

JO, AGE 42
aged 41 at diagnosis

I remember standing in the shower, the night before I went in for my operation, knowing that that breast wasn't going to be there the next time I woke up. But that was OK. I got it out of my system and just went on with it.

JILL, AGE 54
aged 51 at diagnosis

I phoned my husband and he was so busy he couldn't come to the doctor's where I'd just been told. Or he chose not to. I think because, eighteen months previously, he'd been diagnosed with a fairly serious melanoma, he was not ready to be there for me.

CATHERINE, AGE 47
aged 41 at diagnosis

*The awful aspect of it is that you're going to lose a breast—
I think there's no way around that—no woman wants to lose a
breast.*

SUE, AGE 54
aged 50 at diagnosis

Making the Diagnosis

When we're diagnosed with any form of cancer, the world stops
for us. Days continue to pass but initially it's all a bit of a blur. It
feels a little as if time has frozen and compacted and the future
seems a long way off.

You may have found that you have breast cancer in a variety
of ways. Some women, when they find a lump, are immediately
convinced they have cancer whilst others are equally convinced
that it could never happen to them. Some women go immediately
to their local doctor and begin the necessary tests to get an accurate diagnosis whilst others decide to wait awhile to see if it will
go away of its own accord. The problem with this second attitude
is that most women worry until they *do* go and see their doctor.
You're always better off knowing what it is you're dealing with
because then appropriate action can be taken.

Sometimes a woman has an 'intuition' about a lump or thickening and 'knows' that something is amiss. I've known many
women who persisted with diagnostic tests until they *were* accu-
rately diagnosed. Often they were told they were worrying
unnecessarily or, worse still, were being hypochondriacs.

Other women are completely shocked by the diagnosis and
never suspected they would develop such a disease. For some,
there's a history of breast cancer in their family, for others there's
no evidence of cancer anywhere amongst their forebears.

Some women put breast cancer down to an injury they experienced to the precise spot where the lump later developed. Some
doctors acknowledge this as a possibility whilst others say it has
no connection at all.

Some women are told that painful lumps aren't cancerous. One young woman, Madeline, had a large lump in her breast throughout her pregnancy. Her doctor thought it was probably due to hormonal changes within her body. After the birth of her healthy baby she was told to massage her breast to help relieve the mastitis. Four months passed before it was suggested she have a needle biopsy which showed the lump was cancerous.

Women have been diagnosed during pregnancy, just after their baby has been delivered, when they've suckled several children and when they've had an all-clear mammogram. Regardless of how and when the diagnosis was made, whether early in the disease or when it has already progressed, the diagnosis always comes as a shock. If the diagnosis was delayed due to incompetence on the part of your doctor, you will likely experience anger in addition to shock. You may find that anger is directed towards yourself if you were the one who delayed having your health monitored.

The unreality of a diagnosis is often profound. You most probably have been living a healthy, active life with the thought of serious illness a million miles from your mind. Suddenly, you're confronted with the reality of a diagnosis. You may well be swept along in the necessary appointments and arrangements for hospitalisation, surgery and treatment without having time to pause to take in the impact of what has happened to you.

Some women feel frustrated that their doctors ignore them when they tell them about their bodies or the changes they've noticed.

Some women want to get their surgery over and done with as quickly as possible whilst others are desperate for some time-out to assimilate the information and prepare themselves. If you're in the latter group and this book has fallen into your hands before you've had surgery then speak with your doctor. It's rarely necessary for surgery to be performed within hours or even days of the discovery of breast cancer.

Some doctors have the attitude, 'It's best to get it done as soon as possible so that you can get back to your life the way it was before'. Or, 'You have to have it removed, you'll only worry if you wait. Get it over and done with quickly'. This presupposes that your doctor knows what's best for you and knows how you will react. Not all women appreciate this presupposition. Life will never be quite the same *after* cancer as before. Don't let yourself be bullied into hurried decisions if you realistically have plenty of time to make them. A second opinion from another doctor will often give you a different perspective. Take a friend or partner with you to your appointments because four ears are always better than two, especially when yours may not be functioning too well because of shock.

There are so many things to consider. Who'll care for my children? How will this affect my work? What about my career? Am I going to die? Do I tell my friends? Do I need to tell my boss? How and what will I tell them? How will this affect my femininity? Will this be the end of fulfilling sexual relationships?

Often, people think that if you're diagnosed with breast cancer then that's your primary problem. They often forget that cancer visits the homes of those who are unemployed, who are about to go overseas, who are caring for an ailing parent, whose teenager is on drugs, whose spouse is also ill, who are financially dependent on two salaries, whose child has special needs or who are weary of living, and so on. In fact, for most women, breast cancer is an unwanted, uninvited intrusion into an already over-full schedule.

But, here we are, and the question becomes, what next?

Choosing Your Doctors

I think they get really blasé about it because they see so many women with breast cancer. They forget that each time they see somebody it's somebody's life they're playing with. It's not like you're a number, you're not a sheep, you're a human being. But I have to say that my doctor was very understanding, very

11

*compassionate and very helpful and that could be because his
mother had breast cancer.*

MARIE, AGE 32
aged 32 at diagnosis

*I think the very worst time for me was to find the lump and
then having to wait three weeks to get an appointment with the
specialist. I said to my GP, "I've made the appointment, can you
hurry it up—can I have the tests now so I can present them to the
specialist and get things on the road". He said only one in ten
lumps are cancerous and it takes seven years or more to grow. I
said, "I believe I'm the one in ten". Then I tried another doctor
and was fobbed off even more. So I just stayed home for three
weeks with my fear and I think that was actually worse than
being told the statistics later on and being told that my life was
very much in danger.*

LOUISE, AGE 52
aged 51 at diagnosis

*When I finally found the lump in August and went back to
my doctor, he said, "Oh yes, I saw that in April, I meant to
follow it up in June", and by then it had gone into the lymph
glands. And I thought from that moment on, I am responsible
for my medical condition. If anything is wrong with me, I have
to follow it up.*

ROS, AGE 49
aged 47 at diagnosis

It's important to recognise that *you* are in charge of choosing
your medical team. There may be several people on your team
including a general practitioner (or local doctor), surgeon, radiotherapist and oncologist. Choosing your team can give you back
a sense of control. It's essential that you not only have complete
confidence in your doctors' skills but that you also feel comfortable with them. You must feel free to ask questions, have things
explained and that you can contact them when you need to.

It is your right to have a second or third (or fourth) opinion.

Don't worry about hurting the doctor's feelings. Many women are afraid to ask to have copies of their reports, test results or X-rays to take to another doctor for a second opinion. If you feel too overwhelmed by the prospect, ask a friend or partner to attend to it for you. When you're recently diagnosed you can feel totally overcome by the hospital or medical system, a new language with words you never expected to have to articulate and finding your way through the etiquette of referrals. It's good to remember that doctors are in *your* employ to give you the very best of compassionate care and expertise.

Your initial diagnosis may have come from a doctor who was new or unfamiliar to you and you may or may not wish to remain under their care. Perhaps it was this doctor who found the lump or advised you to have a mammogram, biopsy and/or ultrasound.

If you don't have a relationship with a local doctor or general practitioner you might want to ask amongst your friends if they know of a good one in your area. Your local doctor can do much to advocate on your behalf, to answer your questions, to liaise with specialists, to de-mystify the medical jargon and to be there for you when you need support.

You deserve to have the very best doctors for every aspect of your diagnosis, treatment and follow-up. Persevere until you feel confident in your choices.

Sometimes you feel you've found your ideal team right from the beginning. Be thankful and remain open to having a second opinion at any time you feel the necessity.

I mean, no one would ever think she is a GP, she's just so different and she's absolutely wonderful. I can ask her anything and tell her how I'm feeling. In fact, she encourages me. She's totally honest as far as I can tell. When she doesn't know something, she'll say it and says she'll find out for me.

JO, AGE 42
aged 41 at diagnosis

One surgeon's attitude was very negative and the way he related to me I would only describe as punitive. He asked me if I had children and I thought, "Oh, he's all right, he's not as bad as I thought, he's interested in the family". And I said, "Yes, I have three". He said, "Do you have any girls?" and I said, "Yes, I have two girls". He said, "Are you aware that they now have an increased risk of breast cancer?" And I thought to myself, "Why are you telling me this now? Of what relevance is this to me on the day of my surgery? Thank you for making me feel not only a bad person to have this disease but a very bad person to have had bad genes that I have perhaps handed on to my children". He was rough and he examined me in a very rough way.

RUTH, AGE 42
aged 40 at diagnosis

I have my partner to thank for the success of most of our encounters with medical people because, even though I think I'm rather pushy myself, I was often so shocked and reeling at what I was hearing that I didn't know what to say. She was always there with me, helping and asking questions and making notes. Should I depend on these doctors, who are telling me I've got this terrible life-threatening thing? I feel trapped because I feel like my life depends on not upsetting them, not getting them irritated with me so that they'll brush me off or treat me carelessly. It's human nature that they'll neglect me if I irritate them. I'm very lucky to have my partner along who does all that.

JO, AGE 42
aged 41 at diagnosis

Some doctors have a wonderful gift of combining excellent medical skills with compassionate care and respect for you as an individual. They approach you with the appropriate enthusiasm that you can be helped, at whatever stage you might be at with your breast cancer. They listen to you and encourage you in your own efforts to help yourself. They answer your questions with patience, concern and understanding and you feel that you genuinely matter to them.

There are other doctors who aren't quite like that! Some are objective professionals who view you impartially as a medical problem to be solved. They're often excellent at their craft but not necessarily good at communicating with you, particularly if you are feeling distraught.

Some doctors think you need to have as little information as possible and that you should put your treatment entirely in their hands. They're competent experts at judging your cancer and the best treatment for it. They'll be pleased if you respond well to their treatment and will do what they can to continue treating it if you don't respond so well. However, you rarely feel they're passionately on your 'team'; that they care deeply for your welfare and *you* as a valued human being.

There are other doctors who seem to have let us down badly. They may have treated us with disdain or have misdiagnosed and mismanaged our medical situation.

We're wanting more from our doctors than ever before. We're becoming more educated and, therefore, more demanding of our medical services and personnel. If you feel you haven't found the right doctor yet, then persevere until you do. Perhaps speak to other women with breast cancer and find out who they've found to be good.

Healing and Health

I want to clarify what I mean by 'healing' and 'health'. Health is not just the absence of disease. It's a dynamic state of wellness, a state of being deeply at peace with yourself and the world. Healing is letting go of all things which stand in the way of peace. Think of two people confined to wheelchairs with the same injuries; one is a joy to be around and people go out of their way to befriend and spend time with them. The other is angry, bitter and resents their situation and no one enjoys their company. Their injuries are the same, yet one has found peace and the other hasn't resolved the fears and anger associated with their predicament. It's rare to stumble upon peace; it usually takes considerable effort and energy to establish peace within ourselves.

Some doctors have found the only way to cope with their work is to barricade their hearts against the pain. This has been adopted as a valid coping mechanism in order for the doctor to remain objective and professional. Some doctors believe that that is the correct way to practise medicine. It does take a truly special doctor to remain deeply caring, concerned and compassionate towards their patients, to have a respectful relationship with them *and* to combine this with objective diagnosis and treatment regimes. This is what good medicine is moving towards. A healing team joined by the common goal of treating your disease as effectively as possible, whilst respecting you as a multifaceted human being.

I encourage many of my clients to write to their doctors. Thank them for their time and skill and acknowledge the difficulties they must experience in their work. Thank them for answering your questions (even when they don't), because it will encourage them to do so next time. Writing a letter like this helps to establish a good relationship with your chosen doctor.

Sometimes you'll be offered two different treatment regimes according to the particular doctor's preference. This can be quite disconcerting for some women who would prefer that there be one single *right* approach to their breast cancer. It is natural to feel that there should be some all-knowing authority who will decide for us how our cancer should be treated. Often we're tempted to hand over responsibility for our medical management to the experts. However, doctors do have differing approaches and the important thing is to choose a program which will work best for you.

One of the biggest issues for me in having breast cancer is that I realise nobody's managing me. There are so many specialists involved who each have a piece of the puzzle, or they think they do, and they have pieces of each other's which conflict, but you

actually have to manage yourself and that was enormously diffi-
cult for me to come to grips with. I'm not normally a person who
gives over to the other person. I have this real need to know as
much as I possibly can and to make the decision myself. Even
being that sort of person, I found it difficult to not know who was
managing me. And nobody is; I am.

JO, AGE 42
aged 41 at diagnosis

Many women struggle with the feeling that no one is in charge of
their treatment regime. Often the first specialist seen is a surgeon.
Depending on the stage your breast cancer was at at the time of
your diagnosis you may or may not be referred on to either a
radiotherapist or oncologist for follow-up treatment. If you have
been referred on and you embark upon and complete the course
of treatment suggested you can often feel at a loss at the end of it.
Who's looking after me now? Sometimes your local doctor can
fulfil this role but many women prefer to have the ongoing management of their disease looked after by a specialist. It will be up
to you to find out who is the right person for you.

Lois had a whole range of other catastrophes happening in
her life at the time of her breast cancer diagnosis. Her father was
critically ill in hospital, her son was in trouble with the police,
her sister had been diagnosed with breast cancer the preceding
week and her partner was overseas on business. One doctor's
opinion was that she must enter hospital immediately to have a
mastectomy and begin chemotherapy and radiotherapy whilst
another doctor told her that there was no rush and that she
could have a lumpectomy now with follow-up treatment commencing a few weeks later. This second plan proved far more
appealing to her.

Learn to trust your own inner voice or intuition which will tell
you who and what is right for you. Don't be intimidated because
'everyone' says a particular doctor is an 'expert' in your cancer.
We all have different personalities and you may find you clash

17

with someone that everyone else thinks is marvellous. Learning to trust your own judgement is important for your own peace of mind.

Dealing with Decisions and Choices

The mammogram and biopsy proved positive. He said I'd have to have a mastectomy. At first, I couldn't face that as it just went against the grain. I have a great belief in non-traditional medicine. So I set a date ten days away to make my decision. This gave me time to think, meditate, research and make the decision for surgery in a clear way. I decided to embrace whatever treatment was offered, knowing I had made the right decision for me.

SANDRA, AGE 55
aged 50 at diagnosis

It's unwise to make choices and decisions from a place of fear. You may rush into a treatment regime, or a choice of doctor which, in retrospect, didn't serve you very well. Having a methodical way of working through information and arriving at a decision which feels absolutely right for you is another way of regaining a sense of control over your life. The following formula can be very helpful in making those choices/decisions.

Decision-Making Formula

This formula has many applications. It can be used in almost every situation. Tailor the formula to *your* particular requirements, but keep in mind the principles set out here.

1 Make a date with yourself for the decision to be made. Allow a suitable length of time to gather and assimilate your information.

2 Gather as much information as possible about the subject on which you need to make a decision. Talk to others who've had experience, read books, research which facilities are available in your community (perhaps the Breast Cancer Support Service) and which provide the necessary or relevant information.

3 Let this information gradually distil within you. Create some quiet time for yourself each day in which you can begin to feel what is right for you. Remember, within you there's the absolute knowledge of how to establish your own peace of mind. This peace will help create the ideal environment for healing.

4 Make your decision on the date previously decided and make an absolute commitment to the course of action you've chosen.

5 Trust completely in the decision you've chosen, believing it to be the perfect one for yourself at this time.

6 *Believe* that healing is taking place right now.

7 Set a period of time wherein you wholeheartedly implement your decision.

8 At the end of this period of time, evaluate your progress and make any adjustments or additions which appear necessary.

9 Maintain your program whilst listening to the voice within. This allows flexibility in your decisions.

10 Repeat steps 7 and 8 regularly.

For some people the decision-making process is quite new and unfamiliar—and these are *major* decisions being made. So, for those people who have difficulty in this area, be gentle with your-self and concentrate particularly on trusting you've made the right choice.

With this formula, flexibility and listening to the still small voice within, we can find our way through the most awesome and bewildering circumstances and go on with renewed vigour and belief in our chosen path.

It's important to avoid the trap of seeking more and more opinions from doctors simply as a way of prolonging the inevit-able decisions you must make. Write down what it is you want from your doctors and then use the decision-making formula to come up with the best plan of action for you.

Women who live in remote areas often don't have the time to

access further opinions from doctors and that can be a source of frustration in itself. If you feel you have confidence in the medical abilities of your doctor but find no emotional support or willingness to answer questions then employ them solely for their medical expertise and seek your emotional support elsewhere.

The first doctor you're most likely to encounter will be a surgeon. This may be for a biopsy or for a more involved procedure. Remember, you nearly always have plenty of time to shop around for someone you trust and feel comfortable with. Some women prefer to get the cancer out of their body as soon as possible. Others have children, responsibilities or pets to organise or, like Lois mentioned earlier, have other pressures which have an impact on their decision.

Some find they have habitually to wait for long periods for their appointment at their doctor's rooms. Though you can take heart that your doctor is clearly in great demand it can be frustrating if you yourself have a busy schedule or are feeling unwell. You might like to telephone before leaving for your appointment to see what the wait is likely to be so that you can adjust your schedule accordingly. Perhaps you can postpone leaving for your appointment until the waiting room traffic has eased a little.

Many find it helpful to write down questions as they come into their mind so that they don't forget them when they're with their doctor. (Don't forget to write down the answers too!) By the time most of us arrive at a doctor's appointment all the little or (seemingly) insignificant questions go right out of our minds. No question is insignificant and having information adds to your collection of knowledge about your disease. Remember, having knowledge gives you a sense that your disease is manageable. There's nothing worse than being tormented by questions and our *own* fearful answers at 3 a.m!

Sometimes, what you've been told by your doctor might go completely out of your head. It's OK to ask your doctor to repeat it on another occasion. If you feel awkward about doing this you could say something like, 'I'm sure you've told me the answer to this question before, however, I think I must have been in shock at the time because I can't remember what you said. Could you go through it again with me today'? Writing down the answers to questions is a good way to keep an accurate record, especially if you date each list of questions.

Wendie, whose partner Kay had breast cancer, recorded the details discussed at each appointment with the doctor in a journal. This involved keeping a record of the drugs being recommended, other treatment suggestions and any information about her partner's condition or prognosis. In this way they had an accurate record which they could refer to and discuss. Because their doctor was not very forthcoming with information about side-effects of some of the drugs he recommended, Wendie researched this information between visits and felt better informed to ask questions. This diary became a record of their medical journey through breast cancer. It gave them the opportunity to become very educated about the disease and its treatment and to speak to their doctors from an informed base of knowledge. They found that it equalled the relationship with their doctors and they felt more empowered to choose which path to take. Some doctors don't like this approach and find it threatening. It's a good idea to tell them what and why you're doing it. In the same way, it's important that you understand what and why they are suggesting certain treatments.

Some women find it helpful to record on a dictaphone their doctor's responses to their questions so that they can listen to them at a later time or share them with their family. This can certainly help refresh your memory of what *was* said. Again, seek co-operation first from your doctor.

Don't be afraid to ask medical questions of your doctors, nurses or any other therapist you might be involved with. It's OK for you to ask any questions at all. Don't worry about appearing ignorant. This is your life! Make a list of questions and jot down the answers when you receive them. Some doctors wait to see how much information you *do* want before they tell you too much. Remember, your doctors are not mind-readers. If you let them know that you appreciate lots of explanations, diagrams and information then you'll more than likely have that respected. You may prefer that your doctors tell you information as and when you need to know it and not give you too much at once. Let them know that this is your preference.

Usually, at doctor's appointments, our ears are straining to hear any emphasis or hesitation in their words and we often misinterpret the choice of words. You can choose to focus on the positive aspects of what your doctor is saying or you can listen only for the bad news. The choice is yours. I'm not suggesting you should be unrealistic. Sometimes, there *is* difficult news you must hear and comprehend. However, a good doctor will also tell you how they anticipate meeting the problems along the way. You can choose to focus on what *can* be done for your positive benefit.

Many women experience anger at the manner in which they are told their diagnosis. Some women have reported being told in a cold, off-hand manner whilst others have appreciated a direct and blunt approach. To tell a woman that she has breast cancer is an extremely difficult task and there's no easy or pleasant way to do it. To some extent it will be a case of 'shoot the messenger'. No matter how well the news might be conveyed it will be a source of shock, dismay and fear. If at all possible have a partner or friend with you who can support and comfort you. Many women are so traumatised by the initial words uttered by their doctor that they don't hear another word during the consultation. Your companion can help remember what has been said. You might wish to take some time to absorb the impact of the diagnosis and then schedule a second appointment to find out what the doctor suggests for your treatment. Each of us absorbs information at our own rate. It's up to us to know when we're ready to talk about what we *have* understood so far and what we want to know now.

Fortunately, breast cancer has many medical treatment options. If one line of treatment isn't working for you, your doctor can suggest another approach. Some treatments have noticeable side-effects whilst others have very few repercussions. Chapter 6, 'Reach for Recovery', has many suggestions for both minimising the side-effects of your medical treatment and any symptoms you might be experiencing.

If a new line of treatment is suggested, you might find that once again you're confronted by choosing a new specialist. For instance, if you've had surgery and now chemotherapy is being suggested, you may be referred to a medical oncologist who specialises in that aspect of treatment. Again, the advice given earlier applies in choosing someone with whom you feel at ease who will actively support you in your own efforts.

Early Days
Confronting the Scar

The social worker told me that I could go home within two weeks but not until I was able to look at the wound and accept it—a fairly large task. I looked at the long, red scar, not lovingly but at least with resignation and then went home. I decided that as it was up to me I would fight hard to get fit again and resolve the feeling of mutilation as quickly as possible.

JOAN, AGE 54
aged 51 at diagnosis

When the surgeon took the dressing off I looked down and my words to him were, "Well, that's not very impressive", because there was just a tiny little scar and it looked fine, and he said, "What do you want, more"? And I said no, but I thought it might have been worse.

RUTH, AGE 42
aged 40 at diagnosis

I didn't feel mutilated, or scarred or any less of a sexual being by losing my breast. I suppose that came partly from the fact that when my husband's cancer was diagnosed, they had informed us that the surgery would be grossly disfiguring to him and he's a fairly good looking man. It turned out that it wasn't in any way grossly disfiguring. Certainly you can see it. But it's not what I would call grossly disfiguring. So, the cosmetic aspect of it didn't really affect me. And it never has, except for the convenience of having a breast that's attached to the body.

CATHERINE, AGE 47
aged 41 at diagnosis

I could not look at my scar for days. I didn't know what to expect and as I had a round breast, I vaguely expected to see a big round hole.

PATRICIA, AGE 56
aged 52 at diagnosis

Most women feel nervous about seeing the wound for the first time after their surgery. Some women are surprised by the insignificance of the scar whilst others expect to see an open, round wound where the breast once was. Lumpectomy scars can vary according to the size and position of the lump. Some women are deeply shocked by the change in their body image and find it very difficult to come to terms with, whilst others don't find it traumatic at all. Like everything else, there's no right response.

The photographs in the middle of the book show women who have had a lumpectomy, partial, radical and bilateral mastectomies and reconstruction surgery. These photographs have been included to show you some typical results of surgery. However, every woman will heal differently. Also, if you've had radiotherapy treatment to the breast *before* surgery, it could heal differently from skin unaffected by radiation. Many people find they can minimise the effects of radiation on the skin by following the guidelines under Radiotherapy in Chapter 6. This chapter also covers preparing for surgery and promoting post-operative healing.

The first weeks after diagnosis are nearly always a hectic time.

You'll undoubtedly be confronted with many choices. Some women choose not to have surgery whilst others, as mentioned earlier, are keen to be rid of the cancer from their body. For some women, surgery will not be the first line of treatment suggested. Many women feel they're not given any choice or any time to consider what might be best for them and are treated as if it is a foregone conclusion that they'll have surgery. Whatever you decide, your world will suddenly have changed. The following scenario is common to many women.

You find a lump or thickening, you go to your doctor and are diagnosed with breast cancer; everyone is upset. You enter hospital within days, have your breast/lump removed and you recover well from surgery. You're inundated with flowers, cards, love, friends, support and sympathy. You return home and gradually resume your life perhaps with the addition of chemotherapy or radiotherapy. You're upright and on deck, back at the kitchen sink or work and your friends and loved-ones are at pains to tell you how well you look and isn't it marvellous it's all behind you. Six to twelve weeks later you collapse in an emotional heap and feel you're not coping. If you tell someone you're not coping they may well try and cheer you up, usually unsuccessfully.

At this point you might or might not return to your doctor, depending on your relationship with them, complaining of not coping well. You could be told that you have nothing to worry about because the cancer has gone and the (possible) follow-up treatment is to mop up any stray cancerous cells and that you should simply get on with your life and not give it another thought!

The doctor doesn't realise how profoundly your world has been shaken. You may be tormented by questions like:
- Why me?
- How did this happen?
- Do I *still* have cancer?
- Did I *really* have cancer?

- Do I just resume my old life?
- If I go back to being who I was, then will 'it' come back?
- Should I make any changes to my lifestyle to prevent a recurrence?
- How do I face the uncertainty of the future?
- Will I see my children grow up?
- How do I live my life with this hanging over my head?

and for some there'll be questions like:

- Who am I?
- What am I doing with my life?
- Am I having the kind of life I anticipated?
- If not, why not?
- What can I do to improve the quality of my life?
- Who will want me now?
- How will my partner cope with the change in my body?
- How will *I* cope with this different body?
- What can I do to help myself?

Your surgeon may be totally nonplussed by such concerns. What the surgeon might not realise is that through your experience of breast cancer, you've been confronted with your mortality. These questions are entirely natural and normal and it's important that you air them with someone who has a good listening ear and a warm and compassionate heart.

You might find that your spouse, partner or friend can be a good companion on this journey through your feelings. It's important you set aside time where you can really talk about how you feel. Sometimes you can be so confused, depressed or upset that you're not even sure what it *is* you're feeling. Talking about *how* you feel might be something which you're quite unaccustomed to doing. You're not alone! The diagnosis of breast cancer is nearly always a most bewildering experience and many of us have never before had to articulate how we feel. Many of us are confronted with new feelings which are completely foreign to us and for which we don't even have a language to express.

It wasn't until three or four months later that I started to fall into an enormous hole. I felt fairly high when in hospital. Support, love, cards, flowers. A few weeks later when the kids were back screaming at me and the bathroom was left with towels all over the floor, and people weren't doing things for me any more, because the operation was done and finished, it's all over now, being the centre of attention faded and normal was no longer normal for me, and I realised things are never going to be quite the same again.

CATHERINE, AGE 47
aged 41 at diagnosis

Many women complain of a real split between how they feel and how others relate to them. The world sees a woman who's resumed her life, who looks well and seems cheerful enough. On the inside, she might be feeling depressed, frightened, unsupported, confused or uncertain how to proceed with her life. It's good to remember that you *are* extremely competent in many areas of your life and you *will* regain a sense of control. That will happen more quickly if you have the loving support of a friend, partner, counsellor or group.

Many women find their partner, spouse or friends aren't able to provide the kind of support and understanding they need. Frankly, a lot of families react with the attitude that says, 'If she's upright and at the kitchen sink she must be fine'! This attitude usually comes from their great (emotional) need to have you well because facing the prospect of you not being well is simply too painful.

There are some families also who can't cope with you not being well simply because they don't want the disruption to their lives. This can be because they're preoccupied with their own concerns and so long as you look OK, that's how you'll be treated.

Both these attitudes can leave you feeling very isolated in your experience. If this applies to you then seek out appropriate support for yourself. It's not a sign of weakness to feel overwhelmed by feelings. It's a sign of maturity to acknowledge you need some assistance in dealing with the emotional and psychological aspects of breast cancer.

For some women, the diagnosis of breast cancer places them in a very lonely world of fear and anxiety. Even women in a relationship might feel completely alone and frightened. There are times when no matter how much we might be loved, we feel this is our own private hell and no one can really reach us. Other women live a very private life without anyone being close to them. If this applies to you, then you might find it particularly hard to reach out for support and understanding. However, the benefits you'll experience will far outweigh the reticence you might initially feel. No one should have to bear breast cancer alone.

Some women, even when they're not ill, experience terrible and debilitating depression and life hardly seems worth living. The advent of breast cancer precipitates them back into a world of depression which is all too familiar for them. For others, this might be the first time in their lives where they experience depression. The thoughts they have can often be quite terrifying because they may never have felt this way before.

This book will no doubt bring comfort in knowing you're not alone. However, a good counsellor or support group will help ease both the immediate issues related to breast cancer as well as longer term problems. Most states have a Breast Cancer Support Service which will arrange for you to be visited by a woman who has had similar surgery or treatment as yourself. Many of the major hospitals that treat cancer also provide support groups. There's more information about support groups for women with breast cancer in Chapter 4, 'The Company of Women'.

2
Where to from Here?

I put on a facade
But the inside shows through.
A bright morning, new start, brave face,
The cool air, light on water,
Remind me of other mornings,
All brightness,
When limbs were strong
And consciousness untarred by the brush of despair.

I raise a stiff arm
To brush away a tear,
To salute the day,
Breathe in wind's coolness and sun's warmth,
Determined to use this day,

29

To be inspired by the memory
Of hope and an ingenuous childhood.

We are in knowing, caring hands
From, and into, all eternity.
Let it be.

JULIET, AGE 61
aged 46 at diagnosis

My life will never be the same. I look on it now and say that I had an old life and now I have a new one. I still have a way to go but I'm beginning to feel confident that my new life is going to be GREAT!

JUDY, AGE 38
aged 36 at diagnosis

It's just OK to be feeling whatever you're feeling.

JO, AGE 42
aged 41 at diagnosis

When I woke up and found I'd had a mastectomy, I was so shocked and I was certain I was going to die. Back then, the only women I knew who'd had mastectomies, had died. Nobody ever said the word cancer. My doctor never said the word cancer.

MONTY, AGE 69
aged 43 at diagnosis

What most concerned me was not so much the treatment, or a fear of dying, or what I would look like after surgery. My biggest concerns were a tremendous fear of being an invalid, how I was going to cope with looking after a young family and a new job while having treatment and how to tell people because many people seem to gasp for breath and fall over at the mere mention of the word cancer.

BARBARA, AGE 35
aged 33 at diagnosis

I lay in my bed awake all night before I had my mastectomy and kept thinking, "What have I done? Why is this happening to me"? My dog slept close to me all night.

BELINDA, AGE 35
aged 15 at diagnosis

What actually doesn't kill you makes you stronger.

DEB, AGE 40
aged 38 at diagnosis

Life was not quite straightforward for me from that day on. I recovered quickly from surgery and went back to work but some sort of confidence had gone out of my life. I worried about my husband and the boys if something happened to me and agonised for my father who'd lost his wife, my mother, four years before after a battle with breast cancer.

JULIET, AGE 61
aged 46 at diagnosis

The night before surgery, my husband said, "After tomorrow, when I hold you, your heart will be closer to mine than ever".

PAT, AGE 60
aged 57 at diagnosis

I had a very short period of actually mourning the loss, in the sense of the death of that part of my body. It was more of a mourning for the lack of certainty in life and for my youth; it's very hard to explain. It was like that young period of my life was gone and I was moving into another phase where I realised I'm very much a mortal person. Since then, I've now gone back to youth! It's all right to think like that. It's great. But that's the way it seemed at the time, going through the experience.

CATHERINE, AGE 47
aged 41 at diagnosis

At our first interview, Petrea asked me to tell her what kinds of stress I'd been under during the previous five years—it all came tumbling out, starting with the death of our much loved son, aged twenty-four, my mother's cancer and a whole host of other

31

traumas that had been going on. It all sounded incredible, even to me! Somehow through the past twelve months, I have come to terms a little better with these things, and try to think myself calmly through all problems. I try to live as simply and happily as possible.

LYNNE, AGE 55
aged 52 at diagnosis

Breast cancer was not the end of the world for me; in fact it changed my life around in a positive way. I no longer let trivial things matter and I can deal with stress a lot better than I used to. With the help of meditation, I feel very peaceful within myself. It's now ten years since I had my mastectomy and I thank God every day that I'm free of disease.

GERALDINE, AGE 42
aged 32 at diagnosis

When I was told that I had over 70 per cent lymph node involvement and that my future wasn't terribly good, and that I was going to need chemotherapy, that's when the real problems began, because that's when I really had to start sorting out what to do. It wasn't going to be just that little bit of surgery, and then back to work. It was going to be much more than that. I was devastated. To find I had cancer, well, it was the biggest surprise of my life. Because I'd nursed people with cancer. I didn't ever expect to get it myself.

JEANNIE, AGE 54
aged 50 at diagnosis

It was a very very frightening and confronting experience. This is what I was saying about different people handling their cancer in different ways. I didn't think that my husband did any work on himself when he was diagnosed and I thought it's going to come back and hit him. He's got a different attitude. My way of dealing with it was to take it out and look at it from all sides and examine it and see what it was going to do to me and embrace it and throw it away and do all those sorts of things. His

WHERE TO FROM HERE?

way was not like that. His way was, we get on with life, we get on with work, let's put that behind us. And his way is just as valid.

CATHERINE, AGE 47
aged 41 at diagnosis

I did not want people to know I had had an operation, but because of my work, word got around. I didn't want to see the pity in their eyes or have them staring at my body.

PATRICIA, AGE 56
aged 52 at diagnosis

Family, Friends and Loved-ones

Cancer rarely happens to just one person. It also happens to all those who love you. It happens to you *and* your partner. It happens to you *and* your family. Or it happens to you *and* your friends. You might begin to think about those that need to be included in the knowledge of your breast cancer.

Your immediate family will probably already know because of your hospitalisation or change in routine. Family members will react differently according to their individual personality. You might find some deal with their feelings by talking about it whilst others are more introspective and need time alone to come to terms with your diagnosis in their own way. This can occasionally cause clashes amongst family members and is often reflected in their behaviour. For instance, one member might be keen to 'do' something. They might find out about all the alternative/complementary medical treatments for breast cancer and be keen to drag you off to appointments all over the place. Another family member might find all this rushing about 'doing' very hard to take and may think that it is a waste of both time and money.

Sometimes, people are *so* careful and considerate of each others' feelings that nothing useful actually gets said or done! The last thing you want is walled-off communication at a time when openness and honesty will serve you best. There's no right way for any family member to deal with their feelings. We need to offer each other the love and support we would like extended to ourselves.

Everyone affected by breast cancer will need to deal with their fears, frustrations and confusion. This extends to family members, friends or loved-ones who are trying to come to terms with the impact of your diagnosis. They may lash out in anger when, behind their words, there's the fear of losing you, or the frustration of the powerlessness to change your situation. Some family members have difficulty in coping with any added responsibilities they might have to take on. Some teenagers or young adults can become extremely unsupportive and self-absorbed. Mostly, this is due to their inability to cope with the idea of anything being wrong with Mum. It can be particularly difficult where teenagers may already have a strained relationship with their mother. Family issues are addressed in greater detail in Chapter 10, 'My Children, My Life'.

The advent of breast cancer doesn't always bring families together. Dealing with the distress that an unsupportive family can induce can be overwhelming. Seeking support outside the home becomes essential for these women. Some households have been little more than a powder-keg waiting to explode. Adding in the diagnosis of breast cancer is bound to ignite problems. It can be helpful to remember that things weren't perfect before the diagnosis and that it isn't *because* of breast cancer that problems are now flaring. The problems already existed, it's just that now they can no longer be contained.

Even in homes where love and support are tangible forces readily felt, the advent of breast cancer is often cause for re-assessment of roles and responsibilities. Many women find they no longer wish to carry the same responsibilities as previously. This might only be in one area or in many. Discussion will be essential in order to bring about understanding and co-operation. Clearly defining what we each expect of each other will help to minimise friction as some of those changes in roles/responsibilities are implemented. Many of these changes are not at all traumatic and are a natural process of re-evaluation and maturing.

Just moments before I was leaving the house, my twenty-year-old rang and said, "Mum, I'm at my friend's place. Can you come and get me because it's not very nice outside"? I said, "No, I'm walking out the door, I'm going to North Sydney". "Oh Mum". I said, "No Steven, I'll see you when I come back". And I put the phone down and I thought, "My God, I didn't even ask him if he had any money to get home". I mean, normally, it would be the first thing that I would have worried about. And I never even asked him how he was getting home. And then I found myself thinking, "Oh well, bugger him, he can walk"! I'd never have said that before, I'd have felt guilty and gone and got him.

MAREE, AGE 46
aged 45 at diagnosis

Some women become withdrawn and this can make it very difficult for family members to offer help. For many women, it's natural to want some solitude to digest information. However, some family members might find this approach very difficult to deal with. If at all possible, make the effort to explain that you're not rejecting them; that this is your way of coming to grips with what you've been told. Many women have found it invaluable to have some time away from their partner and/or family. This can allow a valuable period of reflection, meditation, re-assessment and the space to plan, decide or think about how you wish to proceed.

It's often helpful to recognise that we're behaving in a *consistent manner* for us. For instance, your usual reaction when under stress might be to seek out and talk to loved-ones where you readily share your tears and fears. Your partner's usual reaction to stress might be to work harder and longer, watch television incessantly, play sport more frequently and not talk about the cause of the stress nor share any fears or tears and perhaps prefer you not to share yours. One partner has always dealt with stress by expressing their concerns and fears; the other partner has dealt with the identical stress by becoming absorbed in something else. This difference in coping styles can be almost unbearable when the cause of the stress is life-threatening. If you can recognise that you are behaving in a typical manner for *you* and that they're behaving in a typical manner for *them*, then some comfort can be taken that you *are* each behaving consistently.

More distant family members or friends will usually find out sooner or later and by including them in your diagnosis you give them an opportunity to express their feelings and to offer their support and encouragement.

Of course, like everything, there *are* exceptions to this! Some women don't want to include particular friends or relatives because they feel *they* would end up supporting *them* instead of the other way around! A family member could be too old, too young, too frail, too emotionally fragile or be living too far away to cope with your diagnosis. Only you know what will be best for *you* so listen to that voice within (or an inner 'knowing' or intuition) which will provide you with your answers. If your cancer has been diagnosed very early on then, of course, your hopes will be that you'll never have to deal with it again in the future. This might be a reason to withhold the information from young children.

The time I had my operation was ten years ago. I was thirty-two. People say, "How did you cope, being so young"? My mother was dying of bowel cancer at the time, and I just didn't have time to think of my breast cancer then. It was awful to go home and tell her that I was going into hospital. All I wanted to do was get home. I just came straight home from hospital and nursed my mother, who died four months later. I felt a bit guilty, that maybe me having breast cancer flared up Mum's cancer again and she got very sick after I had the operation. I believe stress had a lot to do with both her illness and mine.

GERALDINE, AGE 42
aged 32 at diagnosis

There are often other crises happening amongst our loved-ones, or to one's self, when we're diagnosed. These can compound the difficulties and make it very hard to achieve any sense of peace or calmness. It becomes more like just weathering the storm. At such times, hanging on to some sort of affirmation may help. One of my favourites is, 'This too will pass'. Another one is, 'Would you rather be right or happy'? The remembrance of these statements has often saved me from throwing more fuel on a fire that would be better left to burn itself out.

Now that your (possible) surgery is behind you and your treatment options have been discussed and decided upon, you can begin to look at the changes you wish to make to your lifestyle. There are many things which you can do to help yourself. These might include re-assessing your priorities so that you can reduce the amount of stress in your life; learning techniques which will help you to establish a centre of peace and serenity within yourself; improving your diet to support you in regaining and maintaining your health through your treatment time; changing lifestyle habits which are detrimental to your well-being; replacing negative attitudes with a calm and optimistic outlook, and so on.

The Physiology of Hope

Throughout the history of medicine, the recognition of the part the mind plays in a person's recovery has always been acknowledged. In this century, particularly since the discovery of anti-biotics, the sulfa drugs and refined surgical techniques, medicine has taken a more technologically-based view of disease. In fact, medicine is now primarily learnt by studying disease rather than exploring the ways in which health is gained and maintained. There was a time when we all knew that the basis of good health was contentment and peace of mind. When a person was subject to overwhelming stress—either through grief, depression or continued discouragement—it was considered to be the breeding ground for disease.

The place that hope plays in our lives cannot be overestimated. Avoid getting caught up in the statistics available about breast cancer. No two people are the same. Likewise, no two women with breast cancer are the same. Your immune system and genetic make-up are entirely your own. Your will to live and the enthusiasm of your spirit are your own. Your beliefs and attitudes are yours alone. These qualities are a solid foundation on which to build. Hope, love, willpower, belief, faith and spirit: these cannot be calculated into statistics.

Even in the most difficult times there are reasons to hope. Hope for a remission, for a good day, for a restful night's sleep, for the company of loved-ones, for shared moments of love and laughter; hope for a cure, for a longer life or for a better life, here and now.

We do not value a life by its length. It is not how long we live but the spirit with which we live which is of true importance.

It's difficult to live with spirit and enthusiasm if you forsake all hope.

These feelings are not just states of mind. Moment by moment we're secreting from our brain into our blood stream chemicals in accordance with our feelings. These neurotransmitters directly and indirectly affect our immune system. This is cause for celebration because we can change the attitudes, thoughts and feelings in our minds to directly benefit our bodies. You're a unique human being and you can contribute to your own healing by taking control of what goes on in your mind.

If your subconscious mind has only ever received messages of a negative, self-demeaning nature then those are precisely the (chemical) messages which will flow out to every cell within your body. This happens via our nervous and endocrine systems. It's unrealistic to expect your body to be healthy and run smoothly if your mind is chronically full of depression, grief, anger, despair or thoughts of unworthiness. If, silently in our minds, we have thoughts like:

- Life's a struggle, I can't cope
- I just don't have what it takes to meet the standard
- I'll never catch up. I feel constantly overwhelmed
- Nothing ever goes right for me

then it's obvious every cell in the body is going to feel the effects of such thinking through the chemicals our brains secrete. It matters not to the body whether this thinking is in the conscious or subconscious mind. It will still have its influence.

The immune system is extremely complex in both its components and functions. Simply put, its function is to recognise what is 'me' and what is 'not me'. One of the functions of the white blood cells is to recognise foreign cells, like bacteria and viruses, and to recognise imperfect cells, like cancer cells. When it does find these cells—the 'not me' cells—it sends out for the killer and scavenger cells who are then mobilised to dispatch the foreigners.

There's so much we can do to co-operate with our magnificent immune system. We need to provide all the essentials, and then trust it's performing its task perfectly. This means being aware of what we hold in our mind so our body receives positive, encouraging and loving thoughts; that we affirm this thinking by giving our bodies the best and freshest foods and other substances for its health; that we exercise and rest adequately; that we choose appropriate treatments and that we lift and inspire ourselves frequently through the use of meditation and the many techniques within this book. In this way, we create an ideal environment in which healing of body, mind and spirit can take place.

Through the regular practice of physical relaxation and meditation you allow your body to find its own chemical equilibrium. The hormones and chemicals created through stress subside and the body comes back to its 'resting point' where it experiences an internal stability—often referred to as homeostasis. In Chapter 3,

'A Place of Peace Within', we'll explore more fully the means by which we can assist ourselves in the process of establishing this state of equilibrium.

Achieving Peace of Mind

I'm feeling very well indeed, in control of myself, my health and my life. I've had good reports from all my medical checks and have just passed another milestone! I'm more relaxed about things in my life—I try not to worry and fuss, to be more peaceful and serene.

LYNNE, AGE 55
aged 52 at diagnosis

As was mentioned in the Introduction, I encourage people to go all out for peace of mind. When you have peace, you also create the very best of environments for healing within your body.

It might seem a nonsense to talk about peace of mind while you're still in the throes of diagnosis and treatment, however, it *is* possible in time. Ask yourself, 'What stands in the way of me being at peace'? For some women the answer will be a resounding 'Cancer'! For others it will be different. Their reply might have more to do with their self-esteem or with a relationship in their life which causes them pain, or with the future, or a job they find overwhelming, or with the symptoms they're experiencing or with the side-effects of their treatment.

Many a woman has lamented the loss of her energy, her libido or her body image. Many have said, 'I can deal with having cancer, but my hair falling out really upsets me!' Most of us find a change in our body image very hard to come to terms with. The photographs included in this book are there to help alleviate some of the fear many women feel in coming to terms with surgery to the breast. Most women were never given the opportunity to see what a lumpectomy, partial/radical or bilateral mastectomy scar looked like before they had their own surgery.

The Practicalities of Peace

In order to feel at peace with our healing program we must play an active part in making appropriate choices for ourselves. Relinquishing responsibility means relinquishing choice and is the antithesis of being at peace. You don't have to feel like a helpless victim of breast cancer. By directly participating in the creation of a healing program for yourself you leave behind hopelessness and helplessness.

The most destructive feelings we can get stuck with are feelings of being trapped, hopeless, powerless or helpless. Everybody has moments of having these feelings and that's fine but to become paralysed and unable to progress beyond them can become negative. To feel this way also means we're not *expressing* the feelings behind those states of mind. This can lead to resentment and creates a vicious and self-defeating circle.

People sometimes wrongly think that being positive is to only think about the outcome they'd like to have happen. To me, being positive is *being real* with what *is* happening. It's far more positive to say, 'I've never felt so afraid and confused and I don't know how I'm going to get through this. I hope tomorrow is a better day', than to say through gritted teeth, 'Everything's fine', when that isn't the truth.

All feelings are fine so long as they're expressed. When I was younger I was afraid of the depth of my feelings, especially the ones that I'd decided were 'negative'. I used to think that if I allowed myself to feel depressed, afraid, angry, panicky, abandoned or any number of other unenjoyable feelings I'd disintegrate and perhaps never regain a sense of equilibrium. I was afraid of feeling fear! I also felt, if I start to cry, I may never stop. One of the greatest gifts from my experience of leukaemia was that it gave me permission to become 'authentic'. To be myself without all the many filters through which I used to interact with the world. So much of my time used to be spent in trying to figure out what everyone required of me, then trying to *be* that person.

We all need to find a healthy expression of our feelings. For some, that will be through a group or counsellor, for others it will be by talking it through with a loved-one or friend. Others will find that expression through poetry, painting, writing, singing, craft pursuits, sport, being in nature, gardening . . . the list is endless. Expressing feelings doesn't have to be cathartic or done in a professional environment. Find your own creative way of allowing your feelings to be acknowledged and expressed.

In my experience, people who actively participate in their healing process certainly have an improved quality of life. Most of them far outlive their prognosis if they were unfortunate enough to receive a time-frame for their life. Some of them are now completely free of their disease when they had originally been declared terminal.

That is why I believe the word terminal should only be used when talking about buses, trains, computers and airports. We're people living with a life-threatening illness, not dying with a terminal one.

I also believe that in years to come it will be illegal for a doctor to tell a patient how long she has to live, because it will be shown that we begin to secrete the chemicals in our brain which will ensure the prognosis is correct. If modern-day doctors persist in telling a person how long they'll live they keep the ancient Aboriginal practice of bone-pointing alive. In their culture, if one of the Aboriginal community breaks a tribal law, punishable by death, then a bone-pointing ceremony takes place and the Aborigine dies rapidly.

We can override this negative programming by actively participating in choosing our own healing path. I'd have preferred my doctor to have said, 'Petrea, you have a very serious disease and many people die within a few weeks of diagnosis. However, some people don't, and we want to give you all the skills, treatment, support and education so that you can be one of the survivors'. Then I'd have felt like he was on my team.

Being told I wouldn't see Christmas didn't help me to feel hopeful!

Remember, hopelessness, helplessness, powerlessness and feeling trapped are not just states of mind, they are chemicals which we secrete from our brain into our blood stream which affect our immune system. If we're told that our situation is hopeless and we believe it, then the feelings engendered by that statement will have their physical effect upon us.

How do I live after being told I'm going to die? How do I learn to live—how do I try to overcome the doctor's death sentence?

HELEN, AGE 42
aged 34 at diagnosis

I met an oncologist who always refers to me as, "Women like you".

LOUISE, AGE 52
aged 51 at diagnosis

Most of us would agree that a woman who's deeply committed to living, who feels loved and supported by those around her, who feels in control of herself and her world and feels she has manageable and exciting challenges in her life is in a better position to heal than one who feels wearied by life, who feels isolated, abandoned and unloved, who feels she's lost control over her life, who feels all her challenges are overwhelming and, now, is a victim of breast cancer.

We cannot always change what happens to us but we can change the way we respond to what happens to us.

If we believe that life is about a joyful childhood, happy teen years, that we enter the career of our choice and excel, that we meet the perfect partner who adores us in every moment, have wonderful children who always love, honour and respect us, that we find our ideal home and pay it off effortlessly, that life unfolds before us like a dream, our garden's full of butterflies and bliss and that we all go fishing in our old age . . . then we're in for a shock. I'm certainly not having one of those lives and I'm yet to meet anyone else who is.

I believe life's a rollercoaster ride. None of us knows what's over the crest or around the corner and the speed with which it travels is not always up to us, however, it *is* our responsibility to fasten our own seatbelt. Our seatbelt might be our philosophy, faith, spiritual or religious beliefs, music, love, nature, our garden, our meditation practice or whatever deeply connects us to our self and to life. Each of us needs to find the things which help us regain a deep sense of who we are.

Then, when the rollercoaster unexpectedly swings to the right and we could have sworn it was going to swing to the left, we're more easily able to say, 'Aaagh! This isn't the scenery I was expecting'. *But then* be able to say, 'How am I going to respond to this new situation I'm in'? If we don't have a seatbelt then we're more likely to have difficulty in dealing with the unexpected. We can easily then get stuck with 'This isn't fair! It shouldn't have happened! It was meant to be different from this! Why me'? The fact is, it *did* happen and nothing's going to change that. The acceptance of that fact can free us to simply make the journey in the best way possible for us. As Teresa puts it:

Once you accept that you are on a journey, you can simply relax and enjoy it.

TERESA, AGE 42
aged 40 at diagnosis

I'd always felt it was important that people see that you coped. You know, everything was all right and you coped with everything. And I think that was a mistake. We aren't supposed to cope with all the things that come along in life. It's quite OK to say—this is too much for me. And then get some help for it. But I didn't realise those things before.

JEANNIE, AGE 54
aged 50 at diagnosis

I realised I was forever trying to control things in my life. I was in a permanent state of anxiety because things kept happening to me, too quickly for me to deal with. Meditation has led to a deeper understanding of what control is. The only control I really have is over my thinking. I can choose my responses rather than just react to the things that happen to me.

JENNIE, AGE 45
aged 39 at diagnosis

What About My Job?

So began a time of deep thought, meditation and acceptance. One hurdle which remained when I went back to work was to face my male colleagues, whose attitude to boobs was fairly basic.

JOAN, AGE 54
aged 51 at diagnosis

I had taken a year off work because I couldn't work at this time. And I found that the thought of going back to work was really quite daunting for me. And getting back into the mainstream of life was also quite daunting.

My job unfortunately hadn't been kept open for me which was a big disappointment because I'd expected to be able to return there. I then had to turn around and put myself on the open market. And I found that horrendous, because my hair hadn't grown back properly and I didn't feel emotionally ready. And so there I was, out in the marketplace, in my fifties. With my hair hardly grown, trying to get a job. It was just awful, it was just horrendous.

The other aspect was financial. I was a single parent and was supporting the children in tertiary education. I didn't have any money behind me. I had to go on Social Security sickness benefits and I found them difficult. Towards the end, I went for a review with the doctor, and all he was interested in, literally, was whether I could put my hand up over my head. He wasn't interested in the fact that I felt bad about myself, that I was still very

45

tearful, that my emotions still hadn't settled down. It didn't make any difference and I was pronounced to be perfectly fit for work.

Fortunately, I found a position on night duty. I thought that's good: no one can see me. It was part-time and I was able to ease myself back into the workforce slowly and by myself, which was good, because I felt so bad about myself.

JEANNIE, AGE 54
aged 50 at diagnosis

I'm much more game to 'go to the edge', if you know what I mean. If I'm digging into something at work I'm not as timid as I used to be, not that I was ever timid but now I push it further, like it doesn't really matter. You know nothing really matters; life's short and if something goes wrong, well, you get up and go on with the next thing. It's not such a big drama as it would normally have been. I'm more inclined to sort of push some things, and other things I'm less worried about.

MAREE, AGE 30
aged 30 at diagnosis

What should I do about the job I had scarcely started? Resign, and let someone else do it? My boss said, "No. We all agreed you're the person for this job. We will wait and see . . .". I came to the conclusion that while I'm alive I should live, *as fully as possible; so I went on with the job. On another occasion I began a job which incorporated the previous one and greatly added to it. Had I made a mistake? Should I resign now, in fairness to the job, my colleagues, and the team I'd been pulling together? Again, I came to the conclusion that while alive I should live, and continue what I had started. It's impossible to know what the outcome will be, but I'm well, busy, content and at peace.*

JOAN, AGE 67
aged 63 at diagnosis

I've been able to continue working (on a very part-time basis) which has been wonderful—a place to go and be "normal".

JUDY, AGE 38
aged 36 at diagnosis

People didn't want to know about it, they pretended, they would see me knowing that I'd had surgery and chemotherapy and wouldn't *say, "How are you"? or "You're looking quite well".*

RUTH, AGE 42
aged 40 at diagnosis

There are many practical issues to be considered when you contemplate returning to work. Some women have been overwhelmed by the compassion and understanding expressed in their workplace whilst others have been dismayed with the response from their boss or staff. Some have found that they're no longer given the same responsibilities for fear they won't be able to fulfil their function. Sometimes this is done with a view to taking away extra responsibilities but the women generally would have preferred to have been consulted. Many a woman has lamented that it was her breast that was removed, not her brain!

There are no simple answers nor any 'right' way of approaching your work situation. For some women who are self-employed, the prospect of people finding out about the diagnosis may well mean an unwanted reduction in demand for their services.

There may be other very good reasons for keeping your diagnosis quiet. Those in highly competitive jobs may find they're no longer considered to be contenders for promotion. Talking through the issues with your partner, friend, support group or counsellor may help you decide on your best course of action.

Some women find they no longer desire to be in a competitive work environment and may wish to seek employment of a different kind. That can be a challenge in itself—to change careers.

Many women find their work environment not only rewards them financially but they also receive satisfaction and enjoyment from working amongst others. Returning to work can provide both stability and a sense of 'normalcy': 'If I'm working, I must be OK'. Most of us, of course, find the diversion which work provides a welcome alternative to the problems associated with our health. A lot of women don't want a big fuss made of them when they return to work because this is one area of their life where they feel competent and able to function at the same level as everyone else. Returning to work often boosts your self-esteem. It helps you to remember that you're certainly more than just a woman with breast cancer.

It's not at all uncommon for women to resent the good health and seemingly carefree lifestyle of their co-workers. This is a normal human reaction so don't waste time feeling guilty over it!

I couldn't believe how one co-worker got stressed-out over whether her sofa's going to be covered by Christmas. I've been told I won't see Christmas. I'd swap her problem for mine, any day!

BETTY, AGE 64
aged 60 at diagnosis

You might find that some of your work colleagues can't cope with your having cancer. They will either ignore you altogether or will only have superficial conversations like, 'It's nice to have you back; you look well'! and that's the end of the conversation! These people will find it hard to ask you how you *really* feel and will be unable to tell you how *they* feel. It can be quite disappointing if you expected to come back to a warm reception. Many people simply can't cope with your diagnosis. It confronts them with their own mortality and they feel at a loss to know what to say or do. This is particularly so if you're in the under-fifty age group. You present a very scary scenario for them. How would they cope if they were in your situation?

Amongst much of the recent literature there's a tendency to explain away disease as if it's something you created to learn lessons from. This is very tricky territory! Whilst many of us are able to say that we have learnt much from our experience of cancer, that doesn't mean we wished it upon ourselves to gain that wisdom. I can say, without a trace of hesitancy, that leukaemia was one of the best things that ever happened to me, *but* I certainly didn't feel that way when I was in the midst of feeling sick and full of the fear of death. The fact that I'm sitting here now and feeling fine is something for which I feel enormously grateful.

This thinking can be cloaked in many disguises. Some people will want to find fault in you to explain away your cancer in order to reassure themselves that *they* won't 'need' to get breast cancer. Put very simplistically, their fearful thinking can run something like this, 'Julie's never been able to nurture and care for herself and now she has breast cancer. I've always been really good at looking after myself, so I won't need to have that experience'! Or, 'Julie has a horrible relationship with her mother which she's never resolved. I have a really good relationship with my mother, so I won't get breast cancer'.

Most people want to find an explanation for that which causes them fear. This helps them to make more sense of the situation and it can serve to reassure themselves that what happened to you, won't happen to them. However, many of us have been (or are) in situations which cannot be simply explained or rationalised. It can be an insult to have someone give a neat and tidy explanation to what seems completely senseless. That's why my favourite bumper sticker remains, 'My karma just ran over your dogma!'

Spending time trying to figure out *why* you got breast cancer might not be as useful as looking at what you're going to do now that you're *in* this situation.

Sometimes the people we thought would be most supportive are completely unable to be helpful, whilst others we didn't even consider can become our staunchest allies.

Some women have demanding jobs which require physical stamina which they may well not have immediately after surgery or during any necessary treatment. You might like to discuss with your doctor a likely time-frame for your ability to resume your former position.

Many women are financially dependent on their income and this can pose serious problems. It might be best to meet with a financial adviser to see how things could be managed during the time when you're unable to function at your usual level. Many bank managers are sympathetic to clients who inform them of their problem and will negotiate or postpone repayments until things improve.

Some women have had to leave work in order to undergo treatment. This might prove a problem when you're ready to seek re-employment. It's often ignorance and the fear of illness which makes this so. Some companies are concerned to take on someone who may have problems in the future requiring time off. If you feel you're being discriminated against then it's important to speak to a professional person who can give you advice. The people who are most likely to be helpful are your doctor, social worker, solicitor, Department of Social Security, Community Health and Welfare Centre or the Human Rights and Equal Opportunity Commission.

Giving up work isn't always the best solution for anyone who's faced by a life-threatening diagnosis. Many people derive great satisfaction and fulfilment from their work and would miss it badly if they left. The last thing you want is to sit at home waiting for something to go wrong.

Many women experience guilt when they're not working. Jennie describes her situation like this:

I knew I needed time for myself while I underwent chemotherapy. I wanted to have some solitude, I needed to make juices and take care with my diet. Meditation had become a really important tool to help me cope with the stress of surgery and treatment and I devoted two half-hour sessions a day to its practice. In this way, I felt I was doing everything I could to be well, with the ultimate aim of returning to work.

However, because *I looked so well throughout my treatment, people kept saying, "When are you going back to work"? If I worked a day in the garden I'd sometimes give myself a hard time, thinking that if I'm well enough to do this then surely I'm well enough to work. Or, sometimes, if I went shopping, I'd feel guilty in case I met someone from work who'd think I was somehow a malingerer. Perhaps they'd think, "She looks all right to me. How come she's not working"?*

I realised that the work ethic that most of us grew up with said, "Your value as a human being is measured by what you do in the workplace". Given this thinking it logically follows that if you don't work, then you should at least look *sick! It's an ongoing challenge to rid myself of this occasional guilt. Petrea suggested I make as my affirmation, "I* listen *to* myself *as keenly as I listen to others".*

JENNIE, AGE 44
aged 43 at diagnosis

So often we give away what we know to be true about ourselves because we listen to the voice of guilt instead. One of the greatest lessons we can learn in life is to honour and respect what we know about ourselves and to remain *true* to that knowledge.

Cleo found a similar situation in her workplace. She'd told her colleagues that her haemoglobin (the red cells which carry oxygen in blood) was low (7) and that she wouldn't be at work until her situation improved. Each time she spoke to them they'd enquire about her haemoglobin. As it approached the normal range, they expected her return to work, not realising her haemoglobin was *not* the only measure of her wellness. 'Oh good, your haemoglobin's normal; are you coming back to work now?'

The split between how we look and how we feel can lead to all sorts of frustrating situations. People are so often only able to affirm what *they* see as positive without taking into account *your* real experience. I usually say to people, 'Do you feel as good as

51

you look'? as a way of giving people permission to tell you that they feel awful even though they look terrific.

Only you will know how best to navigate the choices or decisions about whether to continue working, whether to take a break or to resign and focus 100 per cent upon yourself. Using the decision-making formula in Chapter 1 may help you to clarify your thoughts.

3
A Place of Peace Within

The most important thing I've learnt from having breast cancer, is what Petrea calls peace, getting in touch with who I am, learning to be real, and taking responsibility for myself. It's been an enormous growth thing for me. You know, I was a real wimp before and most of my real feelings I bottled up inside. Now it feels like I'm alive for the first time in my life. It's great.

TRISH, AGE 53
aged 48 at diagnosis

I live a lot for now, I don't think too far ahead. If I want to do something, I don't put it off. I just do it. I never used to be like that.

ROS, AGE 49
aged 47 at diagnosis

If anyone had told me having breast cancer would change my life in a positive way I'd have told them they were mad. I've resolved a lot of issues from the past, including the sexual abuse I suffered from my father throughout my childhood. I never even realised why I had so much self-hatred and suicidal thoughts until breast cancer made me take the lid off my emotional world.

HILARY, AGE 43
aged 36 at diagnosis

I suppose there was another lesson for me to learn: that it's not only lovely to give but it's also lovely to receive. I hadn't known that before. I think probably as a mother, you're nurturing and that's a big part of your role. And possibly if you've been brought up to think that a woman's role is one of nurturing in all relationships, then this subtle message is given to you. Or you somehow start to think it yourself over the years, that that's what you should do. To receive isn't quite so important. But I've learnt that it is. That's lovely and it's nice for other people; it's nice for you too.

JEANNIE, AGE 54
aged 50 at diagnosis

I've never had a lot of confidence in myself and my opinions. I'm getting it, it's coming.

SUE, AGE 59
aged 53 at diagnosis

Breast cancer has been a positive experience for me. I have grown in leaps and bounds, tapped into new strengths, and started new projects. I've taken charge of many areas of my life. I am more content and life seems such a wonderful adventure and a continuing challenge. Yes, I have changed. I look at myself on many levels now, and try to do something positive in each of them.

JUDITH, AGE 53
aged 52 at diagnosis

Whether I live or die, I think I have found healing.

HELEN, AGE 42
aged 34 at diagnosis

It's a time where I'm discovering a faith that I thought was lost to me. It's a time of great personal struggle and a time of healing spiritually.

DENISE, AGE 44
aged 43 at diagnosis

I have sold my share . . . I had a shop. I loved it in the beginning. I'm a speech pathologist, and I always thought I'd go back to that. But I got locked in. Locked in and locked in and years went by and then I really started to resent it and I thought maybe breast cancer was tied up with it, this feeling of resentment. Again, it's a negative feeling isn't it? So I've booked my fare to Italy and sold my shop and . . .

ROS, AGE 49
aged 47 at diagnosis

I call it something other than meditation. Muscle relaxation. That's what I find I do when I speak to people about it, because I know they're going to think it's mumbo jumbo. But I find that those people who are going to be unsympathetic aren't among my circle of friends any more. It's just a subtle thing that happens.

LOUISE, AGE 52
aged 51 at diagnosis

It's been a fairly huge search for me and it took me quite some time to understand that in many ways I wasn't looking for a cure, I was looking for healing. And I've gone a long way towards finding that and I feel I really have had a miracle in my life.

HELEN, AGE 42
aged 34 at diagnosis

I've left my marriage, I have a new flat, my children are with me, I have a new job, a new car, a new life.

EVE, AGE 43
aged 38 at diagnosis

I found that I could experience insights and bliss in a thirty minute meditation or seated before nature that could hardly be packed into a two-week holiday.

JULIET, AGE 61
aged 46 at diagnosis

I suppose my spiritual journey is through Buddhism and meditation and that's far more accepting of just seeing things as they are and moving towards death with as much graciousness and curiosity as I can.

SHARNE, AGE 45
aged 37 at diagnosis

As a Catholic I had a good background in spirituality. But this was the time when I went more deeply into things, developed my own ways of knowing and put to one side what William James called "a faith in somebody else's faith".

I have read avidly in these years and forget a lot of the detail, but a resonance remains. Every new idea was being tested against my "inner knowing". Listening to music as well as reading became a dialogue with my inner being.

While I had called out in sorrow, while I was neglecting my spiritual life, God came.

I have experienced a healing of the spirit and worry much less about my future health.

JULIET, AGE 61
aged 46 at diagnosis

I feel I'm more happy and contented and serene than I've ever been in my life. Which is a really nice place to be. Without being, you know, smug about it, it's a nice place to be. It's not that I'm not learning. It's not that I'm not "growing" or any of those things. It's just that life is pretty perfect.

There's always little niggly things that worry you, but you put it into perspective. Every now and again you get a jolt when you hear a friend or relative is ill. That brings you back to what's really important; what you've really learnt out of the experience of having cancer. Because as time goes by you tend to get a little bit complacent. And every now and again something really knocks you and you say—wow! I forgot. I'm losing the thread. But I think we're getting to the point where we're not losing the thread any more. We're trying to incorporate all those lessons in our lives.

It didn't change any spirituality that I had, having cancer. It just made it grow enormously. It made me realise the importance of spirituality in my life. Not that I rush off to church or any of those things. But spirituality is something that is deeply personal and intimate and inside me. And it certainly has heightened that feeling.

CATHERINE, AGE 47
aged 41 at diagnosis

After I meditate, I cope just that little bit better. I've found that. My kids have even said, "Mum, you don't explode like you used to. Things just don't upset you as much as they used to". You know, I used to get upset if I dropped a bowl of sugar.

MARIANNE, AGE 49
aged 46 at diagnosis

Unless you have peace of mind and you get rid of all the hurt and anger, healing can't take place. It has certainly helped me enormously, so I give other people that advice.

MARGARET, AGE 61
aged 59 at diagnosis

I'm aware that there have been some changes—a much greater freedom to allow the child within to emerge; to really live in the present; to be much more open to experience of life in all its richness and glory; and an even deeper exploration of the spiritual journey.

PAT, AGE 60
aged 57 at diagnosis

With the help of meditation, I feel a very peaceful person within myself, with the added bonus of making new friends.

GERALDINE, AGE 42
aged 32 at diagnosis

In fact, I'm feeling very well indeed, in control of myself, my health and my life. I have had good reports from all my medical checks. I'm more relaxed about things in my life—I try not to worry and fuss, to be more peaceful and serene. I did try meditation but I still have a way to go there!

LYNNE, AGE 55
aged 52 at diagnosis

Now, for the first time, I live each day as it comes. It took me a long while to achieve and is just one of the rewards of meditation. And I finally came to know what I wanted to do with my life.

JOAN, AGE 54
aged 51 at diagnosis

It is a privilege. It's like being allowed to be older in the head than your chronological age. It's like the grandmother's wisdom, but getting it a bit sooner. Because you see things so differently. You see the importance of very little things. Things that don't cost anything to do. It gives you licence to say "no" to a whole lot of things. I mean, some people say you create your disease so that you can give yourself that licence because you've always wanted to say "no". I don't buy that at all: I didn't create my disease. But our lives are much quieter, in some ways much more serene. Much less frenetic. Much less having to do lots of things. I mean, our idea of a lovely day is to go the beach.

CATHERINE, AGE 47
aged 41 at diagnosis

Stress and Spirituality

For many women, the idea of being at peace whilst living with breast cancer might seem incongruous. No one would expect you to feel at peace in the first days, weeks or even months after diagnosis. As mentioned in Chapter 1, 'From Fear to Fact', women react differently to the diagnosis and it's important that you respect and honour the way *you* feel. You can't simply decide that peace is best and so, therefore, you're going to have it. To establish peace within ourselves usually takes considerable effort! The suggestions within this chapter are guidelines which I hope will assist you in finding *your* way to peace. As you can see from the quotes above, peace is expressed in many different ways but has an underlying common thread throughout.

This common thread is about who we are as women. Are we truly alive and connected to the world in which we live? Are we on track with whatever it is we feel we need to be doing in this lifetime? Have we resolved any grief, pain or hurt from the past? Are our relationships meaningful, nourishing and deeply satisfying? If the answer to any of these questions is 'no' then we cannot experience deep and profound peace and the joy which comes from feeling in tune with our life purpose. Breast cancer presents us with the possibility of healing the past and establishing a joyous relationship with each present moment.

You might find yourself wondering about the stresses in your life, how you've responded to them, and their possible contribution to your breast cancer. For some women that follows on from asking, 'Why me'?

Is there something I've done (or not done) which has contributed to my having this disease?

Many people with a life-threatening illness find that in the six to twenty-four month period before their diagnosis, they were under an unusual and considerable amount of stress. Sometimes the stress goes back much further and it's been a gradual accumulation to the point where the body's defences can no longer cope, whilst for others there was one particular event or series of events which preceded the illness.

We're living in a patriarchy, and it's essentially hostile, by its very nature, to women. It's not easy for women to express their grief, anger and outrage and to act against the oppression of individual men and patriarchy in general. Women are effectively punished for expressing their frustration and rage about what's done to them. So where does it go? If it doesn't have an outlet it stays inside you and it makes you sick. Anything you feel that doesn't find legitimate expression will find another form of expression. The connection between cancer and stress is well known. There are various personality profiles of the kind of people who get cancer. Those people who are very nice, who are in control of their feelings, who put other people first. Who in our society is most likely to have that kind of profile? Women!

DEB, AGE 40
aged 38 at diagnosis

Stress, of itself, is not a bad thing. Stress can also be seen as a challenge and we all feel satisfaction and fulfilment when we overcome challenging stresses in our lives. The problem arises when we feel *overwhelmed* by stress. Many women complain of feeling trapped, powerless or deeply affected by some major event in their lives in the period leading up to their breast cancer. Other women describe a sense of inner emptiness which, when their diagnosis is made, becomes increasingly demanding of their attention.

Most of us are unaware of the powerful influence our thoughts can have on our lives. If we habitually hold negative thoughts about ourselves and/or life it can have disastrous results. Many of us grew up being taught to put others first; that it was selfish to consider our own needs and make sure they were met; that our fulfilment as women could only come after everybody else's needs were met. Women have been expected to take care of everyone else. Many women place their children and partner's happiness or well-being before their own. Or they have a greater commitment to their work than to their own happiness. Our culture has very high expectations of the capabilities of women.

Over the past forty or more years, we've won the right to take on more than anyone, perhaps, could be expected to accomplish! For many of us now, not only do we competently run a household, raise and nourish children but we work full time. Indeed, many women are extraordinarily competent in the workplace.

For those of us who tend to be perfectionists, there's the added strain of having to get it absolutely right both inside and outside the home. This crushing pressure to constantly perform destroys our peace and exhausts our emotional energy.

Many of the quotes from women at the beginning of this chapter, and throughout the book, reflect the changed attitude that breast cancer has brought about; a change in priorities, a deeper regard for the present moment, a greater appreciation for the preciousness of life and each other, a richer understanding of ourselves and an increased awareness of what *is* truly important to us.

To have discovered these qualities within ourselves is a rich blessing. In some ways they give some meaning or purpose to the suffering that instigated these changed perceptions.

Many women find that, for the first time in their life, spiritual matters become important. Spirituality, to me, is about increasing our understanding of ourselves and our relationship to life and gives us a deeper sense of connectedness. For some people spirituality is integral to organised religion and may involve connection to people who are sympathetic to their faith. For others, it needn't have any formal association with a spiritual group or any religious context.

If your religion gives you strength and peace then your priest, rabbi or minister, a sympathetic member of the congregation or a trained pastoral counsellor might be able to give good spiritual support.

Spiritual support might also come through a group, psychologist or counsellor who helps you to understand and know yourself better. When we know, understand, accept and, if necessary, forgive ourselves and others, then we find peace. This isn't as difficult as it might sound.

For people who've never felt any deep connection with their spirituality it could be helpful to find someone who can listen without judgement or criticism and help you to explore your inner world. For many people it means getting in touch with their feelings for the first time. The world of our 'thinking' can be quite at odds with the world of our 'feelings'. Your feelings give a truer picture of how things *really* are within yourself.

Before leukaemia, I was just beginning to incorporate my spiritual beliefs into every aspect of my life. I'd been studying various religions and philosophical ideas since I was a young teenager, but with much greater intensity since the age of seventeen, when I learnt to meditate. Techniques of meditation, contemplation and reflection opened up a wonderful, but often turbulent, inner world in which I began to understand, forgive and accept myself. This process was greatly enhanced by the prospect of my death.

In the eighteen-month period before I became ill I had several stresses which shattered many of my dearly held beliefs. Spirituality became something I no longer dabbled in but was a real and profound force which permeated each moment. My diagnosis came at a time of great distress within my family. My brother Brenden, whom I adored, had just taken his own life, I'd moved to America to qualify as a teacher of yoga and meditation and then I'd separated from my husband within a few weeks of our arrival in this new country.

My life lay like shattered mirror fragments round my feet. In each fragment I saw a part of the picture that was myself. How to make it whole again? Where to turn? How to find healing? How to find peace? Where was wisdom? In looking at the fragments I was constantly reminded that healing lay within myself, that the answers lay within myself, that wholeness, resolution and peace could only be found within myself.

My personal belief is that we're spiritual beings who inhabit a body rather than the other way around. Our body is our spacesuit for planet earth and you can't come here if you don't have one! It's my responsibility to take care of my spacesuit but there'll come a time, when all is said and done, when I no longer need it and I can leave it aside. For me, it gives meaning or a framework in which to create healing; healing of the mind and spirit as well as the body.

Since 1984, many people have asked me to show them the rosy path to healing. They'll say, 'Tell me which diet will help. Tell me about vitamins, juices and how long to meditate. Tell me how not to die'. They want to be told all the things which they must *do* in order to heal themselves of their disease. Mostly, they don't want to know about the inner torment, fears, frustrations, anguish and despair which need to be addressed in order to truly *heal their life.*

If all our efforts are going into staying in a body at all costs, then we may be destined for disappointment. If our efforts go into healing ourselves of all that prevents us from truly living in each moment, then the rewards are certain and abundant.

The beginning of deep and unshakeable healing is to realise that the only question is, 'How shall I live this moment so that I experience peace'? That simple question implies that it's my responsibility to *choose* how to live this moment.

Each of us have the opportunity to embark upon this extra-ordinary inner journey to the heart of peace. For each of us the path will be different, and yet the same.

Prayer, reflection and meditation are avenues which can give us a direct experience of profound peace, love and joy—the hall-marks of spirituality and the basis of healing.

You might find that reading will increase your awareness of spirituality.

The Power of the Mind

Thoughts are powerful and we have thousands of them every day. Even though we think we're in control of our lives, we're often plagued by the incessant activity of the mind. Thoughts drift through in a constant stream. We underestimate the power they have over our lives.

To believe our bodies can be humming along healthily whilst

our minds are full of hurtful or negative thoughts of failure defies commonsense. How can we possibly have a well-functioning and enthusiastic immune system if our minds are full of fears, self-criticism or harsh judgements?

Are you aware of the thoughts you most frequently have? Do you habitually expect the best or worst in any situation? Do you hold judgements or criticisms of yourself, your family, friends and associates—seeing them through an habitual 'veil' of judgement?

Some people are worriers. They weren't born that way, they gradually developed—probably through childhood or adolescence. If there isn't something going on in their lives to worry about they feel insecure, and will often create a worry, just so they can be comfortable with their usual way of thinking.

Some women expect to be successful at whatever they attempt. And, not surprisingly, they are. There are others who always expect to fail. And they do. If you have an expectation of failure, then it's very likely you won't put all your enthusiasm and effort into whatever project is at hand. It's a self-perpetuating pattern of behaviour which ensures your thinking is 'true'. This 'truth' you hold about yourself is not a fixed law for you unless you choose to have it so. It's entirely up to you whether you're willing to make the effort to change. No one else can do it for you.

Imagination is a powerful tool we can use for this purpose. It's not enough for us to say we wish we weren't so negative about something. Often the negative program by which we're living has been in our subconscious since infancy, so to eradicate such deeply held notions requires real dedication.

A life-threatening illness has the possibility, if we're willing to allow it, of showing us how we've lived our lives up until now, and it gives us the opportunity to assess and decide if that's how we wish to continue.

I knew if I began to approach my life with more compassion, understanding and forgiveness then, regardless of the outcome of the disease, every day had the potential to be lived more peaceably. Even if I were to die, the peace and sense of hope this approach gave were clearly going to make the experience of dying as emotionally comfortable as possible.

To change the way we view the world seems a lot to ask, especially at a time when we're already under considerable stress. We might need to find other ways of looking at life because the ways we've been using up till now might not be helping us. They could even have been causing the very problems we now wish to overcome. We can be fearful of letting go habitual ways of thinking or doing things. Sometimes I felt it would be easier to give up my life rather than to let go cherished ways of thinking. In a way, I knew I could 'do' a good death, but I didn't know how to 'do' a good life!

Check to hear when you're putting yourself down, and stop, even if it's in mid-sentence. Change it to a positive.

Here's a list of words that we would all do better without! Letting them go can be a challenge but one with enormous benefits.

- *can't*   (usually means *won't*)
- *but*   (looking for an excuse)
- *if only*   (wanting it to be different from how it is)
- *should*   (who says?)
- *ought*   (who says?)
- *impossible*   (start thinking possible)
- *try*   (just *do* it!)

Instead of thinking what would be good and healing for me each day, I started to 'feel' what would be good for me. Gradually my language changed to include far more feeling words than thinking words. The mind is mostly preoccupied with the future, or chewing over the past, whereas the body is *always in the present moment*. When we bring the attention of the mind to the experience of the body, we're more easily able to enter the realms of feeling.

For many people, change is a frightening thing. The familiar is comfortable. Our negative thoughts are 'ours' and sometimes we'll go to great lengths to protect them, even when they're damaging to us, or at the very least, causing us stress. Sometimes we hold on to these old patterns of thinking because that was the way our mother or father always thought.

No one can claim to understand why any woman develops breast cancer. We search within and outside of ourselves for any understanding of its cause. Perhaps sickness is the body's cry of distress over emotional suffering. Perhaps it has something to do with the enormous cultural pressure to be 'super' women. Perhaps women are grieving deeply for the state of the world and our ailing mother earth. Perhaps, collectively, women are expressing their inability to feel in control of what's happening to them or to those they love. Focusing on the cause of breast cancer often leads women to believe that they're somehow responsible for their disease. These thoughts and the feelings they generate will dictate how we *see* that disease and other aspects of life. I haven't seen benefit experienced from claiming responsibility for *creating* disease, although some people feel that if they 'created' their disease then they're in a position to 're-create' health. I believe it's better to take responsibility for our *response* to having an illness. This is empowering and instead of asking, 'How did this happen to me'? we can ask, 'What can I do now that I'm *in* this situation'?

Many women have, for the first time, begun to address issues from the distant past because of their illness. These have included some terrible traumas of rape and sexual or emotional abuse. Often the memory of these experiences has been completely blotted out. It's only when we begin to investigate the nature of who we are and *why* we are the way we are, that we begin to discover a truer picture of our history.

In order for peace to be practical we must address these issues. We can't experience peace whilst ever there's unresolved turmoil, grief or hurt within. Once we make peace our goal, we begin to confront all the issues that stand in its way. Our history is constantly presented to us in the present moment. By increasing our awareness of our response to each moment, we gain a clearer picture about our feelings and our reactions which are born out of our history.

Depression

I remember at that time I was very tearful. I had no control over my emotions at all. I used to look at other people's lives and think mine was so hopeless; not hopeless, but that my life just didn't measure up. I didn't feel good about my life. Other people's lives seemed less messy, so much easier, they seemed to have a better run than I had. That occupied a lot of my time, when I was feeling negative. And I did feel negative, sometimes, when I was going through chemotherapy. Why had my life not been easier and nicer?

And then, after I finished chemotherapy, I felt terribly depressed. I was still having counselling: I was so grateful for that. Because I really, really felt depressed. I didn't know why, because I had everything to look forward to; the love and support of children, my friends and my family. And I didn't want to go on living. It just seemed too much of an effort. I was on Tamoxifen. I didn't take it for a few days. I just didn't want to keep on living. I don't know why that was, because it was after chemotherapy was all over. It would be so much easier and nicer, I thought, to die.

I find that extraordinary, looking back now. Absolutely extraordinary that I felt like that. It didn't last for a very long time. You see, I'd gone through my life not talking about myself to anyone. Never. Superficially, yes. But never ever talking about the real me. And I was doing this with this counselling.

I didn't feel hungry either. That's incredible, isn't it? So we talked about that and the counsellor said—I think it's because you're completely fatigued, worn out from a whole lot of things and that it's only temporary. Hang in there. Try and think of something in the future that you want to live for.

I couldn't think of anything. I couldn't think of anything at all. Not even my daughter's wedding.

There was nothing I was interested in and I really did want to die. I really did. I felt it would be fabulous to die.

It's only since I changed my life that I really am enjoying it. And I've learnt the value of me, the value of looking after myself, and putting me right there amongst everybody else. And I've learnt that it's the little things in life that are so important. And that you don't ignore them because you've got a bigger problem to think about. I'm talking about seeing friends regularly, the simple little things in life. And being open about myself and letting myself receive support too. All these things I didn't know before.

JACINTA, AGE 49
aged 47 at diagnosis

Depression is perhaps one of the most difficult feelings to live with. This is so for both you and those you live with. We tend to be more prone to depression when everything *isn't* going right. Often our feelings are attached to our test results. If we receive a 'bad' report, we plummet again to the depths of despair. 'I've been doing it all right—why aren't I getting better?' By resolving the issues which surface through our depression, we can make great gains in knowing ourselves. In fact, more healing takes place when we're working through the issues involved in depression, fear, frustration and so on than when we're flying high and feeling good. The depressions I experienced were abysmal, and yet I learnt greatly from them.

Depression is very often a mask for unexpressed feelings. Behind the depression you might well find anger, resentment, feelings of powerlessness, hopelessness, helplessness and being trapped. These feelings need to be accessed and expressed in order to be free of both those feelings and the depression which masked them. One of the finest ways of resolving depression by accessing feelings is through the practice of meditation.

When a sense of hopelessness begins to descend it can be difficult to shake off its influence. For those who experience such dark moments, take heart, you're not alone. It's a lonely road to walk because reaching out to others is made almost impossible by our own paralysing pain.

It *is* possible to change our experience of depression.
- First, we need to acknowledge we're feeling depressed.
- Second, we need to *want* to change our perception.

We can implement small changes to our daily program.
Things like:
- Listening to a relaxation/meditation tape at least twice a day.
- Getting out of bed by a certain time.
- Showering every day.
- Tidying up one small thing each day (for instance, the top of the dresser, a drawer, corner, bookshelf or cupboard).
- Putting fresh sheets on the bed, a clean towel in the bathroom.
- Eating at the table with a tablecloth and cutlery.
- Dusting one room.
- Placing flowers throughout the house.
- Playing music that's new to you or an old favourite.
- Washing the dishes, drying them, putting them away.

These simple things are the beginnings of affirming that we're worthy of love and respect. Don't let yourself become overwhelmed by what needs to be done. Accomplish one new thing each day and acknowledge you've achieved something. Don't focus on what's not right, focus on and approve of your efforts to change. Endeavour to see the glass as half full rather than half empty.

As soon as you feel you can reach out to someone, make a telephone call to a 'help-line', a support group or a counsellor. I know it's scary, and I also know it's possible to pass through the darkest hours but emerge into a brighter way of perceiving life. It takes courage and you have what it takes. You'll notice it becomes easier when you find good company in which to make your recovery.

Positive imaging can bring our desired goals very close indeed and give us confidence to go on believing. Be prepared to give up your unrealistic expectations of yourself or others' expectations of you. This is not a dress rehearsal. You're not warming up for the big event. This *is* your life. This is it, *this* moment, *right* here, *right* now.

What you're living now is the real thing, so feel challenged to take the risks which come with changing your way of thinking. You're perfect and acceptable just the way you are. Give yourself permission to make mistakes. Celebrate your mistakes as a valuable means of learning something. A so-called mistake then takes on a new meaning. If you've acknowledged there's a better way of doing something then you've gained new and valuable knowledge.

Love your imperfections as much as the things for which you allow yourself credit, because they're all part of the same you. Stop judging yourself. One cannot release thoughts of negativity through rejection, only through love. So be nice to yourself and stop scaring yourself. We spend so much time and money on scaring ourselves half-silly. We do this by watching scary movies, reading depressing articles about breast cancer, and so on. Create a safe, warm and loving world around you, not one where you perceive attack lurking around every corner. Many women perceive their cancer cells, as 'out to get them'. Change your perception. Cancer cells are weak, unintelligent wimps who've forgotten how to behave appropriately.

Some people feel there *is* no safe place in which they can freely express their emotions. It's important to recognise that we *have* feelings; then give ourselves *permission* to have those feelings; then find a place in which we can *feel* the feelings. I often need to retreat into the silence of solitude in order to allow these feelings to be recognised and felt and thus released. This is often in meditation or prayer, or it might be in the form of a walk along the beach, a visit to an empty church, time-out in the country or with a friend.

Some women will experience depression while they're having radiotherapy. It can be very frightening to feel so down when you're trying to cope with the treatments. This depression is a direct side-effect of your treatment and is not how you'll always feel. Ask people around you to remind you that this will pass and that it's not how you normally are. The depression may continue for a couple of weeks after you've finished several weeks of radiotherapy (see Radiotherapy in Chapter 6).

The Feel-the-Feeling-Formula

This simple formula works well in almost all situations. The problem with most of our unpleasant feelings is that we *resist* them. *Then* we have to suppress them in order to continue functioning 'normally'. Once we give ourselves permission 'not to cope', 'to feel fearful', 'to feel angry', 'to feel overwhelmed' or whatever else it might be, we find peace once more. By using this formula we can allow our feelings to exist without judgement or criticism. The process goes like this:

1 First we acknowledge the feeling,
2 Then we give ourselves permission to have the feeling, and
3 Then we simply feel the feeling.

For instance, the steps might go something like this:

1 'This is how it feels to be Petrea feeling fearful.'
2 'It's OK for me to feel this way. I've never been in this situation before.'
3 'This is how fear feels for me.'

Paradoxically, to acknowledge that I'm afraid and giving myself permission to feel afraid is the first step towards being released from fear! Likewise, to acknowledge I'm feeling overwhelmed and that it's not surprising I'm feeling overwhelmed, is the first step towards feeling back in control.

The fastest way out of feelings is through them.

Peace is not a wishy-washy state of passive acceptance. It's a dynamic state in which we embrace whatever *is* going on in our lives. If we feel anger, fear, despair, panic, outrage, resentment or whatever, then bring it out in the open, acknowledge it, express it and then you'll more easily be able to let go of it. *This* is what peace is about. It's not sitting on a hotbed of emotions hoping or pretending that they don't exist. Give them your wholehearted permission to come out into the light, to be expressed and understood.

Many people are afraid to express how they feel to someone else because they fear ridicule or abuse of the trust they've extended. It's important to be respectful of our feelings and to choose wisely those with whom we seek to share our vulnerability. This may be with our partner, friend, support group or counsellor.

When we realise our life has been one of self-criticism, doubt or despair and there *is* a better way, it's as if a light has been switched on and we take our first steps out of emotional darkness into our true self. Then we can be comfortable but not complacent with our imperfections.

To find love and acceptance within ourselves is a wondrous experience, and, yet, we cannot find the light of this love and acceptance until we've acknowledged the darkness. By bringing to the forefront of our awareness the unresolved issues of the past, we begin to heal all that stands in the way of us feeling deeply at peace.

There's no room in our lives for ancient history. Forgive the past, release its influence, and move on. Ultimately, we take responsibility for ourselves by dealing with what's causing us pain, ridding ourselves of guilt or any other negative emotion, and proceeding with greater self-acceptance. With self-acceptance comes acceptance of others, and of the events in our lives. When we begin to acknowledge the love in others, we begin to experience more of our own loving nature. Trust in your own ability to find peace, joy and self-love.

I don't mean to oversimplify this process or say it's easy to do. For instance, to deal with childhood sexual abuse is an ongoing process which may involve talking about, re-living or expressing the abuse in some form, feeling the outrage, the powerlessness, the despair or whatever other emotions are bound up with the experience before forgiveness or resolution is possible. *Dealing* with these experiences *is* the path to peace, understanding and wisdom.

Everything in our culture is geared to overload our senses and our minds with information. Actually to stop, listen and feel is a new experience for some people. It embodies the beginning of relaxation and meditation. It connects us with each unfolding moment—each one new, never to be repeated; each one precious and full of potential. The heart understands these words easily. The mind questions, tries to distort, attempts to complicate. The heart is still by comparison. Learn to trust stillness and the knowledge which arises out of it. Allow yourself the luxury of peace. Learn to value it as your most precious asset. With this attitude it's surprising how many worries take care of themselves and never become real.

It's then *our* decision whether now is a good time for us to deal with whatever feeling we might be experiencing, or whether we want to acknowledge it exists and decide to deal with it at another time.

When panic or anxieties assail you, put them on hold and spend some time with the techniques of relaxation and letting go. If they're important concerns or panics, rest assured they'll be there for your attention later. Don't fight them off. Simply use the practice of deeply connecting with the senses of your body through the techniques of relaxation. Having done that, practise being at peace, practise trusting that everything *is* all right, that everything is unfolding in its own perfect time. In the beginning, it could seem an insurmountable task.

Many people find it helpful to develop a little ritual around these fears or panics. Perhaps you could visualise putting them into the basket beneath a hot-air balloon and then loosening the ropes, letting them soar up and away. Or, seeing those fears surrounded in light, melting away into light. Or, place your problems in a small boat at the edge of a river, give it a push until the current bears it away downstream. Find something which seems appropriate for you, perhaps some method which jumps out from your own lifestyle.

I have to rationalise every time I get that very lonely feeling, a deserted feeling almost, and I think, no, this is really good because I have time to myself, I don't have to worry about anyone else, and I can take care of myself, and I do rationalise it in a way, but it does not change the fact that I do feel bereft.

LOUISE, AGE 52
aged 51 at diagnosis

Anger certainly played a part in the beginning. I'd always had this lump in my breast, since I was twenty-seven. It was nothing new. And I'd been very conscientious about having it mammogrammed at regular intervals. I'd gone the year before, and there was nothing wrong. And then that year, I'd been put on hormone replacement therapy, because I wasn't feeling well. I think there's an attitude in the medical profession these days that, for anyone in their fifties, anything that's wrong, put them on hormone replacement therapy. Bingo! You've got a cure for whatever's wrong. So I went on those, and in that short space of time, the lump not only became cancerous, but was very aggressively so. It went to my lymph nodes and it was oestrogen driven, so every time I took a hormone replacement tablet, the cancer said, Yippee! Thank you very much!

I was really peeved about that. Really peeved. It just seemed so unfair. There was no one to be angry at and I got terribly depressed.

But if I hadn't got cancer, then I wouldn't have made changes in my life. So, one can say that it's had a very positive effect. I'd rather not have cancer. I'm not going to be stupid about it. But, having said that, the fact of the matter is, my life is a lot better, and I'm a lot happier than I was.

JEANNIE, AGE 54
aged 50 at diagnosis

Anger

Jeannie expresses really well what many women experience; non-expression of feelings can often lead to depression. The fact is Jeannie was angry, but she didn't express anger. She rationalised it but didn't initially express it. Many women with breast cancer say things like, 'What's the point of getting angry. It's not going to change anything!' That might well be true, it might not change the situation we're in, but to *not* express it means that we end up feeling powerless, helpless, trapped or hopeless, all of which lead to depression and/or resentment. People who can express their anger in a healthy manner are able to recognise that even though their anger mightn't change anything, it's important that it be *acknowledged* and *expressed*. Those who have difficulty in expressing anger tend not even to acknowledge it. It is always better to express how we feel, even if it's only to ourselves. Don't negate or 'put down' how you feel.

I don't know if selfish is really the right word but I care more about what happens to me than what happens to other people. I was a really giving person and I was always listening to people's problems and helping all the time and I got pleasure out of doing that. Only now I do it to a degree, and then I turn around and

75

say, "Sort it out yourself. I've got my own things to worry about". I'm more likely to say what I want and how I feel. I used to worry about nothing to worry about!

I guess there was a tremendous amount of anger. When my husband was first diagnosed with cancer, I felt, because his was cancer with secondaries—and melanoma with secondaries is not good territory to be in. I felt—wow. It's up to me. I'm going to have to bring this family up by myself, because there's quite a distinct possibility that he'll die. So I felt that there was a lot of pressure on me to be healthy. I felt I've just got to survive this. And you know, that was when he was diagnosed.

Then when I was diagnosed it was like—help! Who's going to look after this family? So we made all sorts of plans, we had to, for our own head stuff. We had to make plans so that we knew that there was something in place. The children were very young. So it was a very difficult experience. It made me realise that I couldn't do it all on my own, and I needed some friends and I'd never been very good at making friends, I'm still not to some degree. I'd had a lot of business friends but once I left business I had nothing left in common with them. I had a couple of really good friends who were very good.

When I was first diagnosed and my husband wasn't "there" for me, I was very angry. I didn't recognise it. I mean it took a lot of support group work and things like that to get into what was really bothering me, why I was so angry. And that was probably very good, because through support group work and weekends away with Petrea, you certainly learn to know yourself a lot better. And that's very important to me; to know myself a lot better.

CATHERINE, AGE 47
aged 41 at diagnosis

They are very 'nuts and bolts'—the medical—you do this test and that test. But the terror—you know, I wake at 2 a.m. and I'm lying beside a loving husband and the terror drops into my mind,

"Am I going to die—what's going to happen to me? I've got can-cer". Nobody deals with that.

HELEN, AGE 42
aged 34 at diagnosis

Many of us are afraid of our own anger. I didn't think I had any anger! I thought I was a peaceful person who didn't get upset about things. What I realised was that I was a 'peace at any price' person and I was sitting on a volcano of anger and resentment. I don't think I even knew what anger was and I'd substitute other words like, 'I feel depressed'. Like Jeannie earlier, much of my depression was a shield for anger. I realised that in my childhood I'd never seen healthy anger healthily expressed.

Some people are easily able to transcend their anger through the techniques of meditation and forgiveness, while others need to find suitable outlets to really get their emotions moving. There's nothing negative about experiencing anger. It's a natural emotion. What *is* negative is to keep the anger inside where it can only fester and cause resentment. Anger changes the chemical balance in the body and is detrimental when not discharged.

To find an appropriate way for your anger to flow out is important. In this way you use up the effect of these chemicals. It can be difficult sometimes within our suburban environments to freely express anger without causing neighbours concern or at least raised eyebrows. It's inappropriate to express our anger through physical violence, but there are many excellent ways of getting it out without offence to other members of society.

Many women have great difficulty in expressing anger. It might feel really inappropriate or totally out of character for a woman to express her anger. For these women, the acknowledgement and understanding of *why* they're angry is the beginning of the process of being able to let it go. Often, behind the anger, are tears of grief, hurt, rejection, powerlessness, and so on.

Even though I had blocked off the memory of it, I still had the feelings.

DEB, AGE 40
aged 38 at diagnosis

There are many events in our lives when we feel infuriated and yet we might never have expressed the feelings long held in. What about an ex-spouse who's making things very difficult financially; or in-laws forever interfering with our family; or a boss who constantly derides or puts us down; or a parent who abused us (sexually, emotionally, physically or psychologically) when we were young? These situations are often a potent source of outrage, guilt and feelings of helplessness, and it can be quite confusing to feel murderous rage towards someone for whom you once felt (or feel) love or respect. Many women then feel guilty, ashamed and frightened by the intensity of these feelings. To express the anger in a safe environment is essential to its healthy resolution.

Many find it really helpful to *write* about an experience to which they reacted angrily. This is especially true of women who find it a difficult feeling to express. Writing about an experience can be done in privacy and the written expression gives you a safe avenue by which to get in touch with your anger. To do this exercise, set aside some time when you won't be disturbed. Begin this exercise by writing in a factual manner about the details of the situation which caused you anger. As you recall the situation you will find that you begin to experience the feelings associated with it. Continue with the writing process and, as feelings arise, give expression to them in your writing. Even though this process may be difficult to begin with, persevere until you *feel* the emotions the experience brought to you. Often, this process ends in the healthy expression of tears and the beginning of healing. Very often, behind the anger, are tears of helplessness, grief, sadness, powerlessness, and so on. These tears are healing and, once shed, allow us to live with a deeper knowledge, understanding and acceptance of ourselves and of our history.

If you know you have a problem with unresolved anger, reach out for help and find a healthy expression for it. This could be through a friend, counsellor, support group, through the writing exercise or through a professional you trust.

Guilt

Guilt paralyses our actions and achieves nothing. It brings only oppression and fear of punishment. To feel guilt presupposes we've committed actions not acceptable to the mores of our society, church, family or our self. If we believe we've erred, it reinforces our sense of unworthiness; that we're somehow not acceptable as we are. If we've done something for which we feel shame or are genuinely sorry, then let there be remorse. Honest remorse comes from the heart, not from the mind. Once we've felt, acknowledged and apologised for what we did, if appropriate, we can learn from it and go on enlightened.

Until my illness I felt a terrible guilt because I believed we were meant to be perfect and I knew I wasn't. I tried so hard to maintain an image to the world which said, 'I know who I am; I know where I'm going; I'm a capable, efficient, intelligent person and everything's just fine'. However, I felt a fraud and a hypocrite, knowing none of these things were true. It was far from a happy way to live. On the outside, I tried to maintain the image of coping with everything, while on the inside there was the constant voice of self-criticism.

It has taken a lot of determination not only to become aware of this negative, self-defeating tendency, but also to stop doing it! For some of us accomplishing self-acceptance is a life-long task. Being aware and more accepting of myself helps me to be able to say, 'I know my heart's in the right place, and I'll be out there tomorrow doing my best'. And instead of self-criticism, I can go to sleep with a peaceful heart. I feel more responsible for my life and my actions, and yet I don't feel the weight of the world resting on my shoulders, or that the 'bogey man' (or God) is out to get me. Self-acceptance makes self-forgiveness unnecessary. It's OK to be human. It's OK to make mistakes. In fact, if we don't acknowledge mistakes, we'd just go on making them. When we take total responsibility for our actions we're free to leave the darkness of guilt and to move into the light of self-acceptance and understanding. Guilt is negative and keeps us bound whilst responsibility is mature and liberating. For some of us, the advent of a life-inhibiting disease is the impetus to free ourselves from guilt and fear.

I realised that I *needed* my guilt in order to stop me from living. Once I'd made a commitment to life, to fully living, the armies of guilt were on my doorstep. The first step is that we have to be willing to let go our guilt. I had to be willing to accept myself and my actions as they were. In accepting them, they no longer kept me prisoner. This is healing. To heal ourselves of our past judgements, criticisms and self-hatred we need to be willing to be made new and whole *now*. Healing is the relinquishing of guilt and fear. Health is the experience of peace and acceptance.

Guilt and fear had been my constant companions. To be willing to let them go and replace them with forgiveness, acceptance and love is the healing of my life. We don't have to live a long life in order to be healed. Each moment presents the possibility of healing. It would be more of a tragedy to live to a hundred with guilt and fear as companions than to die much younger with peace and acceptance.

There are two meditation practices on Rainbows to Heal: one for self-healing and the second one is for extending healing to someone else (see Petrea King Products). This tape can be an invaluable tool in self-healing. Details of tapes are given at the back of the book.

Blame
Many people with cancer blame someone or some situation in

their life for their disease. They're often angry with themselves also for having allowed the person/situation to have such an effect upon them.

We use blame for many different reasons but each and every one will come back to us not wanting to 'own' our responsibility. Society reinforces this attitude in many ways. We blame the weather. We blame circumstances. We blame other people. We blame society or the government. We go out of our way to avoid taking responsibility. When we accept our responsibility it means we can decide to make changes in our lives. If we continue to blame outside circumstances, what we're really saying is, 'If only *you* or *it* would change, I'd be happier'.

It can be easy to blame others for the predicament in which we find ourselves. It's often so tempting to believe that the other person made us feel that way. However, no one can make us feel anything. It is our *reaction* to what happens to us that will dictate how we experience any situation. Not taking responsibility for those reactions exemplifies 'victim-consciousness'. Feeling a help-less victim never leads to peace and resolution. It's easy to feel vic-timised and, at one time or another, we've all felt so demeaned. Blaming others is the antithesis of taking responsibility. Thoughts which we hold in our minds will dictate the reality we experience and it becomes our choice as to what we wish to hold there. Victim-consciousness needs to be eradicated from our whole being if the healing of our life is to take place.

Forgiveness

We often believe, mistakenly, that a painful relationship from the past is best forgotten. Yet, more often than not, it isn't for-gotten: the painful memories are just buried deep down inside ourselves. We could say we don't wish to be reminded of the pain it caused us. But the fact is, it's *still* causing us pain and we're therefore *still* in relationship with that person or situation. The person perhaps is no longer physically present in our lives, yet their influence is still there. Quite likely, at the time of being hurt, we made some 'laws' about how we would henceforth live our lives.

Laws like:

- *'I won't let anyone in too close or I'll be hurt.'*
- *'I'd better get my needs met first, otherwise I'll miss out.'*
- *'All men just want sex.'*
- *'If I'm not too ambitious then I can't fail.'*
- *'Life's hard.'*
- *'I'll never get it right.*

When someone in our life has hurt us—even though that person might now be dead—we remain in a relationship with them. It's as if there were a rope stretched between that person and ourselves; we're still holding on hard to our end of the rope. When we let go our end, it sets free a lot of energy previously trapped by the negativity held in that relationship. We might need to let go that rope a hundred times before we're successful in totally forgiving the person, situation or our actions within that situation. We can then learn from the experience and move on. Many people have no desire to forgive those who've hurt them in the past. We can almost savour our hurts as avenues for us to feel righteous indignation. To let go the resentment or bitterness also means to let go the righteous indignation.

By forgiving the past, we can cultivate compassion for others, the compassion which we'd like to have extended to ourselves. We all make mistakes. Recognise them as opportunities to learn something new. They're there for our education, not to carry around with us for an eternity. Acknowledge the resentment, forgive the person or situation, accept it, and move on. In this way, we continue to grow. Held resentments and bitterness cause stagnation and disease.

To forgive is to let go the past. It embodies the ability to respond wholeheartedly to the present without the pain or clutter from the past. Sometimes forgiveness is easy and, sometimes, exceedingly difficult!

We sacrifice the possibility of peace today whilst ever we carry the trauma of the past into each present moment. Allow yourself the opportunity to let go the pain of unforgivingness. It's *you* who suffers whilst ever you hold onto the pain.

Forgiving the person is not *the same as condoning the behaviour or action.*

The behaviour might be totally unacceptable, but that doesn't make the person unacceptable. Perhaps it's easier to understand when we think about a young child who's learning about appropriate behaviour. A child might do something which is very cruel and it's right that we should express anger at their behaviour. To disapprove of their behaviour whilst maintaining love for the child is quite possible. We seem to forget this as people grow older, believing that they should know how to behave. If we believe *they* should know how to behave, we're also affirming that *we* should know also! This may well lay the foundations for further personal guilt and judgement.

To forgive ourselves is perhaps the greatest challenge of all. It's extraordinary to me to see how incredibly harsh and unforgiving I used to be when I made a mistake. If anybody else did the same thing I wouldn't hesitate to tell them that it was OK to make mistakes. Just pick yourself up, apologise if necessary, learn from the experience and move on.

If we constantly drag the past into the present then we're always living our past. And, in so doing, we ensure our future is a replica of our past. To forgive myself means to let the past be buried. In this way we can learn from experiences and then approach each moment as being fresh and new. To constantly judge myself for my past is to sacrifice the present and future to the fears of yesterday.

There are two meditation practices on Gift of Forgiveness: one is for self-forgiveness and the second one is for extending forgiveness to someone else (see Petrea King Products). These practices have proved very useful for many women wanting to develop a more compassionate view of themselves and for resolving difficulties from the past.

Communication

Communication is the life-blood of any relationship. Much of what's discussed in this chapter is about communication. Sometimes that communication is with ourselves, for instance, when we recognise and acknowledge our own needs and feelings. Sometimes it's in acknowledging our feelings and needs to those we love. The intricacies of communication between family members is often very complex. Much is conveyed through body language, lack of affirmative action, intonation and emphasis as with anything which is actually put into words.

For some, communication flows effortlessly. For others, it's a difficult and painful process. Those for whom communication is difficult have often come from families where emotions weren't aired or were inappropriately expressed. If this is your background, be gentle and compassionate with yourself. Don't put yourself down because you feel unskilled in the use of words. Practise with a loved-one. You might need to exert yourself if talking about your feelings is unfamiliar to you. Turn it into an adventure by taking small risks; then acknowledge your accomplishment.

Sometimes shared tears are more healing than all the medicine in the world. It gives us the opportunity to experience a deeper and more profound intimacy when we can communicate our distress and fears. To communicate at such a level is a first step towards healing.

Communication, of course, isn't always verbal. Words are a construction of the mind. More often, it's the subtle inflection, emphasis, posture or gesture which touches or repels us. On occasions, silence conveys more than volumes of clever speech. When we're faced with the pain of another and feel helpless to effect any change, another language becomes appropriate. The language of touch, a meeting of the eyes, a smile or hug can speak more eloquently than words. In such circumstances, if you listen to the language of your heart, it will guide your actions and words, so that they convey love, understanding and compassion.

The gentle touch of a loving hand conveys much to those who are too weary or ill to speak. Hands of love can convey all we've ever learnt of compassion, trust, peace and acceptance. Let your hands become a channel that conveys your wisdom, serenity and faith. Your touch is far more eloquent than mere words.

Visualisation Techniques

Visualisation techniques or guided imagery provide one of the most powerful tools for changing the negative programming in our minds. They use our imagination in a powerful way which can actually bring about physiological changes in our bodies. We have no consciousness of the functioning of our immune system, yet it's still busy about its work without our active participation.

Some people are more visually oriented than others. Some spend hours fantasising or daydreaming; some claim it's better than the real thing! Spend a moment thinking about a holiday on a beautiful tropical island. Think of the golden sands, the vibrant colours in the waters surrounding this island, the vast, clear, blue dome of the sky above, the palms swaying in a soft, cooling breeze, the sunlight enveloping your body in warmth, the sound of the waves flowing gently in, gently out. Probably, at the very least, you experienced flashes of colours and isolated images even whilst just reading the words. Our more visual readers would perhaps have experienced much more. Some probably even smelt the sea air, heard the gentle ebb and flow of the waves and felt the sand beneath their feet! There will be others who found that while reading even these few sentences they took a deeper breath and became slightly more relaxed.

Try another one. Let the image of a lemon, fresh from the tree and warm from the sunshine come into your mind. Now, in your mind's eye imagine cutting it in half, holding it above you and squeezing the warm, lemony juice into your mouth. Imagine the juice running through your mouth. Its astringent freshness waking up your tastebuds. What happened? Did you produce a lot of saliva in your mouth? Here's another. A blackboard with a teacher standing beside it. She looks at you with a mischievous gleam in her eye as she scrapes her long fingernails down the board from top to bottom. What happened that time? This last example probably produced strongly felt but less tangible sensations in your body. An overall shiver perhaps?

These examples demonstrate in a very simple way the connection between your mind and your body. You can see how quickly your body reacts to these images within your mind. The brain produces an instantaneous response to these thoughts even though there is no tropical island, lemon or blackboard in sight. When we hold positive, healing thoughts in our mind every cell 'feels' the confidence and caring that such thoughts bring. Science has now found many chemicals and hormones secreted by the brain which are produced in direct response to these thoughts and feelings. You can send soothing and comforting thoughts or feelings out to needy areas of your body by holding in your mind some suitable image that's calming, and letting the effects of that image flow out. So, also, you can create a dynamic and vibrant feeling throughout your body by holding a more powerful image.

If, in our mind's eye, we're projecting positive, vibrant images then they become our expectation of the future. Choose images from your own inner storehouse of imagination. You'll undoubtedly find the right key to unlock your own particular creative path to healing. Some could say it's not being realistic to project a positive image when we've been told we're dying. Surely what matters is how we live every moment. Believe me, to practise dying all the time gets really boring! People sometimes forget that even though we might have a shortened life-span, right now we're living—not dying.

To be surrounded by beauty uplifts the spirit. A bowl of flowers, a sunset, a child's smile, leaves in the sunshine, clouds, sunlight on water—all these things act as powerful and uplifting images.

We need to be diligent in watching the images which come into our minds. It's useful to have a powerful and positive image to place there whenever we detect a depressing or pessimistic attitude arising.

A very practical way of strengthening this exercise is to spend several sessions each day implanting these images into the mind. Firstly, you must find an image which seems appropriate to you. Many people don't really know what they want. They only know what they *don't* want. They know they don't want to die, for instance. Yet they have no clear image in their minds of how they really want to live. For many people life just happens to them. We experience a richness in our lives when we actually have a goal to aim for and then work towards it.

Many people have difficulty in accepting chemotherapy or radiotherapy as a positive help to themselves. Often it's looked upon as a necessary evil. It's really important to rectify this attitude. If you experience the treatment as a toxic, poisonous substance going into your body, it's very likely to cause you more side-effects than if you believe, and can 'see', this substance as liquid gold pouring its healing power into your body. We *do* have the power to choose what we hold in our minds. If we've chosen to have drug therapy then we can follow up that choice with positive feelings and images about the outcome of the treatment. The same principle applies to radiotherapy. Those rays can be powerful forces of destruction or they can be powerful, shining images of healing light.

Drawing can be very useful in helping to clarify how we really feel about our disease, its treatment and the response of our immune system. Sometimes we can *think* we're positive, and yet when we draw our disease, therapy or immune system, another image might well emerge. Our subconscious attitudes and feelings are easily visible through our drawings. I often use drawings to help people understand what's really going on in their minds. On one sheet of paper the person draws their disease; on another sheet their treatment; and on a third sheet they draw their immune system. These drawings can then be discussed and the fears or anxieties evident in the drawings can be aired.

It might seem necessary to be at least a rudimentary artist to work with drawings. This couldn't be further from the truth. All that's necessary is a willingness to explore. The people in the picture can be very simply drawn though it's better not to make them stick figures. It's preferable to work with white paper and coloured pencils or crayons. Felt-tip pens aren't suitable as no gradation is possible in shading.

Some people have difficulty in actually 'seeing' any images at all when they attempt to visualise. Drawing the visualisation can often be helpful in focusing the mind upon the chosen image.

Another suggestion for those who find it difficult to visualise an image is to work only with light or colour. If you're using a tape which includes a visualisation, then perhaps just go with the sound of the voice or music or the atmosphere of what's being said, rather than judging yourself for not being able to 'see' the picture created on the tape. Self-judgement or criticism is the antithesis of what the visualisation is designed for.

To experience deep peace and love in our lives is healing. When minds and spirits are healed we're creating the very best environment for physical healing. It's up to us how we're going to create peace in our lives. The peace is always there and yet we need to make a conscious decision for peace. Even on the windiest, wettest, greyest day, if you can get above the clouds, you'll find the sun shining brightly in a clear, blue sky.

Several of the tapes I've produced rely on the use of images of nature to instil a sense of peace and profound relaxation. In this state of deep relaxation, your body, mind and spirit know what needs to be done for your healing in each of these levels. We can use these images to work with forgiveness, increasing self-esteem, improving communication, healing and letting go of the stresses we have in our lives. The more we're able to control what goes on in our mind, the more we'll realise the potential we have in being able to choose which thoughts we wish to entertain and which ones we wish to let go of.

Many of the meditation practices listed in Petrea King Products at the back of the book have been found useful in helping people to create an inner environment for healing.

Making Goals

People sometimes experience conflict between living in the present moment and making goals for the future. It's healthy to have short-term, mid-term and long-term goals. Short-term goals might include finishing a particular project, cleaning the house, planting bulbs for the spring, painting the back porch, learning to meditate, and so on. Mid-term goals might include planning a holiday after treatment, studying a course or subject which interests you, completing projects which have been stagnant for too long. Long-term goals might include buying your dream home, planning an overseas holiday, moving to the country, holding your first exhibition of craftwork, attending your son's graduation, and so on.

Meditation

Meditation is the state of being fully aware in the present moment. The *practice* of meditation is any activity which facilitates the experience of being fully aware in the present moment. It's simple to learn and with regular practice brings a great sense of well-being. This can range from greater peace of mind, to a relaxed body. Meditation also releases energy within the body which can be used for healing.

Meditation can give us the impetus to implement and maintain a program for our healing. It affirms our own inner healing power and it activates the wisdom of healing within our body.

More than anything else, meditation will give you the finest energy needed for healing. Your mind isn't separate from your body, your emotions aren't separate from your body. As human beings, each of us is an integrated whole. The thoughts which we hold in our minds affect the functioning of our bodies. The feelings we have, whether acknowledged or ignored, have an effect on our bodies.

One of the most powerful tools for change is the technique of meditation. There are many techniques and the best is the one that works for you. There's no right technique, no higher or lower technique—nor is there one teacher. There are as many techniques as there are people. Allow yourself the freedom to find a right technique and a right teacher that works for you.

Meditation re-establishes the body's own equilibrium. You'll notice your breathing begins to slow down, the heart-rate and blood pressure drop. Your muscles relax and physiologically you come to rest as the mind begins to settle and a sense of ease and peace is experienced. There's no quicker nor better way to allow the chemicals of stress to subside to normal levels than the practice of meditation.

Meditation is like relaxation for the mind. It's very simple. Just as we bring our awareness to the various muscles in our bodies and allow them to soften and relax, so we observe the thoughts and feelings which pass through our mind. Observe and let go. An analogy I often use is that meditation is like sitting deep below the ocean, at rest on the ocean floor. The thoughts are like waves on the distant surface. Each wave dissolving back into stillness. They don't disturb our peace.

Another way to think of meditation is to imagine that your awareness is the 'whole vast dome of the sky'; thoughts, feelings, beliefs, judgements and sensations are like the clouds which drift across this sky. Some clouds are easy to observe the way some thoughts are easy to observe. Others are far more difficult and the mind wants to leap in and have a good 'think' or 'worry'. Sometimes the clouds (thoughts) are little white fluffy ones like, 'What's for dinner?' and sometimes they're big steely grey ones like, 'I get my biopsy results tomorrow!' The art and practice of meditation is to keep your awareness as if it were the *whole* sky. These thoughts (clouds) pass through your mind but you don't get lost in the cloud. The moment you forget your awareness and become absorbed in the thought, your vision and perspective become clouded. Observe and let go. If you find you've started being busy with the thoughts, just let them go again. Do the same with feelings which arise, not judging, not criticising yourself for having them. Let them come to pass. Observe and let go. Be an ocean of awareness, not focusing on any particular thought or feeling. Be patient with yourself throughout your practice sessions. Treat meditation like a new adventure into unexplored territory: a journey within yourself.

When we physically relax our muscles, we 'let go' the body. We find that we can simply observe the body and its sensations. Who *is* this observer? Then, by observing the activity in our mind—its chatter, judgements, beliefs, attitudes, thoughts, feelings—we can also 'let go' the mind. Again, we experience a 'witnessing' of the mind. And again, who *is* this observer? One who watches the body, but is *not* the body. One who watches the mind, but is *not* the mind. We realise that we are *not* our body, *not* our personality and *not* our mind. When we're at one with this 'witness' of our body/mind then we experience a profound sense of 'being'. In this simple state of 'being' lies all peace, silence and bliss.

Meditation also gives us the opportunity to heal our minds of their fears, anxieties and apprehensions. It gives us the chance to *hear* the still small voice within. Many people find their intuitive powers increase enormously with the regular practice of meditation.

Frequently, the benefits of meditation are not experienced during the practice itself. Suddenly, whilst you're driving the car or in the shower, you'll find you have an answer to something which has been puzzling you, or you'll know the solution to a problem you've had for a long time. Inspiration seems to flow more easily and a lightness of spirit seems to pervade your world.

Ingredients for Meditation

You'll need three things in order to learn to meditate. The first one is *motivation*. Those of us who have an illness, feel stressed, panicky or fearful have all the ingredients necessary to provide motivation! The goal of peace of mind is definitely achievable and you deserve to have it.

Secondly, you'll need *effort* in order to put into practice the techniques of meditation. Thinking about meditating, reading about it, hearing of others' experiences will likely inspire your levels of motivation, however, *you* will need to put in the effort in order to experience the benefits of its regular practice.

To sustain motivation and effort you'll need *determination*. Sometimes the 'fire' can go out of our practice and with it can go our motivation. There are often 'dry' patches in our practice when our meditations don't seem to be producing any new or exciting information or experiences. At these times, we need to quietly continue with our practice without making judgements or evaluating our performance.

Practicalities of Meditation

I suggest you practise the techniques of relaxation and meditation regularly, preferably twice a day. You'll need to find out what the ideal length of time is for you; also how frequently you need to meditate in order to feel a real benefit. Some people gain all the benefits in the first ten to fifteen minutes and for them to do a little and often might be best. Avoid falling into the trap of believing meditation is difficult or requires long practice to become effective. It's actually very simple; quite quickly you'll begin to experience the benefits of meditation. Allow your own pattern of meditation to emerge. I find most people can easily start off with two forty-minute sessions of relaxation and meditation per day. After a while it becomes so inviting and enjoyable you might find you need to re-arrange your schedule so you can have longer sessions.

The benefit of having someone talk you through the process (as in the meditation practices listed in the back of this book) is that you're committed to the practice for a prescribed period of time. Unless our motivation is very strong we're often tempted to leave our practice too soon.

Some people worry that they might become dependent on a tape in order to get them into a state of deep relaxation and meditation. Use whatever's available which you find helpful. If you begin with a tape, once you're adept at the technique you can continue with the tape or develop your own particular format for meditation.

There are times when meditation brings to your awareness painful issues from the past or it allows emotions long held in to flow to the surface and be expressed. Many people find they have tears flowing down their cheeks and yet are unaware of their cause. Often, we're in situations where it could be inappropriate to express the emotions we experience. Dissolving into tears in the supermarket isn't considered to be appropriate in our society and, yet, it's in just such places that we can be overwhelmed by emotional pain, grief, panic or other powerful feelings. Meditation gives us the opportunity to release pain, sorrow, anger and fears from our past. Some people are tempted to stop their meditation at that point, but I'd encourage them to continue. By continuing the process of healing, we're actually able to let go the pain, which gives us a sense of resolution and tremendous peace.

Indeed, ultimately, meditation becomes a way of life, of living.

You begin to live all parts of your life with awareness. In this way, we're aware of the patterns of the past, the habitual responses, the fears and apprehensions for the future, and have the opportunity to release them as we live each unfolding moment. Meditation gives us the possibility of being fully present in each moment. The mind is always projecting into the future or chewing over the past. We can strive to be right here, right now, neither regretting the past nor anticipating the future. Just being here, now. Life is made up of many moments. In order to look back at life from our deathbed, whether we're 33 or 103 and be able to say, 'That was a ripper'! means that we actually have to be here and participate *in* each moment.

Some of the benefits of meditation you'll notice include a certain calmness in your attitude, and the things which used to distress you will become inconsequential. Your memory will improve and so will your powers of concentration. You'll also find you're able to accomplish more in your day, you'll have more energy, and you might find you need less sleep. The sleep you *do* have will likely be deeper and more refreshing.

Where Should I Meditate?
Set aside a space in your home for meditation. This might be a whole room, a corner of a room or a chair. Wear loose and comfortable clothing which doesn't restrict your breathing in any way. You could make this corner or room special by placing an uplifting picture of nature or some fresh flowers there. For those who have any spiritual or religious leanings, an appropriate picture or symbol might help to instil a calm and reverential attitude. For some, a cross or rosary is appropriate. You'll probably find you're more comfortable in an upright chair which supports your head. Supplement your sitting position with cushions.

After a time you'll find you begin to relax and become calm as soon as you enter that quiet and special place. In fact, even the *thought* of that place, at times when you're feeling pressured, will help calm you. If you share your home with someone else ask for their co-operation at the times when you choose to meditate. You could encourage them to join with you in your practice if that feels appropriate.

It doesn't matter that there are sounds around you, though it's preferable to practise in a quiet environment. You might like to leave a note on the door asking not to be disturbed, and take the telephone off the hook. Why not let your friends know that you practise meditation at certain times each day? Tell them you consider it to be really important in assisting you in your recovery and ask for their co-operation in not visiting or telephoning you at those times. You could invite them to join you in your practice. If you *do* need to break your meditation, it's not a problem. Just take a couple of long deep breaths, open your eyes, stretch, get up slowly and attend to whatever you need, knowing you'll easily resume the depth of meditation when you return.

Some people worry about the technique, experience, depth, or profoundness of their meditation. You might wonder *how* you will know *if* you're meditating.

The hallmarks of meditation are:
- *The mind becomes much quieter than usual, and*
- *Your breathing becomes very light.*

If that's happening, trust you *are* meditating. You'll find it helpful to begin your sessions with some deep breathing. Begin with some long, slow, deep breaths to release any tension and to bring about a sense of calm and stillness. If you've any difficulty with breathing or coughing, work comfortably within your particular limitations. Sometimes, when concentrating on their breathing, people find that they begin to cough. For these women, it's best to focus their attention on the rising and falling of the abdomen, or right at the entrance of their nostrils, where the air enters the body.

Meditate just as long as you enjoy it and gently begin to stretch the boundaries. Don't give yourself negative messages about the length of time you *should* meditate. You're a unique individual and only *you* will know about the appropriate length of time for your meditation sessions. *Trust* your own knowledge about yourself.

You'll probably need to plan a program for yourself when you first begin. For instance, you might want to begin with two twenty-minute sessions per day. You'll need to have the three ingredients firmly in place to achieve the best results. That is, motivation, effort and determination.

Most people are amazed at how quickly time passes when they're in a deep state of relaxation/meditation. Treat meditation as a wonderful adventure into a new and unexplored world. If you can maintain a childlike curiosity about the process of meditation you'll experience all of its many benefits.

Mantra Meditation

Eastern religions based on meditative practices have traditionally used focus words or phrases called mantras. The Sanskrit word or words which make up a mantra have a spiritual meaning. The benefit of practising with a mantra is that it gives the mind something to focus on instead of the idle chatter which the mind often engages in. The words can be 'attached' to the breath so that they're silently repeated in the mind with each inward and outward breath. You might wish to experiment with a Sanskrit mantra or you could choose something which has meaning for you. It isn't necessary to understand the meaning of the words used. In fact, not understanding the words can be beneficial because the mind has no association with them which might encourage mental activity. Here are a few common Sanskrit mantras:

Om Shanti, *Sri Ram* (pronounced *Shree Rahm*), *Om Namah Shivaya*, and *Ham Sah* (pronounced *Hum Sah*).

There are, of course, Christian based mantras also:

Kyrie eleison, Lord have mercy upon me, Lord have mercy, Christ have mercy, and Gloria inexcelsior Deo.

You can use any word or phrase from the Bible, prayer book or a prayer of your own making.

Other mantras used have no religious or spiritual connection and you might find them more appropriate for yourself. Words like:

Healing Peace, Letting Go, Peace and Calm, and All is Well.

Mantras are used as a *technique* to enter into a state of meditation. The repetition of the mantra is *not* the aim of your practice. It is a tool by which you enter into the realm of peace and stillness.

Breath Meditations

Many meditation techniques focus on the breath. By simply focusing your awareness on the way the breath flows in and out of the body, you're brought into the present moment. You don't have to 'do' anything to your breathing. Simply allow it to flow softly in, softly out.

Some people focus their awareness right at the entrance to their nostrils, others might wish to focus on the rising and falling of their abdomen. You might find that to focus on your breathing at all will cause you agitation, in which case, use the mantra technique.

After a short while of focusing on the breath, you'll notice that your breathing slows right down and becomes more shallow. This is because your body is beginning to relax deeply. This means you require less oxygen and that your metabolism is slowing down. The benefits of relaxation and meditation have already begun as the stress chemicals and hormones in your blood stream begin to diminish.

Music

Many people find that relaxing music, played very quietly in the background, is an excellent way to enter into a state of deep relaxation and meditation. Other people find music a distraction. This is especially so of musicians who've studied musical composition.

Experiment until you find what works best for you. Like the use of a mantra, music is a tool, or an addition to another technique, to enter a state of meditation. Some people find listening to a piece of classical music leads them to a state of stillness. The sole purpose of the music should be to lead you to that place of stillness. To *listen* to the music is not the aim of meditation. To go beyond the music to the stillness from which it arises, *is*.

There are shops which specialise in relaxation music whilst many book stores or health food stores have a smaller selection.

Group Meditation
Most people find they have a much deeper experience of meditation when they practise with a group. I would highly recommend you attend several sessions with a group until you have the 'feel' for what meditation is. If there are no groups in your area, you'll probably find the use of a cassette tape with a guided meditation is invaluable in helping you to establish your practice. Remember, also, that at *any* time you sit to meditate, you're joining with thousands of others around the world who likewise are entering *their* inner sanctuary. Spend a moment thinking about all those in monasteries, tabernacles, churches, hospitals, caves and homes who, at this moment, are immersed in their meditation practice. This can be both comforting and empowering to join with others, especially at those times when you feel isolated and alone.

Meditation in Crisis
Many people have used their meditation technique at traumatic times. For example, they've meditated and remained completely relaxed during bronchoscopies, lumbar punctures, colonoscopies, endoscopies. Some have taken their tapes and headphones into operating theatres. The sound of a familiar voice and technique can bring comfort and reassurance when we're in unfamiliar

surroundings. Remember, it's easier to practise with the *little* crises in life before embarking on the major ones.

Asleep or Meditating

Our bodies are conditioned to fall asleep when we close our eyes and concentrate on letting go and so it might take a little time before we overcome this reaction. It's therefore preferable to learn these techniques sitting comfortably upright in a chair with arms and legs uncrossed, or cross-legged on a cushion on the floor.

For those particularly unwell or on medication that makes it more difficult to remain alert and awake, this can be a problem. Remember, your body could very well need this deep and relaxed sleep and you'll still be benefiting from your practice.

Normally when we go to bed, it takes five hours to drift through our various sleep levels and to reach our deep sleep stage. We stay in this deep sleep stage for a relatively short period of time and then begin to ascend through the levels once more. In your deep sleep level, your brain waves are in the alpha wave pattern. At night, those who are unwell, in pain, restless or need to get up frequently to go to the bathroom, might never get five continuous hours of sleep, thereby missing out on their full deep sleep. It's in this deep sleep that our bodies do much of their healing and repair work. Within five minutes' practice of relaxation or meditation, your brain waves are in the alpha wave pattern and, if you fall asleep during that time, you immediately enter your deep sleep level. This is, of course, tremendously beneficial. Many people find using a relaxation tape as they drift off to sleep helps them to find deep and restful sleep immediately. Alternatively, if you have difficulty in staying asleep, you could use a tape at that time to re-enter your deep sleep level. See also the section Insomnia in Chapter 6, 'Reach for Recovery'.

Some people become very frustrated when they fall asleep regularly during their meditation practice, but all is not lost. You're still receiving something which is of tremendous value to you. You might find you're better to schedule your meditation times when you're fresh. For instance, meditate after a sleep or rest or first thing in the morning.

For those who aren't in pain or on medication and who still fall asleep, the situation is different! *You* might need to change your position or your attitude or sit more upright. Find a way to discipline your mind to be alert during your practice. This chronically falling asleep usually has something behind it. Perhaps not wanting to let go. Perhaps a reluctance to wake up and be present. Explore and experiment. It's preferable to make your regular practice times when you're feeling refreshed and *before* you've eaten rather than after. To try and meditate after a big meal, when you're very tired, whilst sitting on the edge of the bed in your pyjamas, with the electric blanket sending out waves of welcome, is courting disaster. You'll never *find* the time to meditate. You'll definitely have to *make* the time.

There are 168 hours in each week. Not one more, nor one less and *all* of them are yours. Most of us are forever saying, 'If only I had more time,' as if it were something elastic. There are 64 squares on a chessboard. If you were playing chess, you wouldn't say, 'I just need a few more squares on this side, and then I'd be able to win'. Likewise, those 168 hours are all there are and they're *all* yours. You might choose to give them away to other people, you might squander them in things which don't enrich you, but that's your choice. Reclaim your hours and consciously choose how you would like to spend them. If meditation is to be a valuable tool in your healing then give it the priority it deserves.

Meditation and Pain

For those uncomfortable or in pain it might be preferable to lie down. Use cushions to support your body in as pain-free a position as possible. Many people find these techniques tremendously valuable in dealing with their pain. There's much more on pain and its management in Chapter 7, 'Dealing with Recurrence'.

For others, settle comfortably into your chair and allow your feet to rest flat upon the floor. Choose a chair with a high back so it supports your head; place a small pillow behind your neck or head. You could place a cushion beneath your feet if they only just reach the floor. Remove your shoes if you wish. Allow your spine to be as comfortably erect as possible so you're not slouched down into the chair. Tuck your tail right into the back of the chair. Loosen your belt or any tight or restrictive clothing. Let your hands rest comfortably in your lap or on the arms of the chair, in a position where they won't slide off and distract you.

Many people experience strange sensations within their body when they practise techniques of meditation. Some people find that their arms, legs or other body parts feel like they've become enormous, numb, itchy or they've lost touch with their body altogether. Others find they have a spinning sensation or a tilt to one side. Some experience waves of warmth, temperature changes or sweats.

All of these sensations are quite normal. Some people become frightened of letting go of control. You'll probably experience a sense of letting go of the body, then a letting go of the mind, its activity and chatter. This is the beginning of meditation. This happens when we let go of who we think we are and we simply experience a sense of awareness or consciousness which is beyond personality, body, thoughts, beliefs or desires.

Light-headedness

Some people, whose haemoglobin or blood pressure is low, might experience a sense of light-headedness or nausea. It's recommended that these people lie down for their meditation practice. Meditation lowers your blood pressure. If, after the completion of your meditation, you feel a little light-headed, give yourself plenty of time to stretch and arise from your practice in a leisurely manner.

Don't go directly from lying down to standing up. Slowly sit up, dangle and rotate your feet, stretch, breathe deeply and *gradually* return to your activities.

Those who've been taking medication for elevated blood pressure often find that within weeks of commencing a meditation program they become dizzy and light-headed either during, or immediately after, their practice. If this happens, return to your prescribing physician, as it's very likely you no longer require the same level of medication.

Restlessness and Agitation

Some people become very agitated or restless and find it difficult to remain still throughout their practice. It's worth exploring *why* they're restless. The most common cause is a fear to let go of control. Many of us are frightened of letting go into the unknown. We often feel safer if we're controlling life. I encourage you to experiment, be adventurous, take a risk and trust in the spirit within yourself, rather than trusting in your mind.

If, during your practice, you need to lie down because you've a problem which will make it too difficult for you to remain in a sitting position, then do so. During your practice if you need to scratch, cough, sneeze, stretch or shift position, then do so and return to your practice. If you need to have a glass of water nearby, have it! Don't turn your practice into a battle! The intention is to remain passive and still with an intense awareness, not thinking, but simply being.

It's better to meditate with an empty stomach, as much of your energy goes into digesting its contents if you've recently eaten.

Avoid comparing one meditation session with another. You might have a truly profound experience one time and then make the mistake of comparing all subsequent meditation practices with *that* one. Allow each meditation session to be whole and complete in itself. Don't fall into the trap of evaluating or making a judgement about each meditation practice.

Conclusion

It isn't unusual to feel a deep reluctance to leave your meditative state. Sometimes to come back into an awareness of your body feels like putting on a very heavy overcoat. You need to bring yourself out of meditation very gently and respectfully.

Endeavour to let go of any expectations you might have of meditation. Some people expect to hear the Hallelujah chorus with a choir of ten thousand angels! Sometimes we *do* have such experiences but the surest way to sabotage an openness to each unfolding moment is to hold an expectation of what it *should* contain.

Above all else, be compassionate towards yourself in your practice of meditation. Don't fall into the trap of unrealistic standards, lengths of time or depth of practice.

4
The Company of Women

One needs to be reminded of love and friendship.
A smile may do it. A friendly wave.
Pilgrims all, let us realise in all this
Our power to help others.

JULIET, AGE 61
aged 46 at diagnosis

Naturally, there were moments of panic, depression and sad-
ness. At the support group friendships deepened rapidly in the
emotional intensity of sharing the really important things in life.
We shared laughter, tears, pain, love, anger—as we expressed the
full gamut of human emotions.

KERRY, AGE 49
aged 39 at diagnosis

Support group work was very important for me. It took me five or six weeks of going before I was able to say anything about anything that was important. I did develop friendships, and I did feel very safe with the people who were there.

Then I did the facilitator's training course with Petrea and that was a difficult period for me, because I was confronting a lot of the anger that I'd felt. I think the support groups and the facilitator's training were incredibly beneficial. Unbelievably so. I don't think I'd be sitting here, able to analyse it quite as objectively, if I hadn't done that work. That wasn't the end of the work. But that was certainly an opening up. It showed me where the work needed to be done.

I'm a great supporter of support groups as long as they're support groups like Petrea's where you can say anything, where you can rant and rave, talk about treatments and doctors, and things like that. Because a lot of the support groups are run by hospitals and I'm sure they're very good for some people but you can't really get into the anger that a lot of people feel at the medical profession. I think that you've got to have a neutral territory. Because a lot of people have so much anger about their treatment, about things medical. And you can't get into that sort of anger when the doctors, or social workers, or health professionals of that type are there.

CATHERINE, AGE 47
aged 41 at diagnosis

In dealing with illness and death, being with people who are sympathetic and willing to walk with you along this disagreeable path is very important, indispensable.

JULIET, AGE 61
aged 46 at diagnosis

You'll be able to laugh and cry and discuss different problems related to breast surgery and your recovery. If there isn't a group, start one. *It works wonders, and you'll be surprised at how many women out there are travelling the same road.*

JUDITH, AGE 53
aged 52 at diagnosis

It's all right to feel like "this is too much" and it's all right to laugh. It's OK to have black humour and make jokes. I've heard some of the sickest stuff I've ever heard in support groups. People pissing themselves laughing at somebody's expense in the group. If people outside heard us they wouldn't believe it.

GINA, AGE 59
aged 49 at diagnosis

I think it's the presence of such honesty. The presence of a mixture of hope and despair, all at the same time. Because some people go to a group and they're very hopeful and up and bright, and other people are very despairing.

You come away feeling so strong from these people talking about their experiences. You get a tremendous amount of strength from seeing other people cope with their problems. It's an enormous privilege, because people are letting you into their lives.

I did make a resolution that I must put the experience, not behind me, but I must incorporate what I want to from that experience and get on. Because otherwise you just put your whole life on hold. And you don't then progress. I didn't want to put my whole life on hold.

CATHERINE, AGE 47
aged 41 at diagnosis

I was very fortunate that I found out about groups straight away. It made a world of difference because it gave me a positive attitude towards things right from the beginning. There's no way I'd have coped without support groups. You're in the same boat as everybody else around you, and you're learning to cope with something similar and yet you don't always even know what illnesses other people have. In fact, often we hardly spoke of our illnesses at all. Just to know that you're fighting something and you're doing the best for yourself and you were supporting them with their problems, I found it magnificent. I would say I came virtually every week for probably six months or so. Each time I'd meet the same people and we had fun.

SUE, AGE 54
aged 50 at diagnosis

Women are so very strong and breast cancer has made me realise the strength and worth of women which I hadn't realised before. I hadn't appreciated the strength and depth of women. Maybe there was something that I was frightened of. Maybe I was frightened of the feminine side of my nature. But I find them very strong, and in general very optimistic. I think that they're rather wonderful. I think the fact that we organise ourselves and network a lot and use our friends for emotional support, I think that's very healthy for us. Without those things, life would be pretty poor.

CATHERINE, AGE 47
aged 41 at diagnosis

The reason I went to a support group was I needed to feel I had some control over the disease.

CATHERINE, AGE 47
aged 41 at diagnosis

Support Groups

Marianne is a newcomer to the support group. She's pretty, looks healthy and is in her mid-thirties. She looks slightly awkward coming to a cancer support group for the first time, but that dissolves quickly as she feels the warmth and acceptance pervading the room.

The group begins and shortly, after one or two others, Marianne shares her story. She begins tentatively, then feeling she's in a safe place where she can express her feelings without criticism or judgement, her story tumbles out. Six weeks before, Marianne, who has three children, found a lump in her breast where she felt a slightly tender area. She put it to the back of her mind as she had many duties to perform that morning: school lunches to be organised, breakfast to be prepared and cleaned up afterwards, her children to be dropped off at school, the weekly shopping and canteen duty.

The lump niggled at the back of her mind all morning as she shopped, put groceries away and went to the school to perform her monthly duty on the canteen roster. On the way home she popped into her local doctor who assured her that tender lumps were rarely anything to worry about. But because of her family history of breast cancer (her mother had died from it at seventy years of age), he sent her off to have a mammogram as soon as possible.

As soon as possible turned out to be the next day. The mammogram had showed positive, her doctor had referred her to a surgeon who performed a needle biopsy and within three days of finding the lump she'd been scheduled for surgery. She'd awoken from the surgery minus her breast, and with talk about further treatment including chemotherapy and radiotherapy because the cancer had spread into the axillary lymph nodes in her armpit. She'd recovered well and was back home with the children whom she'd missed. They were equally pleased at her return. She'd been overwhelmed by the flowers, cards and loving responses of so many people, some of whom she hadn't seen for years.

Gradually the household returned to some sort of normalcy with Marianne back to preparing school lunches and breakfasts, cleaning up afterwards and dropping the children off to school on her way to the hospital for radiotherapy.

Her husband Brian, who'd been extremely supportive and loving throughout her ordeal, had held the fort whilst she was in hospital and was overjoyed to have her home once more. Everyone said how well she looked. She felt like she was taking radiotherapy in her stride with only a couple of days of feeling off-colour when she had her chemotherapy. Brian had long since returned to work. The children thought Mum looked, and therefore must be, fine as she was back to all her motherly duties.

Now six weeks later Marianne is in tears, thinking she'll never be the same again, and that there's something seriously wrong with her because she dissolves into tears at the drop of a hat. She's trying to keep her despair from her children and Brian because, 'They've all been through so much already'. She feels isolated and alone in her experience and has even wondered if perhaps the cancer has spread to her brain.

By now she's beginning to laugh a little at herself, hearing how silly it sounds. She's beginning to hear her own story; how she's been through a nightmare and that it's no wonder she's feeling a bit down and depressed. By the time some of the group members remind her that she *is* still recovering from the trauma of surgery and *is* having radiotherapy *and* chemotherapy *and* running a household *and* still grieving for an important part of her body, she's able to acknowledge she's been doing fine up until now and that maybe she was setting herself some unrealistically high standards.

After hearing several of the other participants' stories, Marianne looks far more relaxed and at ease. She's found others who've shared in the ordeal of breast cancer and who can recount stories which are almost identical to her own.

It's not that the aim of the support group is to change the outcome of any person's disease, but by joining together we remember the beauty and strength of our common human spirit and we're able to re-establish our commitment to life.

Marianne's story has been heard often in our groups: women of courage living under great pressure who are endeavouring to get on with life. Sometimes we need to stop in our climb up the mountain to enjoy the view; to acknowledge how well we're doing and to re-energise ourselves for the steps ahead.

A similar story is often heard from other women whose doctors have told them there was no spread of their cancer. They've been told there's no follow-up treatment necessary and to put cancer out of their minds. They try to, but often don't succeed very well. What the doctor doesn't understand is that this woman has just been confronted with her mortality in a very unexpected and frightening way. She could feel mutilated, frightened, confused, out of control, angry, depressed, abandoned, isolated and rejected. And *he* says not to worry!

In this situation, the doctor is only dealing with the medical situation, not recognising that anyone who goes through such an experience is likely to feel emotionally traumatised. Not to mention the fact that anyone who experiences the feelings just mentioned on a long-term basis is likely to draw ill health to herself. If you asked him, the doctor would probably say Marianne should be happy it was caught early: two different view points, resulting from poor timing rather than any intent to distress. The day might dawn when she feels happy it *was* found early but right now she needs support of a different kind.

Many women in similar cases struggle to come to terms with their present situation. Do I have cancer? Did I have cancer? How do I know if it will return? How can I live my life with so much uncertainty? Who'll want me now I'm without a breast? Can I safely make plans for my future? Who should I tell? Do I change my diet? Do I change my lifestyle?

Sometimes these women are particularly reluctant to come to a support group or to talk to a health professional because they don't believe they really qualify. After all, 'The doctor says I don't have cancer any more'. Counselling should be offered to *every* woman (indeed, person!) regardless of the prognosis of the disease. We all need assistance to find our way through the confusion and bewilderment.

In 1989, Dr David Spiegel reported in *The Lancet* that women with advanced metastatic breast cancer who attended weekly support groups, which included relaxation and meditation techniques, lived on average twice as long as the control group. In addition, their need for medication for pain was less and their quality of life was improved. Despite this research, little has been done in Australia to *actively* encourage women to attend such groups.

Talking with other women facing the same kinds of issues, choices and decisions can be very helpful in clarifying how you actually *do* feel about something. You don't have to feel alone in your situation. Though your choices will be your own, having a neutral environment in which to talk through your options can help crystallise your thinking. This might not be with a formalised support group. You could have a friend, relative or partner with whom you feel you can share these private thoughts and who won't influence you in your choices and decisions.

A support group, *effectively facilitated*, creates a safe, warm and supportive environment in which any issues can be discussed with complete openness and frankness. Often there are problems or concerns which we feel unable to share with our family or partner, perhaps because it will be too upsetting for them or they can't or don't know how to respond in any really helpful way. Even though we live so closely with family, it's often said by participants in the group that those nearest to them physically don't really know or understand what they're going through. Such groups give us the opportunity to explore and verbalise our innermost feelings and, often, the courage to express them to our loved ones.

If you're seeking to join a support group then be discerning. There are many groups which are really not much more than a social gathering amongst women with the same problem. If at all possible find a *well facilitated* group in your area. Choose a group where there are guidelines for the structure and functioning of the group and where the facilitator has had good training. Ask any questions you might have of the facilitator, before attending the group. One of the most important guidelines in a group is that we don't criticise or judge each other. This guideline is essential to creating a safe, supportive environment in which each participant can talk about whatever they choose. If someone feels miserable, depressed, positive, joyous, peaceful, suicidal or fearful then we don't tell them they shouldn't be feeling that way. If that's how you

feel, that's how you feel! A group which encourages the participants to take an active part in their healing program is essential.

Sometimes a woman has an unsympathetic home environment
where the family might think because she has a good doctor
there's no need for any additional support. One woman, Jean,
said that when she was diagnosed with breast cancer, her husband
retreated into himself and wasn't able to give her any emotional
support. She said *he* looked so miserable she realised she would
have to give *him* a hug. She added wistfully, 'How nice it
would have been if he'd been able to give me a hug'. She wasn't
being critical of him, but she was certainly expressing the senti-
ments of many 'copers'.

The family's attitude can sometimes be, 'If she looks all right
then she must be all right'. This can also be seen when we've a
long or protracted illness where we often don't look particularly
sick. At times when we appear well, everyone else breathes a sigh
of relief believing that everything can return to normal again.
'Isn't it great! You're better now'. It's often at *this* time that the
full impact of what's happening to us hits home. Everyone goes
back to work, back to familiar routines, and we're left feeling
everything is *not* all right at all!

It's often difficult to find the balance between 'Am I a sick person'? or 'Am I a well person'? Often we don't want people asking
us, 'How are you *really*'? Yet there are times when it would be so
nice for someone to enquire how we truly are. It's very difficult
for the support person to know which frame of mind we're in,
and how we'd like them to respond.

Many times the dilemmas we create for ourselves stem from a
simple lack of communication. Sometimes, to raise the issues
which cause us pain or stress is a challenge, because we all tend
to want things to be fine. We don't want to face painful issues.
They *can* sit on the back burner until we feel the heat is so strong
that we're beginning to get singed! Often when we take this
approach, we find we're holding down a hotbed of emotion

which has to break through. Inflamed discussions are rarely anticipated with joy. If we can acknowledge and deal with the small brush fires, we could well avoid the towering inferno.

Communication is the life-line of all relationships but never more so than when we're thrust into a situation which is new and frightening. We need to have our fears heard and acknowledged. We're then able more easily to live comfortably with them, or let them go entirely.

Many a partner has said they're really happy their loved-one has the group with whom to talk over her fears and anxieties. They're extremely supportive and encouraging of the woman's participation in our group.

Our groups are always flexible in content and no two sessions are ever the same. We address whatever issues arise out of each one.

Many who are the least willing to share initially find the most benefit from their participation. The empathy and love generated during the sharing is a powerful and growing thing of itself and a bond which strengthens us to go on. We can gain great encouragement from someone who's further down the track than ourselves and is comfortable and at peace with their situation. Women who come into the room dejected and anxious always leave cheered and ready to face whatever lies ahead. There are many in our groups who are in remission after they'd been told this would be unlikely or impossible. They provide great inspiration and encouragement to those just starting out on their journey.

It's generally surprising to people to find these groups are full of laughter and good humour; there are tears too, and these are freely expressed as the need arises. To have permission from others to have a good cry is invaluable. Very often families don't want to see us cry because it puts them in touch with their own distress. Of course, this is valuable too, but many women then tailor what they want to say to minimise their family's distress. Talking freely without being surrounded by the emotional ties of the family can be very helpful.

We can retreat into a lonely, fear-filled world or we can join with others who are facing the same situation as ourselves and gain courage and spirit from them.

Throughout the treatment I went whenever I could to Petrea's support group. I went reluctantly at first thinking the last thing I needed was to spend time with a whole lot of very sick people who were dying of cancer. Nothing could have been further from the truth and I never met anyone who was dying of cancer. They were all very much alive and often great fun to be around. Being able to talk and have people listen to your experiences was a wonderful and precious experience.

BARBARA, AGE 35
aged 33 at diagnosis

One apprehension newcomers have expressed about participating in a support group, is they might meet people who are sicker than they are, or who are going to die. This certainly happens in our groups; yet we've found that to face death or serious illness together has been a great blessing and strength to us. I don't believe it's a negative thing to look at and discuss death. In fact, looking at my own death and the process of dying was one of the major turning points for me. Once my fears were acknowledged and dealt with, I could begin to focus more fully on living today well.

If we have a life-threatening illness, then one possibility is we might die. *Not* to look at that possibility can sometimes take an enormous amount of energy which would be better spent in healing. Being open to life also means being open to death. Once death has been looked at fully, or as fully as we're able, we can really get on with living. Once I'd accepted the inevitability of my own death, I made a full commitment to life. If I was going to die, I'd do it with as much grace and dignity as I could muster, but whilst I had life and breath, I was going to be doing my utmost to live. And I set about finding ways in which I could affirm life.

To be in a group where someone is exploring their feelings

about dying can be invaluable as a way of gaining insight into our own feelings. Sometimes we're a little nervous about looking at our own feelings, and to hear someone else courageously exploring theirs can help us.

You might feel that death is the last thing on the list of things you want to explore. That's fine. Acknowledge the fact that now isn't the time for you to do that and focus on whatever seems most appropriate for you. Trust and respect what you know about yourself.

I could never face the prospect of a support group. I've always been a very private person and I knew it wouldn't work for me. However, I found counselling very helpful and felt I'd created my own "safe" place for the times when I needed to talk.

LEANNE, AGE 48
aged 47 at diagnosis

Likewise, for some women, the idea of a group is too threatening or foreign because they've never been able to articulate how they feel in front of other people. If you're like this then, perhaps, seek out a counsellor who's had experience and create your own 'safe' place for the times when you need it. Don't give yourself a hard time because, even though the research says it's beneficial, it doesn't seem to suit you. Listen to yourself and respect the fragile part of yourself.

In the support groups we're given the opportunity to air our fears, angers and apprehensions and perhaps gain another perspective. Nothing is more healing than to laugh at something which was once fearful to us but which now has no power over us. There's a silent permission permeating the group, which allows for free expression of whatever emotions are being experienced, be they grief, panic, anger, frustration, depression, regret, sadness, joy, love, fear, guilt, powerlessness, and so on.

When we listen carefully to what a person is saying, either directly or indirectly, it enables that person actually to *hear* what they're saying and gives them courage to explore and discover their own solutions. *My* solutions are always *mine*. They could benefit someone else also, but ultimately we all need to find our own solutions to the problems which arise in our lives. It's not a case of 'Where there is *this* problem, *this* is the solution'. A solution entirely appropriate to one person will be inappropriate, perhaps, for another.

Reaching Out

A lot of support flows outside the formal meeting of the group. It's common when one of the members is going to hospital for surgery, chemotherapy or some other procedure, that several other members of the group will telephone or be remembering them in their own meditations. This feeling of being supported by others is tremendously valuable. It's often said by a participant that even in the darkest night of depression, fear or pain, the remembrance of the group has brought light and comfort.

When we have a life-threatening disease we can feel useless as far as our capacity to be actively involved in the community. Often we need to give up work, sport or other engaging activities and it can easily lead to a feeling of being an observer of life, rather than a participator. We can begin to question our value as a human being, especially when an illness is protracted.

Participating in a support group can allay those feelings entirely. Often those who are sickest and weakest give more strength and valuable insight into another's dilemma and it's only because of their courage and awareness of their own plight that they're able to do so. It has frequently been said by members of the group that they've never felt so connected to other people as they have since their illness. They say they've found a strength within themselves which they've been able to share freely with others in a way never before possible. When we're able to share deeply with others it brings about a completion and healing within ourselves.

What we experience in our groups is spirit reaching out to spirit in love and compassion—and frequently humour—to bring insight, comfort and perhaps a changed perception. The depth and strength of the human spirit has the power to show us the flimsy nature of fear. A situation first perceived as terrifying can, when brought out into the open and looked at in the light, be perceived quite differently—especially with the added strength of others.

A support group can be made up of two people who are committed to self-exploration or discovery and indeed this is how our support group originally began. That first small group was extremely valuable and gave us an opportunity to find out just what *were* the essentials for such groups.

If there's no support group in your area, you could approach the social worker or doctor at your local hospital and express the need for one. Most hospitals within major cities have such groups. Some of these groups are more educational in their structure and these can be very beneficial also.

Your doctor, social worker, nurse or the Cancer Council in your state are likely to know what support groups are available in your local area. Several contact numbers are listed at the back of this book.

5

Good Eating

We're very serious about the juice! I've really seen the diet and vitamin supplements and the vegetable juice as being very important. I enjoy salads and all the different vegetables, so I really haven't felt deprived. If you offered me a piece of chocolate cake I couldn't eat it.

MARGARET, AGE 61
aged 59 at diagnosis

The first step was to visit a naturopath. She smiled at me and said that with the combination of anaesthetics, drugs and deep fear I was very depleted and needed a kick start—and that was exactly what I got. I suddenly felt much better.

JOAN, AGE 54
aged 51 at diagnosis

For the first time, I guess, I was looking at food in a different way. Food before had just been something to put in me, to fill me up, to keep me going. I didn't really care too much about what it was. I was an indiscriminate and sloppy eater and I used to eat a lot of sweets, and then maybe have something on toast for dinner. That kind of thing. Not a good eater at all. So I began looking for nutritious food that was going to be good for me.

JEANNIE, AGE 54
aged 50 at diagnosis

Everyone gives you a cure and the cure is a new diet or a recipe or all sorts of things that you should eat.

SALLY, AGE 58
aged 50 at diagnosis

Before I received the diagnosis I was seeing a nutritionist and I thought I was on a very healthy diet. I was taking supplements, so it was a big shock to find that all the care I'd taken was useless. My first reaction was to go out and have a few glasses of wine!

LOUISE, AGE 52
aged 51 at diagnosis

I must say that I've juiced and all that sort of stuff. When I had chemotherapy three years ago, I didn't have any side-effects at all. I didn't lose a hair from my head, I never had nausea or vomiting. I've just finished six months of Taxol and I've been "wonder woman" on the trial there. They've actually written me up. I didn't get any of the rashes or itching that stopped some of the women from continuing with the trial. I got really angry with the nurses who kept saying, "Oh, well you will get side-effects, Helen. Your hair's going to fall out", and it never did!

HELEN, AGE 42
aged 34 at diagnosis

One thing juicing is doing for me is giving me a sense of control. It's now something that I'm doing for my benefit and I can feel it doing me good.

LOUISE, AGE 52
aged 51 at diagnosis

I see a herbalist and that's helped me enormously. I think there are many things that people can do and finding what you feel comfortable with, and a practitioner who you feel comfortable with, is important. There are quite a few complementary practitioners who are just as authoritarian, bossy, know-all, as the worst doctor. They'll tell you it's your own fault if you don't get better or if you don't do what the herbalist or whoever says. So I think that finding a practitioner who helps you feel good about yourself is very important.

HELEN, AGE 42
aged 34 at diagnosis

I think about the sort of food I eat. I think about the lifestyle I lead, the relaxation, all the things I knew in the past but tended to not have time to do. I like to keep fit, I like to exercise. I eat pretty well. I'm always very conscious of diet, I don't eat a lot of junk food and I still take some of the vitamins that were recommended.

SUE, AGE 54
aged 50 at diagnosis

The Right Diet

Many women are anxious to know what they can do to avoid a recurrence of breast cancer. In addition to treatment, one of the first areas often focused on is what to eat. There seems to be a dietary link in some kinds of breast cancer, but we still don't understand what all the links are. For instance, women who live in Japan have a low incidence of breast cancer. However, when they move to live in America and adopt a different lifestyle, including a change in their diet, their incidence of breast cancer becomes the same as for the American population. A high-fat diet has certainly been implicated in some kinds of breast cancer.

I don't believe the simple equation of diet causes cancer, therefore, diet cures cancer. The cause of cancer is not as simple as that and cancer has, as its cause, several factors including genetic history, lifestyle, response to stress, diet, environmental pollutants and who knows what else?

However, it's commonsense that when you're undergoing rigorous treatments or are under greater stress than usual you'll need to be on a really good nutritional program to make sure you get all the essential ingredients for health from your food. A healthy diet consists of food from a wide selection of fruits, vegetables, cereals, seafood and free-range chicken.

Sometimes, the more books you read, the more confused you become. You can read about diets which advocate garlic until it's coming out of your ears, only to pick up another which strongly advises against its use. One dietary regime prohibits the use of celery whilst another suggests you should have it juiced every day. Macrobiotic or a raw food diet? And so on. In fact, no subject is more open to debate, and it's easy for you to become completely bewildered and frustrated by all the conflicting advice.

You can become so confused as to be paralysed in your endeavours to whip up a quick snack! The premise on which the whole approach of this book is based is that peace of mind is our greatest healer and, therefore, our primary goal. Our choice of an appropriate nutritional program must be in accord with this aim. We need to bring the peace and calmness we experience in our meditation into every aspect of our lives.

From my experience of having worked on a one-to-one basis with tens of thousands of individuals with life-threatening illnesses, I can confidently say I don't believe that diet is the *most* important factor. I've seen people do well on many different kinds of diets. In each case the person chose the diet that appealed to them most. It's the *attitude behind* your eating which is of most importance.

Many women feel, when they change their diet, that it gives them a sense of doing something which can be evidenced and measured. I'm not by any means saying your diet isn't important, but don't turn it into a nightmare. Enjoy your food. Research what you feel might be appropriate for you, and *gently* move in the desired direction at *your* own speed.

Some of the diets advocated for the cure of cancer and other diseases almost require a full-time cook to keep up with the endless preparation of foods and juices. If you have the resources and want to be on such a program, and if it doesn't create a stressful home environment, then it could well be suitable and beneficial. However, if your entire day is dominated by a rigid program of juices and food preparation, and the atmosphere in the home is permeated by stress, then something needs to be changed. Again, it's not the juices or the foods which are at fault, but the attitude *behind* their use.

One of my clients was comparing a book which relies heavily on a strict diet for cancer patients with *Quest for Life*, my first book. She said, 'That diet works for men with cancer who have a wife, *Quest for Life* has been written for the wife'! More often than not, the responsibility of food preparation falls to you to organise. If you have a family, the last thing you want to do is to have to prepare different meals for different family members. You might have to do this if you're unable to eat the usual family fare, but, if at all possible, keep it as simple as you can.

It's the *attitude* of long-term survivors rather than their dietary approach that's most apparent. They're people who've decided to live each day to its full potential with peace in their hearts and joy in each moment. You can't experience peace of mind whilst you're feeling frazzled over which diet to adopt. Keep your sense of humour, it will get you through many a confusing or potentially panicky moment.

To experience peace of mind, with regard to nutrition, it's essential you have a program which:

- You believe is of the utmost benefit to you, and
- Is well within your capabilities to prepare or that you have support in its preparation.

Professional Advice

It's essential for anyone wishing to adhere to a cleansing yet nourishing diet to assist in the healing process, to be under the guidance of a qualified and experienced doctor or naturopath. Choose someone whom you trust and who's familiar with working with women who have breast cancer. When tailoring this nutritional program, it's essential to take into account your emotional and psychological state, cultural background, religious restrictions, physical condition, your personal wishes *and* the amount of support you have at home to assist in the preparation of a special diet. It's important you find a diet which will work for *you*, as opposed to a diet which your therapist believes in but which turns your entire household upside-down in order to encompass *it*!

If your nutritional therapist doesn't ask you lots of questions about the issues mentioned above (that is, tailors the dietary program to fit *your* particular needs), then you're probably with the wrong therapist. Don't fall into the trap of doing contortions to fit the program your nutritional therapist has devised. They should be able to devise a program which is tailored for you.

Diet is only one aspect of an overall approach to healing. Unless wisely guided, people will often put more effort into dietary preparation and other therapies which they've chosen to incorporate, simply because it's something tangible they can do to help themselves.

When we're newly diagnosed with a disease, our tendency, after the initial panic has subsided a little, is to find the things which we can actively 'do' to help ourselves. It's very easy to get lost in the 'doing' and thus overlook the importance of our feelings. A new diet adopted out of fear of breast cancer and its consequences won't be nearly as beneficial as one calmly chosen to assist in your healing. Often members of your family see their most useful role as 'the gatherers of information' with regard to diets and other therapies. This is a valuable and necessary role.

However, it can still be carried out with calmness. There *is* time: time to assimilate, to talk, discuss, share feelings, evaluate information and consolidate your combined strengths.

Once all the factors mentioned before have been taken into account, a program can be designed which allows for healthy cleansing of the body whilst also providing optimum nourishment of a kind which can be assimilated by this *particular* person. Two women, the same age, with breast cancer, might require two very different nutritional programs based on the considerations mentioned earlier. These nutritional programs aren't curative of themselves. All healing power lies within the person. We're endeavouring to provide first-class nourishment of a kind which can be assimilated by the body, so it will be in a position to cleanse and heal itself.

It's of paramount importance that you have faith in your chosen diet and that you *enjoy* the food you're eating. Many people make themselves miserable and create far more stress, by adopting a rigid and unpalatable diet. Others may well thrive on exactly the same foods. This highlights the crux of the matter— find the nutritional program which tastes good to you and which will provide the ideal environment for healing within your body. As has been stated before, the first and most important aspect of healing is the loving gentleness and regard with which you hold yourself. All healing flows from this.

Some people will only experience peace of mind if they feel their diet is a 'tried and true' healing diet. Whilst for others, peace of mind will be experienced by making gentle and gradual improvements towards a more nutritious program.

Many people equate a difficult or rigid diet with the degree to which they want to live. This often reflects a life-long attitude of setting high standards which are almost impossible to achieve. Then we can be self-critical if we don't measure up. Often the underlying thought behind this is, 'If I really want to live, I should be doing everything 100 per cent'. Then it can become easy when we don't 'do the diet perfectly' to say, 'I've failed again'! It's so sad to see this thinking. We can become so depressed by a seemingly insurmountable obstacle, and yet it's an obstacle entirely of our own creation. If this is *your* attitude, it's worth looking at other areas in your life to see if this is a common approach you have. Pick your diet, do your utmost, and *trust*.

Another common attitude behind our dietary choice is one of bargaining: 'If I adhere to a really difficult diet; if I meditate for three hours every day; if I take my supplements and treatments, then maybe I will "earn" my recovery'. It usually stems from, 'If I'm good enough, I'll succeed'. If this applies to you, then let go this harsh and uncompromising attitude and practise loving kindness and compassion towards yourself.

Often when we're sick there are people—such as neighbours, friends and relatives—who offer assistance. We're sometimes reluctant to avail ourselves of their offers as we like to be independent. The partner or support person might well feel they want to do *all* the caring for you, again, as a way of showing their love. If we *can* avail ourselves of their offers to cook, pick up the children or groceries, take care of the washing or ironing, or whatever seems to be most helpful, it leaves your partner or support person more available to spend quality time with you.

So, by all means enlist the assistance of those who've willingly offered their services. They wouldn't have offered if they hadn't sincerely meant what they'd said. When our priorities are right, we can relax and trust healing is taking place.

This principle applies in exactly the same way to the various other therapies which you might encounter. Vitamins, herbals, homeopathics, tissue salts, acupuncture, nutritional supplements, minerals, vitaminB12, essiac, shark cartilage are but a few of the more popular therapies which are available. As well as these various substances which can be *taken* (into the body), there are a host of other therapies which can be utilised: Reiki, shiatsu, re-birthing, regression therapy, meditation, visualisation, tai chi, psychotherapy, float tanks, yoga, Chi Qong, spiritual or psychic healing—the list goes on and on. Don't forget, peace is our one goal. Choose from therapies which come easily into your orbit and are financially possible. Again, it comes back to trusting that the things which you need for your healing are at hand.

In my practice, I rely on sound nutrition tailored to the individual. This nutritional program is tailored to each client, bearing in mind the essentials mentioned earlier. In addition to this, I recommend vitamins, minerals and other nutritional supplements designed to improve overall health and well-being. I use massage, herbals, and homeopathics which I find particularly valuable in alleviating the side-effects of the necessary medical treatments the client might be undergoing, and to relieve the unpleasant symptoms of the disease process itself.

None of the therapeutic substances which I use are designed to cure breast cancer. All of them are to assist women in creating an ideal 'internal' environment in which healing can take place. If we eat a diet which is nourishing and which minimises the stress to our bodies, we're co-operating with our own healing process. For instance, your body could well make excellent use of fish and of potatoes. However, if you eat 'fish and chips'—that is, fried in batter and oil—you're creating an unnecessary stress for your liver. It's not only impossible for your body to digest oils which have been heated to a high temperature, but they're positively detrimental to your liver. Obviously, if you have cancer, it's advisable to assist the liver in its mammoth job of detoxifying the blood stream. It certainly isn't helpful to increase the stress on an organ which is already overloaded. It's simple commonsense to work in accord with your body, which is under stress at the outset. Bear in mind also, that when you're on chemotherapy, your liver is even more preoccupied with breaking down the drugs.

Just as we need assistance in choosing an appropriate nutritional program, so we need to have any other chosen therapy tailored to meet our needs. To find someone qualified to help you in this area, seek out help from other women with breast cancer, your local hospital, Community Health Centre, your doctor or oncologist, your health food store, or ask the Cancer Council in your state or an equivalent organisation which understands your needs. Many of my referrals come from oncologists/immunologists or the Cancer Council who know this approach is beneficial to their patients and that they won't be dissuaded from medical treatments.

As I'm always asked about the 'suitable diet' which I prescribe, the following guidelines are included. These guidelines are such that every individual in the community would benefit from them, regardless of their state of health. They're based on sound commonsense and sensible nutritional information. They're general outlines only and, again, if you're seriously ill, then find a qualified person to help you use these recommendations to your best advantage. Dietitians within the hospital system are highly trained to understand the components of foods. However, they've not trained in the therapeutic effect of various foods. For instance, they can tell you what is *in* orange juice but not how your body reacts to it. Orange juice might contain all sorts of beneficial substances, however, if anything will make you feel squeamish or nauseous, it's orange juice. There's a lot of information about foods to avoid when you have nausea under that section in Chapter 6, 'Reach for Recovery'.

If you have secondary growths anywhere in your digestive tract, then this diet will need to be tailored to your ability to digest these foods.

If you've had breast cancer and:
• You don't have any spread of your disease, or
• The spread does not involve your digestive tract, and
• You're not on treatment which affects your digestion,
then this could be the diet for you.

There are some foods or substances which you're better off

without. These additives or foods are difficult for your body to digest and/or create free radicals (chemical compounds that damage tissue and impede healing).

Foods to Avoid Totally

Avoid any foods containing:
- Preservatives
- Artificial colourings
- MSG (monosodium glutamate—flavour enhancer 621)
- Artificial flavourings
- Emulsifiers
- Stabilisers
- Added sugar
- Cow's milk and its products—with the exception of yoghurt, low-fat cheeses, quark, butter, cream
- White flour
- Any other chemical additive.

Sample Menus

Keeping these guidelines in mind, here are some sample menus. These are for the women in good health with no digestive disturbances. These are only suggestions and you don't *have* to include all the things mentioned. A typical daily dietary program might include:

Breakfast
- Porridge (well-cooked for those with upset tummies) (made with soya milk for those underweight)
- Muesli (to be avoided by those with digestive disturbances)
- Puffed wheat, rice, millet or corn served with soya milk (use sun-dried fruit, soaked overnight, for a sweetener, or chopped banana)
- Lightly scrambled, poached or boiled free-range eggs (if you're experiencing any indigestion do not combine with

any cereal [as above] or bread, toast or muffins)
- Wholemeal bread, toast or muffins

or

- Fresh fruit and yoghurt, quark, leben or low-fat cottage cheese
- Fresh fruit and nuts/pine nuts/sunflower seeds, etc.

Remember these Points

- It's better to eat either grains *or* fresh fruit and nuts or yoghurt, quark, etc. Don't mix fruits and cereals (with the exception of banana which is a complex carbohydrate also).
- Use soya (or light soya milk), goat's or sheep's milk on cereal.
- Always chew slowly, mixing the food well with saliva.
- Enjoy your food, eat with gratitude and joy and be mindful as you eat.
- If you're concerned because you're losing weight, then use cereals for breakfast and keep fruits for snacks.
- If you're concerned because you're putting on weight, then use fruit and yoghurt for breakfast instead of cereals.
- Don't drink with your meal. Drink at least half an hour before the meal or one and a half hours after. If you need to take medication, take it with as little water as possible.

Mid-Morning/Afternoon Snacks

- Banana or other fruit smoothie
- Fresh fruit and nuts/sunflower seeds/pine nuts etc.
- Crackers/pumpernickel and avocado/or salad vegies
- Small amount of dried fruit
- Miso or vegetable soup
- Yoghurt and fruit
- Fresh vegetable juice

Lunch or Dinner

- Always have some salad vegies either as a salad sandwich, a side salad or make the whole meal a salad

- Jacket potato, sweet potato or pumpkin dry-baked in the oven (use yoghurt and chopped chives instead of sour cream)
- Vegetable soups (pumpkin, broccoli, cream of spinach—use soya, goat's or sheep's milk)
- Stir-fry vegies (cooked in a wok so you only start with a teaspoon of oil or a tablespoon of water)
- Grilled, steamed or baked fish or free-range chicken
- Steamed vegetables
- Free-range chicken casserole
- Pumpkin pie
- Lentil, tofu or tempeh burgers
- Pasta and vegetables
- Lentil, split pea, barley, lima bean, etc dishes
- Wholewheat, buckwheat or rice noodles
- Brown rice.

Remember these Points

- Use only cold-pressed oil and lemon juice plus garlic, dried or fresh herbs for salad dressing.
- Use a wide range of salad vegies so you meet your need for vitamins, minerals and enzymes. Include lettuce, tomatoes, cucumbers, capsicum, broccoli, cauliflower, mung and alfalfa sprouts, zucchini, and so on (if you like them).
- Chew your food thoroughly. The first stage of digestion takes place in the mouth when the food is mixed with an enzyme in your saliva.
- If you're having baked chicken, eat the meat closest to the bone. Avoid the fatty areas and skin.
- Use the microwave very sparingly and only for vegetables. When stressed it's better to have food rapidly on the table than to compound the chaos by fiddling around in the kitchen. Don't overcook the vegies.
- Lentil, tofu or tempeh burgers are usually available in the refrigerator of any good health food store.

- Wholemeal pasta tastes pretty awful unless you're creative. Use ordinary pasta made from unbleached flour or freshly made store-bought pasta after having checked its ingredients with the chef. Many of the prepared sauces in good gourmet shops are fine—check the ingredients—avoid oily ones.
- Prepared noodles (often called Ramen) are great to have as a stand-by in the pantry. They're good on their own as a soup or can be added to vegetable, chicken or fish dishes to flavour and thicken. They are available in health food stores and some supermarkets.
- Many unwell people are weary by the evening. If you're weary, so is your digestive system. You might find it best to have your main meals of the day at breakfast and lunch and have just a light meal (like soup and muffins) for dinner at night.
- Don't drink with your meal. Drink at least half an hour before the meal or one and a half hours after.

Recipes

The following recipes are included because of their simplicity and nutritional value.

Banana Smoothies

Banana smoothies are a delicious way to nourish someone who's feeling frail, who's underweight or who's having digestive problems. They're simple to prepare and can be stored in the refrigerator all day without loss of goodness. They're sometimes best drunk with a straw (if the mouth is sore, or the person is feeling a little squeamish) so that it delivers the fluid to the back of the throat. A little and often might be the best approach for most people. Very slightly warmed and taken before bed can help prepare someone for sleep as well as providing extra nourishment. The recipe is very flexible and can have many things added to the basic formula, which is:

- 1 large banana or 2 small ones or other soft, stewed or canned fruit
- 2 free-range eggs
- 1–2 cups of soya milk

Blend the ingredients together until smooth. Cinnamon or nutmeg can be sprinkled on top if desired.

Optional Extras

- 2 teaspoons of slippery elm powder (see page 126)
- a heaped dessertspoon of yoghurt (particularly if the person doesn't like eating yoghurt)
- other soft fruits like peaches, apricots, mangoes
- a heaped dessertspoon of cream or tofu (particularly if the person is underweight).

Juices

Freshly made vegetable juices are an excellent addition to the diet. With vegetable juices you receive an excellent intake of fresh and vital vitamins, enzymes, minerals, trace elements and other substances in a form which is easy for your body to assimilate. They're palatable, easily made and will pick up your energy level more quickly than anything else. For those recovering from surgery or who've been feeling unwell and have become quite run-down, the juices work like a charm. I can say, with complete confidence, that if these women drink three glasses of the following juice a day, they won't know themselves within a week. The juice has a remarkable capacity to kick-start the internal engines! There are very few contra-indications for juices for women with breast cancer. If your liver is affected by secondary growths you might need to dilute the juice. Try it full strength and if you feel it is a bit much, dilute it.

Juices should always be freshly prepared. The vegetables don't need to be peeled, though washing them is essential. Drink the juice slowly, mixing it well with saliva. I believe the following recipe is the best there is:

- 85 per cent carrot juice (chop the top centimetre off the carrot)
- 10 per cent beetroot juice (made from the fresh raw beet)
- 5 per cent green juice (made from celery, spinach, outside lettuce leaves, parsley, beet-tops—not if they're limp).

Some people have difficulty with the beetroot and it's advisable not to go above 10 per cent unless you really enjoy it. I've found this juice will help people to remain as healthy as possible whilst undergoing chemotherapy. It seems to minimise the side-effects to a remarkable degree. I usually recommend three 250 millilitre glasses per day, but it depends a little on the individual's health and ability to prepare them. For anyone about to undergo chemotherapy or surgery, three glasses per day in the preceding week will nourish you well in preparation. Always drink juices at least half an hour before a meal or one and a half hours afterwards. Some people might prefer to drink their juice with a straw. If you don't like the taste of the vegetable juice, leave out the beet-root and see how you go. If you still don't like it, then perhaps vegie juices aren't for you!

Vegetable juices are preferable to fruit juices, especially for those undergoing chemotherapy, other drug therapies, surgery or radiotherapy. Fruit juices tend to bring a lot of toxicity into the blood stream and can cause headaches, dizziness or weakness. Vegetable juices are far more gentle in their cleansing action in the body and these symptoms don't occur with them. For those who aren't feeling ill and who enjoy freshly made fruit juices these can, of course, be included.

6
Reach for Recovery

My oncologist used to think I was crazy because I take vitamins, homeopathics and juices, I meditate and go to a support group. Now he encourages me because he sees I'm doing remarkably well. He says, "Martha, you shouldn't be here! Whatever you're doing, keep it up". He told me I had two years to live, more than six years ago. It amazes me that he never asks for details of what I do or thinks it might help some of his other patients.

MARTHA, AGE 49
aged 40 at diagnosis

I'm very fortunate to have an oncologist who has a remarkable outlook on the powers of positive thinking, meditation, diet and vitamins, so I embarked on a complete change of lifestyle and introduced all of those things into my daily routine.

JANE, AGE 56
aged 49 at diagnosis

135

Looking back now I wish I could have spoken to someone before going in. I had no idea about the scar, the pain, the loss of feeling in my arm as well as no movement. However, a visit from a lady from the Cancer Council in hospital was wonderful. She had her mastectomy thirteen years before and she showed me how she could move her arm and told me how well I'd eventually feel. She also told me about Petrea's book Quest for Life *which I bought immediately. I also had great support and love from my family and friends.*

MAREE, AGE 46
aged 45 at diagnosis

My family were wonderful, with me all the time, my friends were amazingly caring and supportive, some travelled long distances to visit me, I had loads of flowers. The news from pathology was that three nodes in my axilla had been affected by the cancer and that meant maybe chemotherapy after the radiotherapy! I felt very depressed and apprehensive.

The morning I was due to go home, I had a visit from the oncologist at the hospital who was to take over my care. He was very reassuring and positive about my condition—maybe chemotherapy was not necessary at my age and stage in life after all. I was post-menopausal, still teaching small children and active, so he felt that Tamoxifen treatment would be, or could be, sufficient. After several visits, much thinking and talking, I decided against the chemotherapy; he had talked me through all the issues involved in this decision, and continues to give me encouragement and reassurance each time I see him.

LYNNE, AGE 54
aged 52 at diagnosis

Living alone and being sick is never easy, but with breast cancer there's so much fear, anguish and so many changes. I had many tearful nights alone in my unit. Making the bed, washing my hair, doing up my bra, I found difficult while one arm was not fully in use. Putting the washing out was another problem, carrying it down thirty stairs.

136

It has made me a nicer person! I talk, smile and care about people more. I talk to anybody now, in supermarkets, on buses and they talk back! I make more friends, go out much more, my thirst for knowledge has grown. I feel like I've been given a second chance at life and I want to catch up and miss nothing.

PATRICIA, AGE 56
aged 52 at diagnosis

I had a female X-ray person and then this man came up to me and I suddenly just blurted out, "I'm sorry I'm not going with you, I want a woman". He said "Why"? and I said, "Well, I'm sorry, I've had both my breasts cut off and I feel uncomfortable showing myself in front of a man and I want a woman". He said, "You will have a gown", and I said, "I don't care", raising my voice. So he ran away and said, "There's this nut case out here". But I still feel, at times, very vulnerable and very uncomfortable about people seeing my nakedness.

HELEN, AGE 42
aged 34 at diagnosis

The greatest lesson I've learnt has been about people, family and friends. The very ones I'd expected to support and help mostly disappeared. My support came from places unexpected. The local primary school parents have been wonderful in a practical way. At first, it was very difficult to accept that support was not where I thought it should be, but in doing so I've made it easier for myself. I now know where to look and ask for help and have stopped asking in the "wrong" places.

Many of my friends (and family), although fully aware of breast cancer, did not perhaps acknowledge that it occurs in my age group and so found the disease and me very threatening. And the treatment aspect—afraid of what I'd look like—Has your hair fallen out? You look different; Have you lost weight, and so on. Fact is, I've put on weight, still have hair and look pretty good!

But many "friends" have chosen to no longer see me or even contact me.

JUDY, AGE 38
aged 36 at diagnosis

I make the most of every day I suppose. It's really the philosophy that I live by; enjoy what you've got when you've got it. Some people aren't interested in this philosophy. They don't want to come along and get that support. When I was going to radiotherapy I found it very depressing because a lot of those people were very negative about what was happening to them. There was one man who was having radiotherapy and he was complaining about being sick all the time and he was a real misery guts. I think he revelled in being miserable and I can remember thinking how sad that was. There were some people there that were obviously sitting round waiting to die and yet they weren't dying. I just don't think they had the opportunity or the support to try and be positive about it.

SUE, AGE 54
aged 50 at diagnosis

I do say to him, I think holistic medicine is important and I'm letting you know I'm still taking the vitamin supplements and I'm still going to meditation and I'm still going to my support group and he just sort of poo-poos that, and says it won't make any difference. But I guess most of the oncologists are like that. In the main, doctors are amongst the most intelligent, best educated people in the community, and I always thought that one of the characteristics of a well-educated person is that there would be this openness of mind.

MARGARET, AGE 61
aged 59 at diagnosis

This chapter covers many aspects of breast cancer and the side-effects which might be experienced from your treatments or from the illness itself. It also covers many of the practical things which you might like to incorporate into your healing program.

I encourage you to read the whole of the chapter even though you won't experience all of the listed symptoms or difficulties. You'll find there are many overlapping suggestions amongst the alphabetically listed subjects and that there's a wealth of information to absorb. Take from these suggestions those things that seem to be right for you.

Complementary medicine concentrates on increasing the health, fitness and well-being of a person so they're vibrantly healthy in mind, body and spirit and would therefore also be an unsuitable host for any disease.

Much of the following information is based on simple commonsense, the use of home remedies and the addition of nutritional and herbal supplements. The problem with commonsense is that it is one of the rarest commodities in our society today and it's most elusive when we're in the midst of a crisis.

The ideas, suggestions and recommendations in this chapter are a result of years of working with women who've suffered not only the symptoms of their disease but the many discomforts that their treatments sometimes cause. None of the remedies mentioned in this chapter will in any way interfere with your medical treatment. The information is not intended as a prescription and you're encouraged to speak to your doctor before implementing these suggestions and to give them feedback as to the results. You could also benefit by consulting a naturopath or doctor trained to tailor a nutritional and natural therapy program to your specific situation.

The remedies and guidelines within this chapter are in no way designed to *treat breast cancer*. The intent is to give you some information about minimising the *symptoms* of breast cancer or the *side-effects* of your treatment. Very often, your doctor is more interested in the treatment of your disease and is less interested in the symptoms you might experience. If you complain about a lack of appetite; hot flushes; weight gain; a mouth full of ulcers; chronic squeamishness; restlessness at night; indigestion; lymphoedema; memory, weight or hair loss; watery eyes; nightsweats, or any of the myriad discomforting things which may occur, they might well show little interest because they're more concerned about the treatment of your primary condition. This can be very disconcerting. In fact, I find most people will say, 'I can cope with breast cancer but my hair falling out really gets to me' (or gaining weight, or lack of energy, or living with uncertainty).

In the health food store, you mightn't be able to replicate the exact formulations mentioned in this chapter. However, there'll be formulas which closely resemble them and I suggest you seek the assistance of the proprietor in deciding which is most appropriate for you.

Where it's suggested that a remedy be taken at regular intervals, it is with the understanding that you *don't* need to wake up at night to continue the process. For instance, when there's severe indigestion it's recommended that digestive enzymes be taken at two hourly intervals. It might be necessary to continue this right up until bedtime, but once sleep has been achieved, enjoy it!

To eliminate repetition, when a remedy is mentioned for the first time, an explanation of what it is will also be given. Subsequently, when that remedy is recommended, there'll be a note as to the section heading where it was first mentioned.

Throughout this chapter you'll see that homeopathics are referred to frequently. Homeopathic healing is based on the principle that 'like cures like'. For instance, in the homeopathic mixture for nausea there's a plant called ipecac. If you ate ipecac in large amounts it would *cause* nausea. In minute amounts, ipecac *cures* nausea. It's a little like a vaccination process; a tiny amount of infective material will set off the body's reaction to curing itself of the infection. The medicinal substances used in homeopathic medicines can be of animal, vegetable or mineral origin. It's not completely understood *how* homeopathic remedies work but the important thing is that they *do*!

The Formulas

When a homeopathic formula is suggested in this chapter, you'll see that after every ingredient there's a number with an 'x' following. For instance, Bryonia 2x; the number and the 'x' refer to the strength of the homeopathic. Homeopathics are available in some health food stores or through naturopaths. If you have difficulty in procuring any of the formulas, or any of the other supplements referred to, please write to the address given at the front of the book. Your feedback and experiences will help to develop and expand this knowledge so it can be made readily available to all those who share your path to healing. Please write and let me know if you've found remedies or solutions which have assisted you in your efforts to improve the quality of your life so they can be passed on to others.

Anaemia

Anaemia means that there aren't enough red blood cells to carry oxygen around your body. You need oxygen for energy and for the many processes which your body is engaged in. Anaemia can be caused by a number of things. If you've lost more blood than your body can readily replace, you become anaemic. Some drugs can depress the bone marrow's ability to produce sufficient red blood cells. These drugs include many of the chemotherapeutic drugs. As you can see from these causes there's not a great deal *you* can do about your haemoglobin (the oxygen binding protein in the red cells in your blood stream). The most likely symptoms of anaemia are:

- Low energy level or general weakness.
- Exhaustion or breathlessness on exertion.
- Giddiness or light-headedness on rising.
- Headache.
- Increased pulse rate.
- Pallor of skin.

It's essential that the cause of your anaemia is found. Your doctor will be the best person to find the cause and evaluate the appropriate treatment. However, the following suggestions have been found to be useful by many people. These are foods rich in iron and other essential nutrients which help to form red cells in the blood.

Remember these Points

- Drink the vegetable juice detailed in Chapter 5, 'Good Eating', three times daily, particularly in the week leading up to chemotherapy.
- Take a supplement which contains iron, zinc, folic acid, vitamins B12, B6, C and E.
- Drink a glass of stout before the evening meal or before bed.
- Eat meats which are rich in iron.
- Include leafy greens in your diet (or juice).

The benefits of adding these foods or substances to your diet will depend very much on the cause of your anaemia. If you're bleeding continuously from an area of your body, then drinking juices and not attending to the haemorrhage would be worse than useless. However, if nothing can be done to prevent the bleeding, or if anaemia is a side-effect of your treatment, then by all means use everything available (including blood transfusions) to ease the situation.

It can be very disconcerting to mentally prepare yourself for chemotherapy only to be told that your haemoglobin is down and your treatment will have to be postponed. I have found that women on chemotherapy who are taking vitamins, are on a good nutritional program, who meditate and who are using the vegetable juices (in particular) rarely have a problem with their haemoglobin. The section under Chemotherapy in this chapter has further guidelines on how to prepare for it.

Appetite, Loss of *see* Loss of Appetite

Bloating

Some women feel very bloated whilst going through or after chemotherapy or antibiotics. This is usually caused by a combination of factors. As always, it's essential that the *cause* be determined so that appropriate action can be taken.

When you take chemotherapy or antibiotics a lot of your good little gut bacteria in the intestine are destroyed. These bacteria are essential for you to be able to break food down so you can assimilate the nutrients into your blood stream. These bacteria keep in check yeasts which also reside in your intestines. When the chemotherapy or antibiotics destroy the bacteria you get an overgrowth of yeasts in the intestine and these yeasts cause fermentation, gas, discomfort and a feeling of bloatedness. The yeasts thrive on sugar and many women find that a sugary meal will cause havoc with rumbling and gas. In order to re-establish a healthy balance in your intestine it's essential that you eliminate sugar and replenish your gut bacteria. Reduce sugar to only that which you get from fresh fruit.

Many women over the age of fifty have a reduced capacity to produce gastric enzymes. This can also lead to your food not being properly broken down and the formation of gas and bloating.

In small amounts which are easily passed, gas isn't difficult to deal with. In large amounts that rumble within the convolutions of the bowel, it can become very uncomfortable and an embarassment. This kind of gas will usually respond to the addition of a low-fat yoghurt and/or gastric enzymes and an elimination of all sugars with the exception of the sugars found in fresh fruit. You may also want to simplify the combinations of foods at any one meal, so that you're not making it too difficult for your body to digest.

Occasionally, some women experience another kind of bloating which has nothing to do with chemotherapy or the taking of antibiotics. This bloating is caused through a build up of fluid in the abdomen. This fluid generally collects in the peritoneal cavity.

The peritoneum is a fine double membrane that lines the abdominal cavity. Fluid might collect between the membrane if cancer cells start growing on it or the build up of fluid can be caused by secondary tumours in the liver. This fluid is called ascites and won't be improved by the above approach. Your doctor is the best person to diagnose and treat ascites. Often indigestion is experienced *because* of this bloating and this can certainly be eased through using the guidelines in this section and in the one on Indigestion.

Chemotherapy

I likened that first experience of chemotherapy to feeling like I was in a concentration camp. The sisters wore white overalls with aprons which I hated and they put on two pairs of gloves. And I remember thinking, how horrible, how poisonous is this stuff they're injecting into my veins if they're too scared to get a drop of it on their skin. But once it was over, the actual physical experience really wasn't that bad.

RUTH, AGE 42
aged 40 at diagnosis

Perhaps Ruth's situation was made even more acute by the fact that she's a doctor and is more familiar with administering therapies rather than receiving them.

The thought of having chemotherapy really frightened me. All the horror stories. I was lucky, not many side-effects. Halfway through the treatment I looked awful. I hated my body—I looked like a freak, my hair was very thin and I felt everything feminine was being taken away from me. My boyfriend coped with it very well, but I couldn't.

PATRICIA, AGE 56
aged 52 at diagnosis

At the conclusion of my treatment I felt as if I'd fought a heroic battle, and won. I have every intention of being around till I'm

1. Lumpectomy

2. Simple mastectomy
with skin folds left for
reconstruction

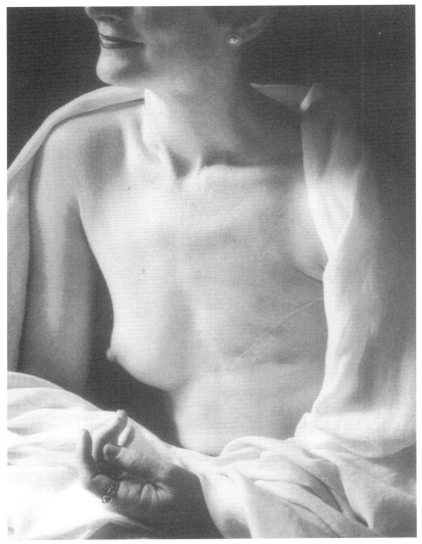

3. Modified radical mastectomy

4 and 5. Modified
radical mastectomy
with incomplete
reconstruction

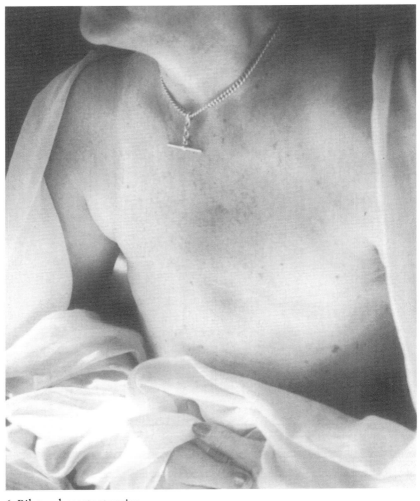

6. Bilateral mastectomies

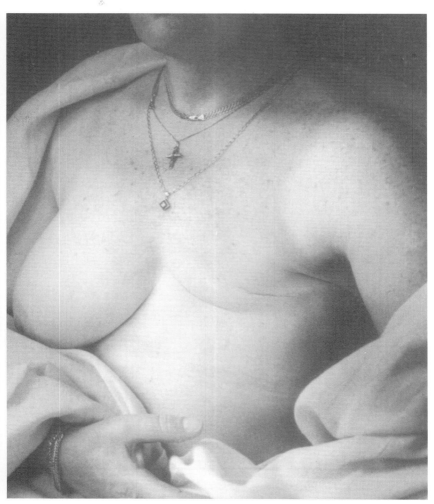

7. Simple mastectomy

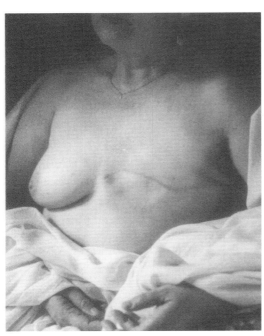

8. Modified radical mastectomy after 6 months

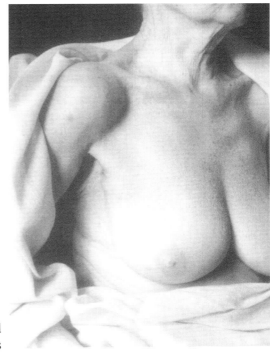

9. Lumpectomy and axillary nodes

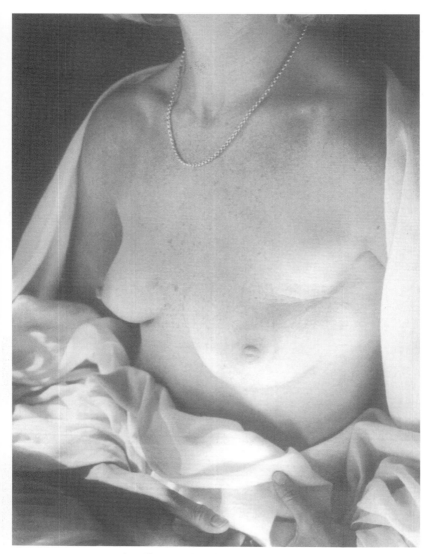

10. Lumpectomy and axillary nodes after 3 months

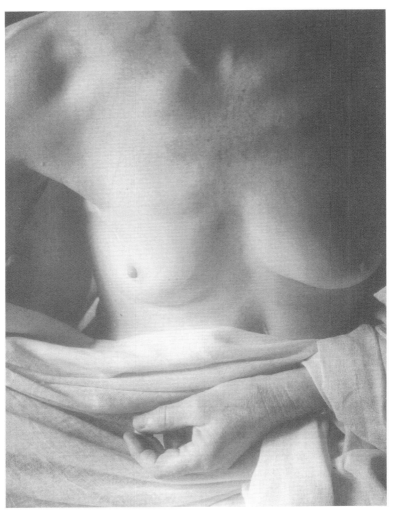

11. Lumpectomy

93, and am confident that I will. The wonderful things that I experienced in the meantime will live with me forever. It re-affirmed my belief that life is about giving and receiving love, for I received an almost endless torrent of loving deeds, thoughts, cards, flowers and support.

FIONA, AGE 34
aged 33 at diagnosis

I had the breast removed and the glands, as these proved malignant also. It was suggested that I have chemotherapy. Six months later after feeling really sick for the whole time (nausea, hair loss, bad nails, mouth ulcers and general disorientation) the chemo was finished.

LIZ, AGE 49
aged 47 at diagnosis

The chemotherapy lasted four months, and was tough. I came and went from my job overseas between treatments. The radiotherapy was comparatively easy, contrary to warnings and expectations, with minimal side-effects. During and following treatment I carried on my somewhat intensive life and work style.

JOAN, AGE 67
aged 63 at diagnosis

At four months I just stood outside the hospital and said to my husband, "Do I really have to go in there again"? And he said, "No, you don't". And the way he said it gave me a choice. And I said, "Oh, I'd better finish it, hadn't I"? and he said, "Yes, if you want to".

ROS, AGE 49
aged 47 at diagnosis

It was hard for me to imagine that this insignificant little lump could lead to my death. I was fit, happy, busy and I felt proud of the health of my family which I felt I'd helped to create. To agree to chemotherapy was a huge challenge because it seemed crazy to take something which would actually make me feel sick, when all

I started out with was a little lump. I'd always thought I'd never have a toxic treatment like chemotherapy. I felt like my beliefs were shattered.

MARILYN, AGE 41
aged 38 at diagnosis

All the stories I'd ever heard about chemotherapy rang in my ears. I was terrified of the stuff. I'm a complete wimp and I got myself into quite a state before I had it the first time. I waited and waited for the awful reaction to the drugs. It never came! I used to say, "I'm having Clayton's chemotherapy"! Seriously though, I believe counselling beforehand and the nutritional program, meditation, juices and vitamins all helped to make me feel more positive about chemotherapy.

JACKIE, AGE 53
aged 44 at diagnosis

Having used vitamins, juices and meditation with such success during my chemotherapy, I started on a similar but more intensive program when a bone marrow transplant was suggested. My oncologist was amazed at how few side-effects I experienced and I was out of hospital quicker than most. It also gave me a real sense of helping myself rather than just hoping for the best. The days of relative isolation passed without too much tedium, mostly because the techniques of relaxation and meditation helped keep my attitude positive. It's been over a year since my transplant and I feel on top of the world.

MARION, AGE 43
aged 40 at diagnosis

For many women it's very hard to come to terms with the idea of having chemotherapy. For some, it seems incongruous to embark upon a treatment which is likely to make them feel unwell when they didn't feel sick in the first place. It seems so unlikely that such a small lump or thickening can be life-threatening. This sense of unreality can be quite profound. Others are grateful that there *is* something they can do and are anxious to begin chemotherapy.

I've met many women who've been very frightened of chemotherapy; some who've been terrified; some who are a little reluctant; others who are resigned to it; and still others who feel comfortable and positive about the treatment they're starting on. The majority of women will do whatever it takes to rid themselves of cancer and give themselves the best chance for a remission or cure.

If you're one of the women who feel absolutely terrified of having chemotherapy, then speak to someone before you start treatment. Here are some suggestions:

- Perhaps you could ask your doctor to put you in touch with another woman who has completed the same suggested treatment program.
- By participating in a support group, you could air your feelings, and gain strength from others who've been through chemotherapy.
- You might like to find out more about the particular drugs they want to use and what are their likely side-effects. (Or, you might be like a friend of mine who says, 'Don't tell me the side-effects because I'm bound to get every one of them—even before I start the treatment!')
- You might want to get a second opinion.

If at all possible, resolve your fears *before* you embark upon treatment. Many women find the only way to get through chemotherapy is to listen to a familiar relaxation tape (with a Walkman) whilst they're having the treatment. Often, a familiar voice helps us to remain calm and positive. Several practices are suggested at the back of this book. These techniques can be harnessed to help you maintain a positive attitude towards your treatment. You can view your treatment as a highly toxic poison which is bound to make you sick *or* as liquid sunshine, light or healing which is designed solely for your benefit. It's up to you.

Some find that the company of a friend/partner is essential, whilst there are others who prefer to go alone and be left undisturbed. One of my friends found chemo so traumatic that she preferred to go into hospital and get 'knocked out' on medication so that she was completely unaware of the twenty-four hour period of her reaction to it. Do whatever works for you! There's no right way to cope with chemo. Find supports for yourself then use them without guilt or regret.

When peace of mind is our major goal then we can look at the suggested treatments with this view in mind. The vast majority of women feel much more at peace adopting the chemotherapy program suggested, than in choosing *not* to have treatment. If, in choosing not to have treatment, you have a little voice always in the background that says, 'I hope I'm doing the right thing. I wonder if I'm covering all my bases'? then that little voice becomes very undermining to our peace.

Obviously, no one looks forward, with enthusiasm, to chemotherapy. But most women feel far better to be actively doing something to rid themselves of cancer. In fact, many women feel a sense of 'abandonment' when they finish treatment. They feel, 'I'm alone with it and nothing "outside" is helping me. It's just me and the breast cancer'. This is usually mixed with the relief of finally completing treatment!

Some women find chemotherapy particularly taxing and, in discussions with their doctor, decide not to complete the full course. Talk to your doctor if you're feeling overwhelmed by your particular treatment program. It may well be that you can have a break from treatment or change it in some way.

There are many different chemotherapeutic drugs. Some have very few side-effects whilst others leave you feeling frail for a couple of days, and others knock you around more. However, the most common side-effects of chemotherapy include:

- Nausea, squeamishness or vomiting for the first forty-eight hours.
- Varying degrees of hair loss.
- Temporary cessation of periods in younger women. In women close to menopause, this may result in permanent cessation of menstruation.
- Constipation or diarrhoea.
- Depression and fatigue.
- Symptoms of menopause, for instance, hot flushes.
- Mouth ulcers.
- Weight gain/loss.
- Excessive bleeding or bruising if any injury occurs during the treatment period.

Slippery Elm Powder

Slippery elm powder is made from the inside bark of a tree and has been used for centuries by the Native Americans as a gruel for their babies to soothe upset tummies and to nourish them. It puts a slimy or mucilaginous coating over the whole of the gastro-intestinal tract. This substance is very soothing to the smooth muscle of the stomach and small intestine and promotes healing to damaged tissue. It tends to regulate the bowel and is useful for those who suffer with nausea, diarrhoea or constipation. Slippery elm is readily available from any health food store and has no side-effects.

Slippery elm is best used in powdered form as it's the most readily utilised/assimilated. It's also available in capsule or tablet form and, for problems occurring lower down in the bowel, these can be used instead if powder is unavailable. Frankly, I always prefer to use it in powdered form. The powder itself can be mixed with water but the easiest way to ingest it is mashed into a little low-fat, acidophilus-based yoghurt or soft, peeled, stewed fruit or banana. You can have it as frequently as seems necessary for you and, in fact, many people have virtually lived on slippery elm and yoghurt and fruit for one or more weeks.

Slippery elm is very soothing to the bowel wall, calms irritated and raw tissues and promotes healing to those surfaces traumatised through surgery, infection, antibiotics, chemotherapy or radiotherapy.

If you're having chemotherapy, you might like to take slippery elm powder an hour or two before your treatment is administered, and again a couple of hours after. Slippery elm mashed into whichever medium feels right for you might be the only food which sits happily in your tummy for a day or so around chemotherapy time. This will vary enormously from person to person and will depend also on the side-effects of the chemotherapy. Some women find very well-cooked porridge (rolled oats) with soya milk serves them well for their first meal after chemotherapy. Porridge for dinner mightn't sound appetising; however, it can be very soothing for a nauseous tummy.

Not everyone emerges from chemotherapy feeling exhausted and debilitated. Many women come through their treatments extremely well indeed. In my experience, women who are:

- Practising meditation, visualisation and relaxation techniques
- Participating in a support group
- Feeling positive about their treatment
- Well nourished
- Taking vegetable juices
- Taking vitamins

fare far, far better than women who feel negative about their treatment or who feel they're helpless to help themselves.

If you have two or three weeks before you begin your chemotherapy program, then use that time to prepare yourself physically, emotionally and psychologically. There is much that you can do to make sure you come through your treatment as well as possible. The sooner you begin on the diet recommended in this book, the juices, meditation, and so on, the better you'll cope with the treatment.

Rarely do any of the women, who take this approach, need to have a blood transfusion because their haemoglobin has been affected by their treatment. Generally, they remain in good health (and spirits) throughout their chemotherapy. Again, I'd recommend you visit a good naturopath or doctor who specialises in nutritional medicine, to have a vitamin program tailored to your individual needs.

There are many sections in this chapter which will be relevant to the woman on chemotherapy. I suggest you read through the whole of the chapter so that you'll know where to turn to if, in the future, you encounter any of the symptoms listed.

Chewing and Swallowing Problems, Mouth Ulcers, Dry Mouth and Thrush

Some kinds of chemotherapy can interfere with the health of the delicate tissue in your mouth. Radiation which affects your oesophagus can make swallowing difficult. Some analgesics, like morphine, dry out the secretions in the mouth. The problem doesn't necessarily stop at the discomfort and inconvenience of having a dry mouth. The saliva serves a valuable function in maintaining the oral hygiene within the mouth and gullet area and, with these secretions missing, infections, mouth ulcers, increased sensitivity, bleeding gums and thrush can all become a problem. Having a mouth which feels and tastes like the bottom of a bird-cage is no fun either. With a sensitive mouth it becomes increasingly difficult to eat.

A *dry mouth* at night can be very distressing as it interferes with your sleep. To awaken gagging from the dryness can be awful. Always keep some fluid nearby. Artificial saliva can be useful for this as it evaporates much more slowly than water. Your chemist can order in artificial saliva if they don't have it in stock. Five to ten drops on the tongue is usually sufficient to give relief. You might need to use a little more at night to keep your mouth lubricated whilst you sleep. Your dentist or chemist can also supply you with a chewing gum which increases salivary production. There are some excellent ones available.

Ice chips of peppermint, lemon or lemongrass tea can be both soothing and refreshing to the mouth. Do not use lemon tea if the lining of the mouth is raw or sensitive. In severe cases where the mouth is very sensitive or raw a liquid spray or gel local anaesthetic will bring relief. You can apply this a few minutes before eating to minimise discomfort.

If *thrush* is present then your doctor will prescribe a liquid for the mouth or some lozenges for you to suck. Thrush can be very painful and can make swallowing difficult, particularly when it extends down the oesophagus. Your doctor will prescribe some further medication if this is the case. Thrush sometimes develops after a course of chemotherapy or antibiotics.

Many people find rinsing the mouth and gargling with diluted tea-tree oil is helpful in keeping thrush at bay. Take 5 drops of tea-tree oil in a quarter of a cup of tepid water, rinse, gargle and spit out. This might sting a little if there are any broken areas. You can reduce the tea-tree oil to 1 or 2 drops if that's more comfortable. It's very helpful for bleeding gums, mouth ulcers, thrush, cracked or sensitive mouth linings (in addition to, or replacement of, any prescribed medications).

I've known other people who swear by using Coca-Cola for the same purpose. They say it gets rid of thrush in no time! Use it undiluted, rinse, gargle and spit it out. As a naturopath, it makes me squirm but I'm all for what works!

Zinc lozenges which contain vitamin C and lysine are also very helpful for any *mouth ulcers* or broken areas in the mouth.

Propolis is a bee product which contains many nutrients which are readily assimilated by your body. It's also a valuable antibiotic against anaerobic germs which live in our mouths and throats and which extend right throughout the digestive tract. Propolis is very helpful for people who have recurring infections in the mouth and throat.

Those with *chewing problems* will find it easier to eat moist, soft foods and might even benefit from a liquid diet of nutritious foods drunk through a straw. Smoothies, soups and vegetable juices can all be ingested in this way. This delivers the food to the back of the mouth and minimises any irritation.

Remember these Points

- Use artificial saliva (available from chemists) or chewing gums which increase salivary output (available from dentists and chemists).
- Eat soft, tender and bland foods such as pasta, noodles.
- Eat cool, moist foods such as stewed fruits, yoghurt, cold soups.
- Make ice blocks of peppermint and/or chamomile/lemon or lemongrass tea and suck on the chips.
- Drink non-acidic juices such as peach or apricot nectars, grape or apple juice (you might need to dilute them with water).
- Rinse your mouth frequently to keep mouth and gums clean, put a fresh taste in the mouth and prevent infection.
- Avoid highly acidic, spicy or salty foods such as citrus fruits or juices, tomatoes, strawberries, pineapples, pepper and chilli powder.
- Very hot foods can be irritating, cool/cold foods can be soothing.
- Avoid chewy foods or hard to chew foods like fresh fruits and raw vegetables.
- The warm liquid from a nourishing chicken casserole might be tolerated quite well.

- Tilting the head back to swallow might ease the discomfort.
- Use a blender to prepare soft, smooth foods.
- Drinking through a straw delivers food to the back of the mouth. Suitable foods to be consumed in this way are soups, smoothies, vegetable juices and yoghurt.
- Relaxation or meditation techniques practised before eating can allow swallowing to be more easily tolerated by those who experience pain in their oesophagus.
- Use Coca-Cola (as a last resort!) for stubborn thrush plus whatever your doctor suggests.

Cold Bones

Many women with breast cancer find they experience a coldness that seems to come from the bones out. No matter what they put on in the way of extra clothes or even if they sit right in front of a fire they *still* feel cold. This is something that many sick people feel and isn't associated with breast cancer in particular. I used to feel as if my bones were made of ice, even though it wasn't particularly cold outside! The only remedy which I've found helps is ginger tea. This is made by thinly slicing a quarter of a cup of fresh ginger root, simmering it for fifteen minutes in 1litre of water. Let it cool to body temperature, strain. You might like to add a little honey for sweetening. Drink a small cupful every hour or two or before bed.

Cold Sores *see* Herpes Simplex

Constipation

Constipation can create intense pain and discomfort. You're constipated if your motions are hard and you have difficulty passing them. All sorts of things can cause constipation and, like everything else, it's essential to find the cause.

We all know some of the things which cause constipation—lack of exercise, insufficient fluid intake, most analgesics (pain-killers), lack of fibre, not eating enough, and some foods like cheese, fried eggs, and so on. Constipation is only the symptom of a problem. Once the problem has been established, appropriate treatment (if any) can be planned. If possible, don't wait until you're really badly constipated before doing something about it.

If the constipation is caused through the necessary intake of analgesics then you'll need to take a laxative. Most analgesics, in addition to relieving you of pain, also cause constipation. They do this by slowing down the peristaltic movement of the bowel and by drying out its contents. These two things in combination cause you to develop constipation.

Your nurse or doctor will know what's causing *your* constipation so ask their advice. The community and palliative care nurses are also experts at managing constipation. They'll recommend to you an appropriate laxative which contains a softening agent. The addition of extra fluids, prunes, slippery elm (see under Chemotherapy in this chapter), bran and so on can be helpful but if your constipation is due to the intake of analgesics then you'll almost certainly need to take a laxative as well.

It's important to drink plenty of fluids and to exercise to the extent you're able. Sometimes a massage to the abdomen or the application of warmth will be sufficient to stimulate the bowel (in addition to your laxative). This warmth can be applied in the form of a 'hot-water bottle'—an electric heating pad or small towel soaked in hot water and wrung out, then placed gently over the abdomen. If massage is used, always massage in a clockwise direction, starting with the downward stroke on the left side of your body. Slow and gentle massage with a warmed and perfumed oil can be very soothing and can stimulate the bowel to function.

Your nurse might also suggest the use of suppositories or enemas. These days they're extremely easy to give (though some cause a burning sensation) and are very effective. Be guided by their advice.

See also Diarrhoea.

Coughs

Any cough should be checked by your doctor so that they might discover its cause and establish the appropriate treatment. There's one particular cough about which I want to say a few words.

Some women develop metastases (or secondary growths) in the lungs. Occasionally, these small tumours can interfere with the nerve receptors which can cause a constant and irritating tickling sensation in the upper part of the chest. You might develop a frustrating cough which can be exacerbated by talking, stress, trying not to cough, physical exertion, laughing or lying down.

Sometimes, these tumours can be effectively treated by radiotherapy or chemotherapy so it's essential you speak to your doctor. There are some medications for pain which also suppress this tickling cough. If there's no recommended treatment you might like to try the following homeopathic remedy which has worked effectively in many cases. This formula isn't intended to treat the cause but to alleviate the effect of the nerve irritation and it can be taken in addition to any medical treatment:

Ipecacuanha	6x
Bryonia	3x
Drosera	4x
Spongia	6x
Coccus Cacti	6x
Belladonna	5x
Corallium rubrum	12x

To alleviate cough: Take 10–15 drops in a couple of teaspoons of water every half to one hour. Hold the liquid in your mouth for a few seconds before swallowing.

If the cough is particularly persistent: Take 70 drops in half a glass of water. Sip every 2 to 3 minutes, holding each sip in the mouth for a few seconds before swallowing, until the cough settles. Then reduce the frequency to every 5, then 10, then 15, then 30 minutes. Resume frequency if the cough returns.

Though this remedy will alleviate the cough in many cases, it doesn't do anything to the cause of the cough. It doesn't work by reducing tumour size or by treating infections, but it does seem to affect the irritation to the nerve receptors. It's also a beneficial formula for those who develop an irritating cough when under stress.

Cramps

Leg cramps can ruin a good night's sleep and leave you feeling sore the next day. They can sometimes be related to medication you might be taking so it's important to let your doctor know that you're having cramps in your legs. If they're not related to your medication (and even if they are) try this simple remedy. It might sound crazy but it works! Take 10-12 wine bottle corks and pin them in a piece of cotton, such as a large handkerchief, and place in the bottom of the bed. That's it! It's best if the corks came from their bottles in the last three months but *you* don't have to drink the wine first. Your local restaurant will probably oblige by giving you theirs.

If this 'remedy' sounds too unscientific for you, try a supplement which contains vitamins B1, B3, B6, E, biotin, calcium, magnesium and potassium.

Diarrhoea

Diarrhoea involves passing loose motions often and usually with urgency. In other words, 'when you gotta go, you gotta go!'

For women with breast cancer, the most likely cause of diarrhoea will be chemotherapy. Other possibilities include infections, nervous tension or the effect of medications. Again, the cause must be determined in order to find the appropriate form of treatment.

If your diarrhoea is caused by an infection then it must be

treated. If your diarrhoea is caused through your chemotherapy, the treatment could either be adjusted by your doctor or you could adopt the very successful plan outlined here.

Remember, diarrhoea often occurs after a course of anti-biotics. If this is the case, it means in addition to the 'bad' bacteria, the antibiotics have also killed off the useful bacteria which live in your gut and they need to be replenished with either yoghurt or *lactobacillus acidophilus* in capsule or powder form. This might in itself be sufficient to remedy the situation.

It's important you don't become dehydrated if you have diarrhoea. Make sure you continue to drink plenty of fluids during the time when you have diarrhoea. At least eight 250 mL glasses per day of fluid. Peach and apricot nectars are particularly good because they're high in potassium which is lost when you have diarrhoea.

There are some excellent medications available for diarrhoea and you might wish to speak to your doctor about these. The problem with some of them is that they stop up the system only to have it let go with a vengeance at a later time. If this is the case, then the approach suggested here could save the day. Please discuss these guidelines with your doctor before following them. The information here will also be helpful to anyone suffering with erratic bowel function.

In order to soothe and comfort the lining of the bowel, you can't find a more efficient and calming substance than slippery elm powder (see under Chemotherapy in this chapter).

The bowel wall needs to be soothed in order for you to assimilate the nutrition from your food; you can have the best diet in the world but if the food passes through your body too quickly, you'll be unable to absorb its goodness. The treatment of diarrhoea, as set out here, involves the slowing down of the bowel function and the addition of substances which will ensure that you have the necessary enzymes and bacteria to assimilate the food you're eating.

For any bowel irritation, I suggest one or two heaped tea-spoons of slippery elm powder mashed into a little low-fat yoghurt or very ripe banana or soft or stewed fruit, taken four times daily before meals and before bed. Use it as often as every one-two hours if the diarrhoea is very severe.

This simple remedy will be beneficial in conjunction with a commonsense diet for *any* bowel disturbance including diarrhoea, constipation, and so on. It's important to use it in conjunction with the diet.

Foods to Avoid
The following foods should be avoided completely if you have diarrhoea:
- Cheese, cow's milk, cream, butter, sour cream or any other dairy product with the exception of yoghurt. Replace with a 'light' soya milk.
- High-fat substances such as fried foods, gravy, creamy soups or sauces.
- Seeds, whole nuts, bran, muesli, grain husks, whole grains, most unprocessed foodstuffs, salads.
- Caffeine, Indian/China tea, carbonated beverages.
- Cabbage, broccoli, cauliflower, onions, beans, peas, corn.
- Sweets, chewing gum, sugar, honey, molasses, golden syrup, cookies, chocolate, cakes or any other sweet substance with the exception of those listed below.

Suggested Liquids
- Water, broth, clear soups.
- Apple or pear juice, apricot and peach nectars.
- Herb teas (without honey), dandelion coffee.
- Vegetable soups.

It's also important to replace electrolytes with high potassium foods such as bananas, potatoes, apricot and peach nectars.

The use of homeopathics is also highly recommended. These will need to be supplied by a homeopath/naturopath or health food store. The most beneficial homeopathic formula I've found is:

Diarrhoea Drops

Oleander	6x
Phosphoricum acidum	3x
Tincture chamomilla	4x
Tincture colocynthis	6x
Tincture veratrum album	6x
Rhus toxicodendron	4x
Ferrum phosphoricum	8x
Mercurius corrosivus	5x
Baptisia tinctoria	4x

To prevent diarrhoea: Take 10–15 drops in a couple of teaspoons of water four times daily before meals and before bed. It can be taken as often as every hour. Hold the liquid in your mouth for a few seconds before swallowing.

Taking the drops this way *before* having any treatment which you know will give you diarrhoea helps to minimise its effect. If you still develop diarrhoea then take the drops as follows.

To alleviate diarrhoea: Take 70 drops in half a glass of water. Sip every 5 to 10 minutes until diarrhoea begins to subside, holding each sip in the mouth for a few seconds before swallowing. Once the diarrhoea has settled, then reduce the frequency to every half hour, then every hour, then two hours, then three, and so on until you're back to taking it four times daily. If another wave of diarrhoea appears, resume the prescribed frequency. Homeopathics work best not by the strength of their dosage but by the frequency with which they're taken.

Many women with breast cancer develop an intolerance to cow's milk. This often happens as a result of using chemotherapy, especially in women over the age of fifty. If you have intermittent diarrhoea/constipation or one or the other try leaving out cow's milk altogether. Replace it with soya, goat's or sheep's milk. The addition of gastric enzymes can also be very helpful for these women. Choose a formula like the one listed under Indigestion in this chapter.

Remember these Points

- Note the foods to avoid.
- Keep up your fluid intake.
- Make ice blocks of peppermint and/or chamomile tea and suck on the ice chips.
- Drink fluids through a straw if it makes it easier for you.
- Well-cooked porridge (oatmeal) is often tolerated. You can add slippery elm powder to your oatmeal.
- Try small meals, frequently, served at room temperature.
- Try low-fibre foods such as stewed apple (without the skin).
- Try puréed or grated fruits or cooked vegetables.
- Don't drink with your meals—drink thirty minutes before or at least ninety minutes after eating.
- So long as the carrot-based vegetable juice listed in Chapter 5 doesn't increase your diarrhoea, it's an excellent form of nourishment.
- Have your food neither too hot nor too cold.
- The herbal relaxant (see the Insomnia section in this chapter) is often very helpful for a bowel in spasm.

Many people find the following recipe good for stopping diarrhoea in its tracks.

1 cup of cooked white rice
1 large mashed banana
1 grated peeled apple (left to go brown before adding to this mixture)
1 heaped dessertspoon of slippery elm powder
cinnamon or nutmeg to taste
Mix all the above ingredients with Gastrolyte or the equivalent (available from the chemist) to the desired consistency.

Intermittent Constipation and Diarrhoea

Another very common problem is constipation which alternates with diarrhoea. This can be caused in a number of ways. Women often experience this problem after a course of antibiotics or during or after chemotherapy. Following the guidelines set out here will help in regulating the bowel function. They will not *cause* constipation.

Irritable Bowel

Irritable bowel can also be helped by following the guidelines suggested here for controlling diarrhoea. Slippery elm is particularly helpful, as are the homeopathic drops. Eliminating all sugars except fruit sugars is essential.

Experiment until you find *your* perfect solution. Techniques of relaxation, visualisation and meditation are very useful and should be incorporated on a daily basis.

The herbal remedy mentioned under Nervous Tension, Fear and Anxiety (this chapter) is also invaluable.

Exercise

I used to walk 6 kilometres a day before I was diagnosed. I miss it. I want to get back to walking. I think it would help if I felt strong enough to have the exercise.

SALLY, AGE 58
aged 50 at diagnosis

Initially I missed playing competition tennis, but now I enjoy the relaxed and easy-going atmosphere of social tennis. It was hard for me to give up the competitiveness and yet, I think I'm a happier and more peaceful person, and I like the changes in myself.

RACHEL, AGE 40
aged 36 at diagnosis

Sport has been a major feature of my life. I swim regularly and play squash twice a week. The exercise for my arm has been good. I can't play at the level I used to but I'm working on it.

BRONWYN, AGE 39
aged 38 at diagnosis

Exercise is a treasured part of many women's lives. For some, it's a major source of enjoyment, perhaps through sport, and for others, it might be the morning walk with the dog or attending to a garden. We often take for granted many of the activities, routinely performed, which provide us with exercise. For some, it may be yet another area in which they experience loss.

Many women are involved in work which requires physical stamina. You may need to discuss with your doctor and your employer a likely time-frame for your return to increased duties.

It's easy to fall into the trap of comparing yourself now, with who, and how you were before breast cancer. Accepting the fact that you're not as physically fit as you were before and that you'll have to gradually increase your level of exercise, can be a challenge in itself.

We all know that exercise is a really important activity for everyone. However, it's essential that you find a balance between pushing yourself to stretch your limits and being gentle with yourself if you're recovering or if you're not well. You may well have to let go of some cherished activity and embark upon a gentler regime of exercise until your body becomes stronger.

Even if you're confined to bed, it's important for your own physical comfort, that you don't become stiff and immobile. Gentle, passive exercise where somebody helps you take your limbs through a range of movements will help your circulation.

As Sally above says, we often *need* energy in order to be able to exercise. It can be very sad and frustrating to want to be more physically involved and simply to lack the energy to follow through on that desire.

If you're physically fit and enjoy exercise then it would be good to aim for at least four periods of exercise a week. This exercise can be walking, swimming, running, tennis or whatever you enjoy and ideally is sustained for thirty minutes. It needs to increase your pulse rate and have you breathing more deeply. Physical exercise is essential to prevent osteoporosis.

Fatigue—Too Tired to Prepare Meals

Feeling exhausted can be very depressing and once depression sets in, it can become difficult to motivate yourself enough to prepare healthy and nutritious meals. It's important, as always, to find out the cause of the fatigue.

It could be because your haemoglobin is low; it could be because your lung capacity is restricted for some reason and the red blood cells can't pick up sufficient oxygen; it could be because your body is undernourished; it could be the overall effect of debilitating illness or depression.

Once the cause is understood and treated as effectively as possible, then you'll need to find practical and simple ways to nourish yourself with a minimal requirement of energy. Many people find difficulty in actually asking for assistance and, in other cases, there *is* no one to ask anyway. If there are friends, neighbours or family who've offered their assistance, now is certainly the time to reach out for help. They wouldn't have offered if they didn't genuinely mean for you to take them up on it. It gives them the opportunity to do something truly constructive to assist you.

A supplement containing methionine, tyrosine, asparagine, iron, folic acid, biotin, vitamin C and manganese might prove helpful. Some people benefit from vitamin B12 injections on a regular basis. Speak to your doctor about whether they might help.

Co Enzyme Q10 can be beneficial in reducing fatigue, depending upon its cause. This substance, available through health food stores and many chemists usually gives quick results. It has other benefits as well for the immune system. Most people need to take 40–80 milligrams per day. It *can* take four to six weeks for the full effects to be felt.

Remember these Points

- Prepare meals ahead of time when you feel well and freeze them in individual servings.
- Keep easy to prepare foods on hand, such as frozen dinners, canned tuna, salmon or sardines, free-range eggs, noodles, frozen soups, muffins, muesli bars, healthy snack bars.
- Eat small meals frequently.
- Accept offers of family, friends or neighbours to help prepare meals.
- Take advantage of healthy take-away foods.
- If someone offers to make vegetable juices and you find you can tolerate them, accept with as much enthusiasm as you can muster. Vegetable juices will pick up your energy level more quickly than anything I know (depending on the cause of your exhaustion). If you can manage three freshly made glasses of juice (see the recipe in Chapter 5) per day, you won't know yourself in a week.
- Take advantage of home delivery services.
- Use Sustagen, Ensure (a soya based formula) or a similar supplement to provide a nutritional base.
- Take vitamin/mineral formulations to meet your essential needs.

Hair Loss

There are some kinds of chemotherapy where you'll be told you'll lose all your hair. There are other kinds which result in hair loss of an indeterminate amount. For the women in the former category, it's heartening to remember not everybody loses all of their hair; in the latter category, many women on a good diet, drinking vegetable juices and taking vitamins and other supplements, lose only a minimal amount of hair or none at all. These women also tend to grow their hair back more quickly.

Many women notice a 'hair ache' in the days before their hair begins to fall. They describe it as if the hair roots are hurting. Some women decide, rather than let their hair fall, to shave their head. This has given them a sense of them being in control. Others have decided to cut long hair very short to reduce the weight on their hair roots.

Everybody's hair grows back after chemotherapy, sometimes with a wave in it, sometimes even curly, thicker and often of a slightly darker shade than before, though not always. One of my clients, aged fifty-two, who had long, straight, black hair before chemotherapy grew the most wonderful, curly, silvery hair afterwards. She looked very elegant and was delighted with the change.

Just about everybody finds it difficult to come to terms with losing their hair. It can be very disconcerting to wake up and find hair all over the pillow or to see it going down the drain in the shower. The emotional impact of losing the hair will vary from one woman to another. For some, it can be quite devastating and will feel like the worst part of having cancer. Reassurance is necessary as the self-esteem often falls with the hair!

Hair lost through radiotherapy to the head usually grows back unless the dosage has been very strong. For many, particularly young women, the challenge of learning to live with bald patches can be almost insurmountable. Our self-esteem is nearly always connected to our self-image. Special consideration and encouragement are needed to ensure safe passage through the traumas of such hair loss.

Many major hospitals run programs called 'Look Good, Feel Better' in which women are given guidance on how to maximise their self-esteem through tips about dress, hair and make-up.

Manufacturers provide a wealth of information and samples for women to try.

Wigs

Some hospitals or cancer support associations provide a wig library, from which you can borrow a wig for as long as you need it.

The constant wearing of head scarves, wigs, turbans and hats has its own tedium. Some wig companies will make a wig fringe attached to a light cotton scarf. This gives the impression of hair whilst letting the scalp 'breathe' more easily than if it were confined under a full wig or turban. This is, of course, particularly relevant in summer when a wig can feel hot and 'foreign', especially as hair regrowth begins.

Fingernails

Women often find that their fingernails thrive on chemotherapy and become (and stay) much stronger than before! Occasionally, women find they have all sorts of trouble with their fingernails. The following supplements for the hair will prove helpful for nail re-growth as well.

The essentials for strong hair re-growth are folic acid, silica, biotin and cysteine. These can be taken in a formula and are available from your local health food store, naturopath or doctor who specialises in nutritional medicine. If you are using the dietary program recommended in this book you won't need to take a supplement as you'll be getting everything you need from your food.

Herpes Simplex (Cold Sores)

Ulcers which form around the outside of the mouth in the lip area usually respond very well to diluted tea-tree oil. Most people who develop herpes simplex are aware of a sensation of numbness or tingling *before* anything actually shows up on the skin. If you apply tea-tree oil diluted 50/50 with almond, grape seed or apricot kernel oil, twice a day as soon as any numbness or tingling occurs, the herpes rarely appears or is very minor when it does. If a sore is already present then the juice from leeks, applied to the sore, will often alleviate the pain.

All this applies equally to genital herpes. Many people find they have an outbreak of herpes either during or immediately after their course of chemotherapy, antibiotics or other drug therapy. This only occurs, of course, in women who have the herpes simplex virus in their system. Usually, it is when your body is under stress and your immune system is depleted that herpes will flare up.

The homeopathic drops mentioned under Shingles in this chapter are also helpful for herpes.

If you're prone to attacks of herpes (either genital or in the form of cold sores) you might like to try a supplement containing lysine, folic acid, zinc, vitamin B12 and the B complex. You should also avoid chocolate and nuts, both of which contain arginine which the herpes simplex virus thrives on.

Hot Flushes

I've had two years of the most horrendous hot flushes. The only thing that eases them is the homeopathic drops.

MAREE, AGE 46
aged 45 at diagnosis

My kids at school must think I'm totally weird. I'll be sitting reading them a story and all of a sudden I have to put down the book and grab a tissue. In summer it just drips down my chin and my glasses slide down my nose and I'm still reading them this story. They must think I'm nutty.

LYNNE, AGE 55
aged 52 at diagnosis

Many women experience early menopause either through surgical removal of, or radiation to, the ovaries, or through the use of drugs which interfere with the action of oestrogen. The symptoms can be very mild or they can be quite annoying. In fact, it can be

168

one of the most exasperating of all symptoms to cope with. It serves as a constant reminder of breast cancer or menopause.

It's important to point out the difference between hot flushes and night sweats. As the name implies, night sweats are usually only experienced at night, aren't associated with an increase in temperature and don't necessarily have a hormonal aspect to them. Hot flushes are experienced regardless of the time of day or night and are generally accompanied by a feeling of increasing heat though one's body temperature doesn't rise.

Many people whose immune system is not functioning well experience night sweats. Often the dampness is experienced in the shoulder, chest, neck, upper back and head and not in the usual places at all. See Night Sweats in this chapter for the remedy.

The following homeopathic remedy, Climacteric Drops, assists most women in bringing hot flushes under control. It consists of:

Climacteric Drops

Cimicifuga racemosa	4x
Sepia	4x
Sanguinaria	4x
Lachesis	12x
Sulphuric acid	4x

To control hot flushes: Take 10–15 drops in a couple of teaspoons of water four times daily before meals and before bed. Hold the liquid in your mouth for a few seconds before swallowing. Once the flushes have gone or are greatly decreased in frequency or intensity, reduce to three times daily, then twice daily and stay on once daily until you reach the end of the bottle. If the hot flushes are very stubborn, increase the frequency to every one to two hours.

Occasionally, when hot flushes are really severe and usually of long-standing, the above drops are insufficient on their own. In this case there are some extra drops, Potentising Drops, which can be taken once a day in addition to the others which double the strength of any homeopathic.

Potentising Drops

Nitricum acidum	12x
Phosphoricum acidum	12x
Sulphur iodatum	12x
Ferrum iodatum	12x
Calcarea iodatum	12x

They're taken in the same way as the Climacteric Drops, except they're only taken once a day, preferably in the morning.

Most women find that these drops greatly reduce their hot flushes if not eliminate them altogether. The addition of these drops will not interfere with any medical treatment you might be using.

Vitamin E can be helpful in reducing the intensity and frequency of hot flushes. Speak to your naturopath or nutritional doctor about the right dosage for you (usually around 500 international units per day). Likewise, a good quality vitamin B complex helps many women (see the section in this chapter on Vitamins).

Tamoxifen, a non-steroidal anti-oestrogen, causes flushing in some women whilst others experience no side-effects at all from this treatment. Some women take medications prescribed by other doctors for problems unrelated to breast cancer. Make sure your oncologist knows all the medications you're taking so that any which may be increasing the symptoms of menopause can be changed or eliminated.

Some women find that spicy foods increase the intensity of hot flushes and you may be better off avoiding these foods altogether. Avoiding synthetic mixes in both night clothes and sheets is also recommended.

Indigestion

The mucous lining of the mouth, oesophagus, stomach, intestines and other internal organs have a high proportion of rapidly

dividing cells and are therefore affected by most forms of chemotherapy. For instance, the cells forming the lining of the mouth are
replaced every twenty-four hours. Most chemotherapy drugs
interfere with this process and so the mouth can become raw or
sensitive and can form ulcers. Chemotherapy targets rapidly
dividing cells so the surface of the digestive tract will be damaged
and will take several days to recover.

Many women develop indigestion when having chemotherapy
or other drug treatments, particularly those over the age of fifty.
This might be in the form of burping repeatedly after eating, a burning sensation just below the sternum or a feeling of bloatedness.

From experience, I believe that some forms of chemotherapy
and some other drug treatments interfere with the body's ability
to secrete hydrochloric acid and gastric and pancreatic enzymes.
The addition of hydrochloric acid and digestive enzymes in conjunction with an appropriate diet, can eliminate these distressing
symptoms altogether. Many women have a diminished ability to
produce digestive enzymes. Sometimes this inability to produce
sufficient digestive enzymes is evident in women who:

- Are over the age over fifty.
- Are having or have recently had chemotherapy.
- Are unwell.
- Have had major surgical procedures to the digestive tract.
- Are recovering from *any* major surgery.
- Are having or have had radiotherapy to the stomach/
  abdominal area.

The formulas which I prescribe contain:

Betaine HCL	400 mg
Pancreatin 4NF	200 mg
Bromelain	100 mg
Pepsin	100 mg
Glutamic acid	100 mg
Trypsin	30 mg

One or two tablets of a formula like the one above with or immediately after each meal should be sufficient to alleviate the above symptoms. Some women find they need to take digestive enzymes and hydrochloric acid any time they ingest any food or fluid, with the exception of water.

Do not drink any liquid for at least thirty minutes before a meal or at least one and a half hours after eating (with the exception of minimal fluid to take the digestive enzymes).

The reason why you shouldn't drink whilst eating is this. Imagine you eat a piece of toast. Your stomach responds to this complex carbohydrate and begins to secrete the hydrochloric acid and gastric enzymes to digest it. At the far end of your stomach there's a little muscle which will only relax and allow food to pass into the small intestine when the contents of the stomach are liquid. The contents should be liquid because the food has been mixed with digestive enzymes and hydrochloric acid. If you've had a glass of water, juice or a cup of tea or whatever with the meal, then the food in your stomach is mixed with *that* and dilutes the digestive enzymes and hydrochloric acid. For most people, that is not a major problem but if you are frail, under-weight or undergoing treatment then it's important that you get the goodness from the food you're eating.

The exception to this is wine. Wine actually stimulates the production of gastric enzymes and can be included on special occasions, but not if you suffer with indigestion or have liver secondaries which decrease your tolerance for alcohol.

Chemotherapy, antibiotics and some other drug treatments destroy the 'good' bacteria that normally reside in the intestines. These bacteria are essential because they help break down the food you eat so your body can assimilate the nutrients.

I recommend you eat 2 dessertspoons of an acidophilus-based low-fat yoghurt per day during the time you're having chemotherapy/antibiotics, so you replenish the gut bacteria which the drugs destroy.

Keep that up for at least two months after you've completed treatment. If you miss a day, of course, it's no problem. If you want to eat more than two dessertspoons a day, that's fine. The yoghurt must be based on the acidophilus lacto-bacillus. Several low-fat cow's milk varieties are available as well as goat's milk yoghurt and sheep's milk yoghurt. Most people find the cow's milk varieties the most palatable and readily available. Yoghurt, quark, leben and natural cheeses are generally the *only* kind of dairy food which I recommend for women with breast cancer.

If you can't stand yoghurt, mix it into a banana smoothie (see Chapter 5) or take acidophilus lacto-bacillus in powdered or tablet form.

Swedish bitters stimulate the secretions within your stomach, your liver and pancreas and can be very helpful with indigestion and as a general tonic. Take 3-5 millilitres diluted in water about twenty minutes before eating.

For the first few days after chemotherapy your body won't be able to fully assimilate the foods you eat no matter how nutritious they might be. The main objective in the first few days is to replenish gut bacteria and maintain your physical comfort as much as possible.

Insomnia

Sometimes I think, oh I'm too tired to play a tape tonight, but I still find that every time I play a tape I sleep better. It forces me to really breathe deeply and switch off and think about nice things. On the tape Petrea gets me to imagine beautiful places and because I like travel I sort of go back and think about some beautiful scenery like the Canadian Rockies and I just drift off, and I sleep much better when I have really turned my mind off at night. No matter how physically tired I am, the sleep is a dead sleep when I play the tape first. All those things that I was

introduced to have made a very big difference. An enormous
amount.

SUE, AGE 54
aged 50 at diagnosis

Anyone who's unwell has an increased need for sleep. And yet, it's at this very time when sleep might be disturbed or elusive. You might need to implement correct sleeping patterns if they become disturbed through hospitalisation, pain, worry or some other factor. The worry of *not* sleeping can, in itself, keep sleep at bay. Lack of sleep is nothing to be overly concerned about. We *can* catch up. A good day's worry is far more exhausting than a good day with an axe. When we've had a good day working with an axe we fall into bed and sleep like babies; when we've had a good day's worry, we twitch all night. This applies doubly if we're going to spend our nights tossing and turning with fruitless worry. I'm sure you've had the experience, as I have, of everything seeming far worse at 3 a.m.! I call them the 3 a.m. freakies! In fact, I made a rule for myself about 'thinking things through' in the middle of the night. I could see that every time I decided to think things through at 3 a.m. I'd get myself into a real state and I'd make decisions that would never stand up to the light of day. I simply decided that I wouldn't allow myself to be coerced into thinking about problems in the middle of the night.

If it's pain which wakens you through the night, you might want to check with your doctor or nurse that your pain medication is adequate before you retire in the evenings. See also Chapter 7, 'Dealing with Recurrence'. Many techniques which could prove useful for those with pain can be found there.

Some women who normally sleep well have difficulty for a few days around their chemotherapy time. This is often not due to the chemotherapy but is a side-effect of an anti-nausea drug which is often prescribed at the same time. If you're susceptible to the side-effect of this particular drug, Maxolon, you'll feel jittery and restless and settling into a comfortable position may be very difficult. If this is your problem, speak to your doctor about changing your anti-nausea medication, and see the section in this chapter on Nausea.

Other women sleep restlessly because they're *anticipating* chemotherapy in three or four days time! These women will particularly benefit from the regular daily practice of relaxation techniques and following the guidelines set down here.

For women living alone, the nights can be very long and lonely when you feel unwell or apprehensive. Some women have fears and anxieties which keep them from nodding off at night, whilst they've no difficulty in falling asleep during the day. These concerns are best talked about with someone you trust. This might be a friend or a family member, or you might prefer to speak to your nurse, doctor or counsellor.

Many women find that even though the medically prescribed drugs make them sleep, they don't wake up feeling refreshed in the morning. The 'hypnotic' family of drugs allows you to wake up feeling refreshed, but they're effective for only four hours. Instead of sleeping the night through, many women wake up the moment the drug has worn off. You might like to use the following program in addition to your medically prescribed drugs or in place of them. If you've been using medically prescribed drugs for sleeping for a long period, I suggest you don't just suddenly stop. Use this program in addition to your medication and then gradually reduce when you no longer have a problem sleeping.

Using a relaxation or sleep tape as you drift off is really helpful. Normally, it takes us five hours to drift down through our various sleep stages to our deep sleep level. This is where our brain waves are in the alpha wave pattern. Our bodies do most of the healing and repair work when our brain waves are in the alpha wave pattern. This is the level where children do most of their growing. For many women, five hours of uninterrupted sleep is unrealistic because they're uncomfortable or need to get up to go to the bathroom.

Within five minutes of using a relaxation tape, your brain waves are in the alpha wave pattern and, when you fall asleep, you go straight into your deep sleep level. In this way, you get the very best from your sleep.

When you follow the guidelines listed below I'm sure you'll find deep and refreshing sleep. For those who have a chronic sleeping problem, be patient; it may take three to four days or even a week before you notice an improvement. Here's the program:

- Affirm, throughout the day, that you'll have no difficulty at all in falling asleep easily when you go to bed. Every time you're assailed by thoughts of yet another sleepless night, gently put them aside.
- Take two tablets of a herbal sedative formula (there's one listed below) with dinner and two tablets one hour before bed. This formula has no side-effects and won't make you sleepy, just very relaxed. It helps by relaxing the muscles of the body and tends to quieten down the activity of the mind.
- During the evening, engage in quiet activities. No riveting television, no mystery or adventure stories. Perhaps do some tapestry or other craft work; listen to relaxing music; read some inspirational or encouraging books.
- In the hour before bed, have a warm bath or shower (if practical), drink a cup of warm chamomile or valerian herb tea (a good complement to the herbal sedative formula), then go to bed.
- Settle into a comfortable position, then play a relaxation tape.

Sometimes, a gentle massage from your partner or someone else will settle and soothe an aching body or an agitated mind. Use grape seed, almond or apricot kernel oil mixed with a few drops of lavender or geranium oil. Even a gentle massage of hands, feet or head can bring incredible relaxation.

If your difficulty isn't in falling asleep, but in staying asleep, then have the relaxation or sleep tape ready for when you awaken. Go to the bathroom (if that's your habit), go back to bed and play the tape immediately before your mind becomes active. The use of a relaxation tape as you settle into bed can be helpful in getting the mind focused and the body relaxed, allowing sleep to come as it will.

I've recorded a relaxation practice for people who have a sleep problem and the use of this practice can help to re-establish healthy sleep habits. The sleep practice can also be used when you feel anxious or physically uncomfortable (see Petrea King Products at the end of this book). I can say, with (almost complete) confidence, that no one's ever heard the end of this practice!

Try this herbal sedative formula, or a similar one, available from most health food stores:

Herbal Sedative Formula

L-Lysine	50 mg
L-Glutamine	50 mg
Magnesium orotate	50 mg
Valerian	50 mg
Passionflower	50 mg
Nicotinamide	50 mg
Hops	25 mg
Pyridoxine hydrochloride	5 mg
Chamomile	5 mg
Oats	5 mg

The sleep achieved through this formula is usually deep and refreshing and is a valuable ingredient in a program to re-establish better sleeping patterns. It isn't addictive or habit-forming and has no side-effects. This formula is also particularly good for women who are anxious, fearful or distressed. Two tablets can be taken as often as every three hours without any side-effects. If you know you're going to have a tough day because of beginning a new treatment, or visiting a doctor to get results or having some unpleasant procedure done, then you may well find this formula really takes the edge off feeling apprehensive.

Dealing with Addictions

I've often used this program with women addicted to sedatives, alcohol or other drugs. Many women started taking sedatives because they were having difficulty in sleeping. Perhaps this was because they had some emotional or psychological pain they needed to address, but didn't know how. Instead of being helped to deal with the real issues, they've been prescribed sedatives. Before long, sleep becomes impossible without them and the unresolved issues become buried more deeply within.

For those who are addicted to, or dependent on, sedatives, I highly recommend that you find a support group wherein you can deal with the painful issues in your life. You use sedatives (or alcohol or other drugs) to dull the pain which exists within yourself. Deal with the pain and you deal with your addiction. I'm not saying it's easy, but it's certainly possible. Deal with the issues which stop you from fully living.

In the meantime, you could find it useful to take two tablets of the herbal sedative formula every three hours *in addition* to your drug of addiction. Then gradually reduce the amount of the drug. You might need to reduce it by half a tablet at a time until you're off them altogether, and it could take weeks or months depending on the degree of your addiction. This program will only work if:

- You're deeply committed to wanting it to, and
- If you're dealing with the painful issues which are unresolved in your life.

Libido

Many women experience a decrease in their sex drive during their illness. There are many possible explanations ranging from the effects of fear, illness, depression and worry through to side-effects of treatments or surgery. Most people are reluctant to talk to their doctor or nurse about a decrease in their libido. In fact, most doctors and nurses are reluctant to talk about sex at all! This can leave the patient in a very isolated situation.

Sex is a very important part of most people's lives and to lose one's libido can be quite distressing. Your doctor will be able to ascertain what's caused your decreased libido. Talking things through with your partner can help in dealing with the fears, depression or anxiety. A decrease in libido is very commonly experienced by those on chemotherapy. Rest assured, once your treatment program is complete and you've recovered from its debilitating effects, your libido will increase.

For many women, their sense of identity and self-esteem are strongly attached to their sexuality. In addition to the trauma of having your breast or a part of it removed, to lose your libido can feel like the last straw. It can be most traumatic to feel a loss of identity at a time when you're also feeling unwell and perhaps facing other issues around purpose and meaning in your life. A safe, supportive environment in which these fears can be aired and explored is invaluable.

Instant menopause can also lead to dryness in the vagina and the use of a lubricant will become essential to enjoyable sex. When you're coping with so many changes it's not surprising that your libido suffers. The most important things are to be gentle with yourself, decrease your expectations and talk about the issues involved with your partner or a sympathetic health professional. There's far more about sexuality issues in Chapter 8, 'Body Image and Sexuality'.

Liver Metastases

As you know, breast cancer can spread to other parts of the body. One of the most frequently affected organs is the liver. It doesn't mean that you now have liver cancer in addition to breast cancer. It's still breast cancer. Metastatic disease in the liver might, or might not, cause pain and discomfort. Many people believe that cancer, particularly cancer in the liver, is extremely painful. It can be, but I've known many people who've experienced no pain at all. Sometimes pain is experienced in the right shoulder area rather than around the liver itself. This can be 'referred liver pain'.

If you're experiencing digestive problems because of your liver then appropriate dietary choices will be important. The symptoms might include vomiting, nausea or squeamishness, burping, and so on.

Swedish bitters can be very useful in resolving some of the digestive upsets as they stimulate the production of gastric, liver and pancreatic juices. 3–5 mL taken twenty minutes before each meal will often aid the digestion of food.

There are some foods which your liver finds difficult to digest. These are best eliminated altogether from your diet.

This means avoiding:

- Oranges and orange juice.
- Fats, oils, butter, margarine (fried fatty foods).
- Alcohol.
- Fried eggs (poached or boiled are usually fine).
- Cheese, cream and all dairy products with the exception of yoghurt.
- Complex combinations of foods.

There are some women with liver metastases who love orange juice and who seem to suffer no side-effects from it. In this case, keep on enjoying it. It seems to depend very much on the location of the tumours in the liver. For others who love orange juice, but have a chronic squeamish feeling in the tummy, it's definitely worth leaving it out altogether for a couple of days to see if it's the juice which is the culprit.

If anything *will* make you feel squeamish, it'll be oranges or their juice. Most people find they can tolerate grapefruit, lemons, mandarins and limes without any discomfort whilst others are best to leave out all acidic foods—including strawberries, pine-apples and tomatoes.

Digestive enzymes are also beneficial for many of these people, particularly if there's burping and discomfort in the upper part of the digestive tract. The formulas listed under Indigestion in this chapter will very likely bring relief. One to two of each of these tablets can be taken any time food is ingested. If there's discomfort further down the intestinal tract, then incorporating the guidelines under Indigestion will be helpful.

Remember, if *you're* tired by the end of the day, so is your digestive tract. Make your main meals breakfast and lunch and have only a light dinner, for example, soup and muffins or stewed fruit and yoghurt.

Loss of Appetite

Loss of appetite has been referred to, here and there, in the previous pages. It can be quite depressing to lose one's appetite, particularly for those of us for whom food has played a major role in life. Now we look upon it with disinterested eye and jaded palate. We wonder if life's worth living if we cannot enjoy the tasty morsels of the past. Loss of appetite can stem from many causes. It could be the side-effect of a treatment we're on, it could be a result of our disease or it could simply be the product of depression or anxiety.

Many women find that chemotherapy will destroy their taste for food and subsequently lose interest in what used to be enjoyed. Some complain that all foods have a metallic taste after chemotherapy. This diminishes as you recover from the treatments. Some find they crave salt, whilst others can't stand anything salty, and so on.

Whatever its cause, the results can be a worry, unless we started off being well-covered in the first place. As with all symptoms, it's important to seek out and, if possible, eliminate the cause. If anxiety, depression or fear are causing loss of appetite, then it's essential these feelings be dealt with. This can be done with a friend, support group, caring nurse, doctor or counsellor.

Once any psychological, physical or emotional stresses have been removed, it's possible to stimulate the appetite in a number of ways. Again, homeopathics can be helpful in stimulating the appetite and in improving the function of the tastebuds. Ask your homeopath or health food store for a formula which contains homeopathic dosages of:

Sulphur	30x
Lycopodium	30x
Ceanthus americ	8x
China	6x
Ferrum muriaticum	6x
Aranea diadema	30x
Arsenicum iodatum	6x

These drops can be taken as often as every hour or two. Take 10–15 drops in a couple of teaspoons of water. Hold each sip in the mouth for a few seconds before swallowing.

Some women find that a glass of sherry or cold white wine stimulates the appetite if taken a half hour before eating. Two to three pieces of ginger in its crystallised form is excellent for calming a squeamish tummy and stimulating the appetite. 3–5 mL of Swedish bitters taken twenty minutes before a meal stimulates the appetite and acts as a general tonic.

Remember these Points

- Take 3–5 mL of Swedish bitters twenty minutes before a meal.
- Eat small frequent meals five to six times throughout the day.
- Schedule eating times every two to three hours and stick to them.
- Keep high-calorie snacks available for nibbling between meals. For example, nuts, seeds, yoghurt, dried fruit, soups, crackers.
- Make eating a pleasant experience by eating with friends.

- Make your food and surroundings attractive.
- Choose your favourite foods to stimulate your appetite.
- Prepare foods that have a pleasant aroma such as simmering soup, baking bread, casseroles.
- Give all food a chance; what's unappealing one day might be appealing the next.
- Prepare foods at times when you're feeling 'up'.
- Always have in the refrigerator foods like banana smoothies (see recipe in Chapter 5).
- Use dried or fresh herbs, garlic or spices to enhance flavours.
- Avoid low or no calorie foods such as coffee, tea or clear soups.
- Try two to three pieces of crystallised ginger twenty minutes before eating (if you like ginger).
- Don't skip eating times; treat them as you do medications or other therapies.

Lymphoedema

I went to a rehabilitation place for a month for treatment. My arm was as big as a football and now it's just a little swollen. I had to wear an elasticised sleeve all the time and then they teach you how to do the massage yourself.

SALLY, AGE 58
aged 50 at diagnosis

I find that nurses and doctors hardly ever talk about lymphoedema. After the person gets it they say, "Oh yes, you shouldn't have sat out in the sun and got your 'bad' arm sunburnt". I've had it on both sides.

HELEN, AGE 42
aged 34 at diagnosis

Whenever I travel long distances I get near the window and keep my arm up.

SALLY, AGE 58
aged 50 at diagnosis

I'm a professional viola player and lymphoedema was a real fear for me. There is some swelling and I'm fortunate that I can use the hand and I think I'll be able to play again.

LOUISE, AGE 52
aged 51 at diagnosis

Don't let any well meaning individual (particularly doctors) ever tell you not to worry about lymphoedema. Get it treated quickly. You'll save yourself an awful lot of heartache.

FIONA, AGE 34
aged 33 at diagnosis

I find the thing that I have most problem with is my arm. I've got through all the stages of discomfort with the breast after the radiotherapy, but my arm is a constant reminder. Some days it's really painful and stiff and other days it's OK. My right arm was slowly becoming more usable and less painful, but at the end of the radiotherapy treatment, the arm and hand began to puff up and become very uncomfortable with lymphoedema. The specialists more or less said that I'd have to live with it, "It wasn't too bad"! but I had great help and support from Petrea and a massage therapist she recommended. My husband Kevin gave me daily massage and once a week I visited the therapist who also prescribed a herbal mixture. With good care my arm is much better now, almost "normal".

LYNNE, AGE 55
aged 52 at diagnosis

Because I have my arm properly massaged it gives me minimal discomfort and doesn't look too ugly. But it's still a reminder every single day. I don't wear a stocking. My husband massages it every day and I get it professionally done once a fortnight.

MAREE, AGE 46
aged 46 at diagnosis

Lymphoedema is the retention of lymph in the tissues. It can appear in the arm of a woman who has had all or some of her lymph nodes in the armpit removed or irradiated by radiotherapy.

Lymphoedema affects about 10 per cent of women who have had these procedures done to them and it can occur many years later. It's always better to avoid lymphoedema than to treat it.

As the lymph nodes are responsible for protecting the arm from infection, you need to take extra care not to burn, scratch or cut the affected hand or arm. This means no sunburn, saunas or very hot water. You need to take care when sewing, gardening, cutting your nails and shaving under your arm. You should avoid wearing tight bras, restrictive clothing or tight jewellery. Avoid medical procedures to the affected limb. For instance, don't have your blood pressure taken on that arm, don't have chemotherapy or other injections or have blood removed from that arm. Avoid carrying heavy weights with that arm.

If you do injure your arm, clean the wound thoroughly with antiseptic and see your doctor if you're at all concerned. The doctor may want to treat you with antibiotics to prevent infection. Most doctors will tell you the only things which can be done about lymphoedema are taking diuretics (fluid tablets), wearing a support stocking or bandage on the limb and keeping it elevated. These are certainly of some benefit but don't do a great deal for women who've a really major problem with lymphoedema.

Proper lymphatic drainage can make an enormous difference. The kind of lymphatic drainage referred to here is a very specialised one and proper training must be undertaken in order to practise it effectively. This isn't the kind of lymphatic drainage which is available through beauticians or most massage therapists. It must be done by someone who understands breast cancer and its treatments, and has a good understanding of the lymphatic drainage system throughout the body and who's been trained in the technique. This training is becoming more widely available in Australia and I urge you to speak to your oncologist, and ask them to find out the nearest clinic which can teach you and/or your partner how to do it. Very often it isn't until you ask for something to be done about a particularly annoying symptom, that it gets addressed. Often doctors are preoccupied with your medical treatment and a symptom like lymphoedema is of no importance to your overall medical management (in their view).

Occasionally, lymphoedema disappears with time but more often than not it becomes permanent. Some women find that elevating their arm on a pillow at night or, better still, having it supported so that it's above your head so that it can drain through gravity will help reduce the swelling. Physiotherapists often recommend the use of an elasticised sleeve or bandage up the length of the arm during the day. This is most effective when it is combined with the massage technique mentioned earlier.

Memory Loss and Lack of Concentration

Many women complain of memory loss and/or lack of concentration after they've been diagnosed with breast cancer. Most often this is due to the effects of shock, stress and a change in priorities and will certainly improve with time. Many a woman has ascribed her poor memory or concentration to a more sinister cause—secondaries in the brain! These are not the symptoms of brain tumours! They're simply the outward show that major shifts in priorities have occurred and the mind is gradually catching up.

It's important not to have high expectations of yourself when you've been through the trauma of your diagnosis. You'll undoubtedly find your priorities change. This might show itself in simple and yet aggravating ways. For instance, you might find that after being introduced to someone, you completely forget their name; or you're forgetful of where you left your keys; you might forget telephone numbers or where you put your glasses (even when you're wearing them!), and so on. This can extend to forgetting what your doctor told you and, in some cases, forgetting to take your medication. It can be very frustrating, and sometimes worrying, to find you no longer are functioning at your usual level of competence. Remember, you're under considerable stress and you need to be gentle with yourself.

A formula containing vitamins B1, B6, B12, choline, tyrosine, serine, iron and glutamine could be of benefit.

If at all possible, enlist the support and assistance of your loved-ones. For instance, most people benefit by having someone familiar with them when they visit their doctor. Remember, four ears are always better than two. You might need to make lists which will help you remember things and to establish a place where you *always* leave your keys/glasses, and so on. A tablet dispenser which has compartments for each day might be helpful. Some people record their consultation with their doctor on a small tape recorder. Others write down their questions and seek their doctor's co-operation in writing down the answers. This is then a future reference.

Some people find a herb called Gingko Biloba very helpful. It's been used for centuries by the Chinese as a remedy for memory loss and poor concentration. It increases the blood flow to the brain. Start off with one tablet or capsule a day and gradually increase to between three and six per day.

Monilia Vaginal Thrush

Many women on chemotherapy or antibiotics experience monilia or vaginal thrush. This aggravating complaint can be quite difficult to treat. Most women will find an improvement if they follow these guidelines:

- Totally avoid all sugars in your diet; this means no cakes, sweet drinks, cookies, honey, chocolate, maple or golden syrup.
- Eat at least 2 dessertspoons per day of an acidophilus low-fat yoghurt.
- Add 60 drops of tea-tree oil to the bath water.
- Soak a tampon in a solution of 90 per cent almond, grape seed or apricot kernel oil and 10 per cent tea-tree oil.

- Take 6 drops of sandalwood oil each day. Use a small piece of bread to soak up the sandalwood or have it in water. Continue for at least another week after all signs of thrush have gone.
- Add 4 drops of lavender oil to 2 each of rose and bergamot oil and add to 1 litre of warm water for a douche.

Muscle Pain and Weakness

Many women experience muscle pain during their illness. This can stem from inactivity, tension in the muscles due to anxiety or pain in the region, or to the drug treatment. When muscles are held in tension they produce lactic acid which is very irritating to the tissues. This irritation leads to greater tension and the cycle is perpetuated. In addition, I believe that many of the by-products of the chemotherapeutic drugs are lodged in the tissues and this can make them very sore.

Massage can be very helpful in easing the pain and can often increase the mobility of the area. I've seen many women who think they have a secondary growth from a cancer because they're experiencing pain in their back, neck or shoulder area when, in fact, it's only muscular tension. A supplement containing biotin, inositol, selenium and the vitamins B5, B1 and E could also be of benefit in this situation.

See also Chapter 7, 'Dealing with Recurrence'.

Nausea

Many women encounter nausea or an unsettled feeling in the stomach at some stage during their illness or its treatment. This nausea could be induced by chemotherapy, radiotherapy or some other treatment, or it could be part of the disease process itself. The important thing to find out, as with all symptoms, is what's causing the nausea. It can be directly related to the illness itself, for instance, if there's a secondary tumour in the liver. Anxiety, fear or depression can be responsible for, or increase, this nausea.

It could be the result of an infection, over-indulgence in food/ alcohol, a stomach ulcer, gastritis or something that's been eaten.

Don't forget, you probably experienced nausea occasionally before you had breast cancer! Once we're diagnosed, we tend to think *everything* is related to the disease or its treatment.

There are numerous myths surrounding chemotherapy. There's a vast array of chemotherapeutic drugs. Some of these are extremely mild and create minimal side-effects whilst others produce nausea, squeamishness or vomiting. Radiotherapy to the abdomen or surrounding areas can also produce nausea.

Women will respond individually to their treatment so comparing yourself and your reactions with someone else could be totally inappropriate. If your treatment involves the kind of chemotherapy that creates nausea, your doctor will also have prescribed an anti-nausea drug. Some people find they can control their nausea without requiring this medication. Others prefer to take their anti-nausea medication as they begin their chemotherapy, whilst some prefer to wait and see if they actually become nauseated before taking theirs. Often these anti-nausea medications are given automatically at the same time through the intravenous drip that delivers the chemotherapy.

If your anti-nausea medication is to be taken by mouth, the sooner you start taking it, the better will be its effect. Halting mild nausea is easier than when it's really giving you a hard time. Some women find the side-effects of the anti-nausea drug more difficult to deal with than the nausea itself. If so, speak to your doctor who'll review your treatment program and perhaps suggest another drug in its place. Others find they feel very jittery or restless after chemotherapy and this interferes with their sleep and emotional well-being. If this is the case for you, speak to your doctor. It's very likely a side-effect of the anti-nausea drug, which can easily be changed, rather than the chemotherapy.

Sometimes, after a long period of treatment, or after a strong reaction to chemotherapy, *anticipatory* nausea can be a problem.

People might experience this in the days leading up to their chemotherapy, some even at the sight, thought or smell of the hospital or clinic in which they receive their treatment. Some people think they're being weak or have gone a little crazy when they experience this. Not so! The mind and body are interconnected and your body has learnt a conditioned physical response to a mental process. Some people feel squeamish or even reach the stage of vomiting just by driving on the same road which leads to their place of treatment.

Chemotherapy is broken down in the body by the liver, so it's a good idea to adopt a liver-friendly diet during this time. If the cause of the nausea cannot be removed then you'll need to implement a program or treatment plan to minimise its effect on your life. Nausea is nausea no matter what its cause and there are some helpful guidelines which are worth trying to alleviate this problem.

Many women find their taste for food is disturbed during chemotherapy treatment and their food has a metallic taste to it. This will gradually disappear once the treatment has stopped. Some find they cannot tolerate salty or sweet foods whilst others crave them. Some women thrive on chemotherapy and continue working or maintaining their usual lifestyle without interruption. Taste changes can occur regardless of the treatment schedule. Don't force yourself to eat foods which you no longer enjoy, simply because you think they're good for you. Find a suitable alternative.

Some find the side-effects of the chemotherapy increase (or decrease) as the treatment program progresses. Some grow weary of the side-effects and might wish to discuss with their doctor the possibility of a break from treatment or a change to a less intense treatment program. Hand in hand with nausea goes a lack of appetite. This is often distressing when weight or energy loss is also present. (There's more information about lack of appetite under the heading Loss of Appetite in this chapter.) Some people find eating dispels nausea. All of these responses are normal and individual. Avoid comparing yourself with others.

Women sometimes feel they'll never return to their usual healthy selves again. It's an understandable fear and yet many people who've been *very* sick with their treatment feel on top of the world within weeks of its completion. Those eating a nutritious diet, taking appropriate supplementation of vitamins, drinking vegetable juices, meditating and maintaining a positive outlook, seem to suffer only minimal side-effects from their treatments.

There are naturopaths who suggest a low-protein diet if you have cancer. I've found people who adopt this kind of diet often suffer with debilitating weariness. Remember, whilst you're having chemotherapy or radiotherapy treatment which destroys both cancer and some healthy cells in your body, you'll have a higher demand for protein. Proteins are the building blocks of the body. You might prefer to get your proteins from beans, nuts, seeds, soya products, fish and free-range chickens and decrease, or preferably eliminate, red meat.

Foods to Avoid

There are some foods to avoid when you're feeling squeamish in the stomach, or are about to have chemotherapy. They are:

- Oranges, orange juice.
- Fats, oils, butter, margarine.
- Fried fatty foods.
- Alcohol.
- Fried eggs.
- Cheese and all other dairy products with the exception of low-fat acidophilus-based yoghurt.
- Complex combinations of foods.

There might be other foodstuffs which make *you* squeamish whilst another person could tolerate them easily. Listen to your own body. If anything will make you feel nauseous it will be oranges or orange juice. Sometimes, we think we're doing the very best thing for ourselves by having freshly squeezed juice, when in fact it could be *causing* the nausea. If your liver is upset (as it will be with most chemotherapy) avoid oranges or orange juice. It's a mystery to me why orange juice is served in hospitals to cancer patients whilst they're *having* their chemotherapy. The liver seems to tolerate grapefruit, lemons and limes, but dislikes oranges. However, some people find that grapefruit, strawberries, tomatoes, pineapples, lemons or any other acid foods will increase their nausea. Listen to your own body and heed its messages.

If you're feeling nauseous, probably the last thing you feel like eating is food containing fats or oils. Likewise, most people will want to avoid red meat entirely. There are exceptions, some people crave red meat at this time. Similarly, most people lose their interest in alcohol when feeling nauseated. Cooked eggs are best avoided during treatment, though raw eggs in banana smoothies (recipe in Chapter 5) are often tolerated very well. Some people tolerate soft boiled, poached or lightly scrambled eggs.

Cheese isn't recommended as it's too high in fat to be tolerated easily. Even low-fat cheeses aren't recommended. Most women who suffer from nausea don't tolerate foods containing lactose. Use soya milk instead. There are some very good 'light' brands of soya milk available. Goat's and sheep's cheeses are often tolerated well and can be included.

Keep foods very simple when suffering with nausea. Perhaps as simple as only two or three foods (without additives) at one meal. There is more information about chemotherapy and its effects in the section earlier in this chapter called Chemotherapy. See also Nervous Tension, below.

Radiation Treatment

It's unusual to experience nausea with radiation treatment unless it's to the abdominal area or to the brain. If this is so, all that has been said about nausea applies equally. You might need to use a system of trial and error in order to find what works best for you. If you've had radiation to the abdominal area, it's almost inevitable that you'll experience diarrhoea, or at least looseness of the bowel motions. Please refer to the section on Diarrhoea earlier in this chapter.

Nervous Tension, Fear and Anxiety

Stress affects the body in many ways. One of its favourites is to make us feel nauseous. If you feel that stress plays a part in your feelings of nausea, then don't just worry about it! Find some constructive ways of dealing with stress so you can channel your energy into more useful directions. For instance, talk about your fears or anxieties with a friend, support group, nurse or caring professional counsellor. They'll help you deal with the situation and assist you in finding constructive ways of minimising your stress. Learn the techniques of relaxation, visualisation and meditation and *practise them at least twice daily*. These techniques will change the way you view life and your illness. Find the things which bring you joy and make sure every day you have those things present. This may be solitude; the company of good friends; inspiring books; the company of your pet; music; nature; exercise; a walk along the beach; your favourite craft or pastime. Whatever it is that brings you peace, include it in each day.

With clients who are particularly stressed, I often use a herbal formula which works to help calm them. This formula does not make one sleepy, only relaxed, and tends to quieten down the chaos in the mind. It's particularly good for helping people to relax so that sleep comes. Ask at your health food store for a formula as close to this one as you can get or write to me at the address in the back of this book:

L-Lysine	50 mg
L-Glutamine	50 mg
Magnesium orotate	50 mg
Valerian	50 mg
Passionflower	50 mg

Nicotinamide	50 mg
Hops	25 mg
Pyrodoxine hydrochloride	5 mg
Chamomile	5 mg
Oats	5 mg

For people very frightened, agitated or distressed, two tablets can be taken as often as every three hours. For others less distressed, one to two tablets every four hours are sufficient.

For those who wish to ensure a night's sleep by using this formula, I suggest they take two with dinner, and then two tablets one hour before bed (see Insomnia, earlier in this chapter).

Slippery Elm Powder

Slippery elm powder is a wonderful substance to counteract nausea (see details earlier in this chapter under Chemotherapy). Try mixing two heaped teaspoons of the powder with yoghurt, banana or stewed apple and have it three times daily, about twenty minutes before each meal. You can have it as frequently as seems necessary for you.

If the slippery elm doesn't control or alleviate the nausea by itself, the addition of homeopathics is nearly always effective. You'll need to get these from a homeopath, naturopath or health food store. The homeopathics which I use for nausea are:

Vomisan

Veratrum album	30x
Aesthusa	8x
Colchicum	12x
Cocculus	12x
Ipecac	12x
Petroleum	12x
Nux vomica	12x
Apomorphinum muriaticum	12x

This formula is in liquid form and can be taken in two ways.

To prevent nausea: Take 10–15 drops in a couple of teaspoons of water four times daily, before meals and before bed. Hold each sip in your mouth for a few seconds before swallowing.

To alleviate nausea: Take 70 drops in half a glass of water. Sip every three to four minutes until the nausea begins to subside, holding each sip in the mouth for a few seconds before swallowing. Once nausea has settled, reduce frequency to every five to six minutes, then every 10, then 15, then 30, and so on until you're back to four times daily. If another wave of nausea appears, resume the frequency as mentioned above.

Homeopathics can also be in pilule form; these are like sugar pills the size of a pin-head. Because they dissolve easily under the tongue they're suitable for use by children as well as adults. They're marvellous for travel sickness or for the low-grade squeamishness which so many women experience during chemotherapy.

Note: Those who've been using slippery elm powder for a while to counteract nausea may find that even the *thought* of taking slippery elm could make them feel worse! You need to be flexible and perhaps alternate the powder with the homeopathics or find creative ways of disguising its taste. Because you're often nauseous when you take slippery elm powder you can easily develop an aversion to its taste. Some people blend it into their carrot juice or banana or paw-paw smoothie. Just because slippery elm works wonderfully for treating nausea doesn't mean you have to make yourself sick by eating it!

Ginger Tea

Ginger tea is very helpful in settling upset stomachs. Thinly slice about a quarter of a cup of fresh ginger and add it to 1 litre of boiling water. Simmer for fifteen minutes, then allow to stand until lukewarm or cool. Strain. You can add a little lemon juice or honey to sweeten if desired. Sip very slowly.

Dietary Approach to Nausea

As well as avoiding certain foods, there are other factors which need to be taken into account when one is trying to minimise or eliminate nausea. Experiment with the following suggestions so that you find what works for you.

Remember these Points

- Take a moment to calm yourself before eating by practising some deep breathing.
- Eat *slowly*!
- Two to three pieces of crystallised ginger eaten half an hour before a meal will often settle the stomach and stimulate the appetite.
- Eat more food during the times you feel better.
- Salty foods are often tolerated well; try soup and crackers.
- Avoid foods that produce a strong odour when cooked.
- Make sure your cooking area has good ventilation.
- Have only two or three foods at one meal. For instance, porridge and soya milk, soup and muffins, yoghurt and slippery elm, yoghurt and stewed apple.
- Avoid foods that may produce gas; for example, onions, cabbage, broccoli, cauliflower, cucumber, beans or green (capsicum) pepper.
- Chew food thoroughly so that it's mixed with saliva; the first stage of digestion begins in the mouth.
- Avoid your favourite foods during the times when you experience nausea to keep from developing an aversion to the foods you enjoy.
- Don't drink with your meals—your stomach knows it's done a good job of digesting its contents by how much liquid is in there. If you drink with your meal, the little sphincter at the far end of your stomach interprets that your stomach has done its job and relaxes to let the food pass into the small intestine for further digestion. If you've had a cup of tea, water or juice, the stomach's interpretation will be that the

food is digested, when really it's only been mixed with the fluid you drank. For most people this won't be a problem but for anyone with a fragile digestive system, *it is*. Drink thirty minutes before or at least an hour and a half after a meal.

- It's better not to eat fruit with meals unless the whole meal consists of fruit. The exception to this is bananas used as sweetener on cereal in the morning. Bananas, like cereal, are a complex carbohydrate and will be digested in the same manner.
- Peeled and well-cooked vegetables are preferable to raw or fibrous ones for those with nausea.
- Small, frequent meals tend to be tolerated better than three larger meals each day.
- Presentation is important, make the meal look attractive.
- Use slippery elm powder in yoghurt or banana plus homeopathics before eating.
- Drinking soups, flat lemonade and smoothies (recipe in Chapter5) through a straw might be better than having food around the mouth. A straw can deliver the food straight to the back of the mouth.
- Have food neither too hot nor too cold. Warm or tepid are best.
- Moist foods are often better than dry foods for those who suffer with a dry mouth in addition to nausea.
- Dry foods, such as toast or crackers, might be better for those who don't suffer with a dry mouth.
- Don't lie down after eating unless you've found that to be helpful in the past; recline with your head elevated.
- Don't become overly preoccupied with nourishing yourself in the first days after chemotherapy.

Conclusion

The suggestions contained in this section aren't in any way intended to be a prescription. They're suggested only as an effective, natural means of controlling nausea or squeamishness. They're totally without side-effects and, in this way, can be very useful. Some people have quite a marked reaction to some of the medically prescribed anti-nausea drugs. There are new nausea drugs which are marvellous and which have very few side-effects. Talk to your doctor about them. You might find a combination of both prescribed and natural substances works best for you.

Night Sweats

Some women experience the unpleasant effects of night sweats at some time during their illness. These sweats aren't associated with a fever and their cause is unclear. Sweats can be frustrating and depressing because they interfere with sleeping. They can be very mild where you barely wake with them, or severe, where the pyjamas and bed linen might need to be changed several times during the night. They can often be set off by the taking of antibiotics or analgesics (pain killers). The following homeopathics work wonderfully in stopping these sweats. They're also effective for those who perspire excessively during the day. Many people with cancer are troubled with night sweats and these drops have been amazingly successful in stopping them. The formula consists of:

Antihydrosin Drops

Nitricum acidum	12x
Tincture veratrum album	12x
Belladonna	12x
Sepia	30x
Larchesis	30x
Kali carbonicum	6x
Pilocarpus	4x
Salvia officinalis	30x
Sambucus nigra	4x
Tincture sanguinaria	6x
Tincture jaborandi	4x
Tincture sambucus nigra	4x

For night sweats: Take 10–15 drops in a couple of teaspoons of water four times daily, before meals and before bed. Hold the liquid in your mouth for a few seconds before swallowing.

When sweats have greatly diminished (or disappeared) reduce to three times daily, before lunch, dinner and bed. If there are no more sweats for three nights, reduce to twice daily, before dinner and before bed. If there are no sweats for another three nights, reduce to once daily, just before bed.

You might find the sweats will return if you begin a course of antibiotics or start taking some new analgesic medication, in which case you might need to repeat the above procedure with the drops.

Occasionally, when sweats are really severe and usually of long-standing, the above drops are insufficient on their own. In this case there are some extra drops which can be taken once a day in addition to the others which double the strength of any homeopathic. They consist of:

Potentising Drops

Nitricum acidum	12x
Phosphoricum acidum	12x
Sulphur iodatum	12x
Ferrum iodatum	12x
Calcarea iodatum	12x

They're taken in the same way as the drops above except they're only taken once a day, preferably in the morning.

Sweats and Fevers

The following remedies work very effectively when there are sweats *with* fevers which don't respond to any medical treatment. The following combination of homeopathics has been used many times both inside and outside hospitals with excellent results. The Antihydrosin Drops are used with the addition of the following homeopathics:

Inflammation Drops

Belladonna	4x
Apis mellifica	4x
Lachesis	30x
Mercurius corrosivus	5x
Baryta muriatica	6x

Take the Antihydrosin and the Inflammation Drops in the following manner (do not mix together in the same glass):

1 Take 10–15 drops of each remedy in a couple of teaspoons of water four times daily before meals and before bed. Hold each sip in the mouth for a few seconds before swallowing.

2 When sweats and fevers have subsided, reduce to three times daily (before lunch, dinner and before bed).

3 If, after three days, there are still no sweats/fevers, reduce to twice daily (before dinner and before bed).

4 If, after three days, there are still no sweats/fevers, reduce to once daily (before bed). Continue taking the remedies once a day until the end of the bottles.

5 If sweats/fevers return, increase the frequency of the doses as in (1).

Overeating

For all those who've a problem with eating too little, spare a thought for those whose problem is eating too much. Some treatments, containing corticosteroids like prednisolone, stimulate the appetite. For these women, the novelty of having an appetite soon wears off as they begin to put on extra kilograms they'd prefer not to have. Most of this extra weight is retained fluid and so, fortunately, with the completion of treatment, the appetite and size, return to normal. There is more information on unwanted weight gain under that heading later in this chapter.

Oxygen at Home

One of the most frightening feelings is not being able to catch our breath. Those who become very breathless on exertion might benefit by having access to oxygen at home. For some, getting up and showering can be an exhausting process. Likewise, any small exertion can result in complete collapse. The value of oxygen nearby is that you can spend ten minutes receiving oxygen *before* you attempt your shower or other activity. You'll need to discuss your particular situation with a visiting nurse or doctor who'll be able to advise whether the use of oxygen would be beneficial. Your doctor can arrange for a cylinder of oxygen to be delivered to your home.

I've had many clients who've been able to maintain their independence by having oxygen available. One lady, Sophie, had a very small portable cylinder which enabled her to continue coming to groups. The oxygen gave her a sense of security whenever she had to exert herself.

International air travel from Australia always involves many hours of flying. For those who've difficulty with breathing, it might be worthwhile organising to have oxygen made available on the plane. (The oxygen which is standardly available through the masks in an emergency is of a different quality to medical oxygen.) Your doctor will need to organise this. Several of my clients have continued very rigorous international schedules when they have a secondary spread or scar tissue from radiotherapy in their lungs. It's easy to organise oxygen on the plane and it has meant a great deal to them to be able to continue their work, visit family or have a holiday.

Pregnancy

Most doctors recommend that you avoid pregnancy for at least two to three years after having breast cancer. Your doctor will want to give you a full examination before you become pregnant. If your doctor finds any active cancer cells, you'll almost certainly be counselled to avoid or postpone pregnancy. As many breast cancers are oestrogen receptive and the level of this hormone increases during pregnancy, it could activate the cancer cells.

Pressure Areas

People who are confined to bed for more than a few days must be careful of the areas on which their body rests. These areas are principally the heels, hips, buttocks, sacrum, shoulder blades, ears and elbows. This is especially necessary for those fairly inactive in bed, since the constant pressure can lead to the skin becoming very thin and perhaps breaking. This frequently happens with the elderly or with those who've retained a lot of fluid in their tissues because of their medication.

A daily intake of 1 gram of vitamin C has been shown to increase the healing of bed sores, however, they're best avoided altogether if possible.

Regular gentle massaging of the areas at least every two to three hours, and changing the position of the person so other areas take the load on an alternating basis, will help in alleviating this problem. Sheepskin rugs also help to distribute the pressure of the body as do ripple mattresses. These are mattresses which have compressed air forced through alternating channels.

One of the most effective substances to rub into the area in order to maintain the integrity of the skin is chickweed cream. A dear friend of mine, Rosemarie, who started off as a client, moved into my home when she was very unwell. Rosemarie had very fine, papery skin and at this time was very thin and frail. She spent a lot of each day in bed and it was a miracle that she didn't form any broken areas in her skin. Every two hours during the day we would massage in, very gently, chickweed cream. The visiting nurses were also very impressed with the state of her skin because, potentially, she could have had a real problem. One doesn't have to be particularly sick for these areas to become a problem, it happens whenever we're in the one position for too long.

Prostheses

Back then the nurse said, "Just stuff some stockings in your bra, dear".

MONTI, AGE 69
aged 43 at diagnosis

The next step was being fitted for a prosthesis. I had been a "large woman" and I found the only danger associated with the prosthesis was in dropping it accidentally on my foot as I was sure it would do great damage—it was so heavy. But it realised the aim of the surgeon, the nurses and the bra fitter that I would look "just the same" and "no one would ever know"—but I knew.

JOAN, AGE 54
aged 51 at diagnosis

There's some inconvenience having to use a prosthesis at times, but it's an inconvenience I've got used to.

CATHERINE, AGE 47
aged 41 at diagnosis

I would very often forget my prosthesis. I actually left it at Grace Bros on the seat once while trying on a bra. I had to go back and ask if they'd found it.

JOYE, AGE 50
aged 42 at diagnosis

Finding a breast prosthesis was another pain. I'm fed up with that too. I'm going to try and invent one myself. I'm so sick of them. A man must be inventing them. They are just ridiculous. I've got a birdseed one that a girlfriend made. I ditched the one I bought at the shop. It falls out all the time. It's nothing like my other breast and it just makes me angry and frustrated. This birdseed one, it fits in quite nicely and it looks pretty much like the other one.

I had this great fitting from this shop, and yes dear, that's the best size. It was nothing like the other one. I thought, oh well. I bought this bra that was supposed to be especially tight fitting and so on, and I kind of half slipped in the shopping mall. And *as I was coming up I saw this man looking at me, and I looked down and I had this mound in the middle of my chest. I was so angry and embarrassed.*

I thought—is this the best they can do? So I got a little shoulder pad, and put that inside. Of course it didn't match the other side. And I pinned it all around. But then I had this big thick ridge where all the pins were around my bra. So now I've got a birdseed one and I'm quite happy with it. But then you know, what if you're dancing with a man, or up close, and he bumps you or something? I heard a really funny story about that. This woman was with this guy, dancing with him, and he was sort of a bit all over her, and he was wanting to feel her up while they were dancing and she lost her block and said—here, if you're so bloody obsessed with it, have it! And she took it out and gave it to him!

JEANNIE, AGE 54
aged 50 at diagnosis

"You'll feel good when you get your prosthesis, you'll feel much better", so I said "Oh, good, I'll look forward to that"! So the time came and I got the prosthesis, and I have pretty much kept it under the bed since then, because I'd got used to the temporary one and the thought of this piece of rubber or whatever it is, just brings up the loss of the breast, which is the image I guess. It just brings it up for me a lot and I didn't expect that. So I've just put that aside—I can't deal with it yet.

ROBIN, AGE 44
aged 44 at diagnosis

I keep it with me all the time, and I don't put it in the box. It's part of me, so it's always under the pillow when I go to bed. I never wear it to bed, but I feel it's something that's part of me now. And I have four sons and when I first bought it, they had a lovely game around the kitchen, throwing it and poking it. The boys are in their twenties now, so it was OK for me.

LYNNE, AGE 49
aged 44 at diagnosis

The only time I'd really like to have a bosom is when I get up and wander around in my nightie. The kids always have people staying and I go downstairs and there's someone asleep on the sofa and there I am in my nightie with one bosom. I get so annoyed. Then I've got to go back upstairs, put on the bra, put the nightie on again, put the dressing gown on and then go back downstairs and I feel irritated.

ROS, AGE 49
aged 47 at diagnosis

I spoke to a woman who said she took hers out and threw it at the garage door in an absolute rage. There are lots of stories about women who do that.

LOUISE, AGE 52
aged 51 at diagnosis

To get a mastectomy swimsuit you need to be married to the Aga Khan, or else be a top barrister pulling in that sort of money. It's so simple to make mastectomy swimsuits, because whenever I think of going to buy one, they say, "Oh, we had a lovely range but they've all sold to women who don't have mastectomies because they don't notice that they are for women who've had a breast removed". Why can't all swimsuits be made with a simple little slit in the side to put in your prosthesis? There are a hell of a lot of us in Australia who need that sort of thing and it would be so simple. I just think the manufacturers should be encouraged to make all their swimsuits accessible to women with mastectomies.

I'm going to go to the swimming pool this summer, I'm really going to get fit and lose the weight I've put on through the Tamoxifen. And even that's a big effort, to think I'm going to be seen in public. Will I wear the prosthesis to the pool or will I put it in when I get there? Then to find it's hard to get a costume, it's just another way of making you feel you're not a normal whole person, making you feel like a woman with a disease who needs special things all the time. At times I find that difficult.

HELEN, AGE 42
aged 34 at diagnosis

I love to swim and with the extra weight of the prosthesis, I go down to the beach looking like a whale before I get into the water. I was with one of my gay male friends and we went into the surf. I was on top of a wave about to break, and I thought, "Oh no, my prosthesis," because it was just sitting inside my costume and I came in on the wave and sat down, no prosthesis. I couldn't decide which was worse, getting out of the water or the loss of my new $350 prosthesis. I felt very upset and I didn't know what to do.

I called to my friend and he ran to get a towel, thinking I'd split my costume. I thought it was gone and suddenly I saw two teenage girls poking at something with a stick on the edge of the sand. I knew straight away it would be my prosthesis, from the way they were looking at it and so I called to them and they very tentatively picked it up and brought it to me, giggling because I think that was the way they handled it. They gave it to me and I said, "I just hope you don't get breast cancer". I felt just terrible and I had to leave the beach. I just wrapped myself in a towel. I just couldn't stay there. It took me some hours to feel OK again. I can laugh about it now, but it was awful.

LYNNE, AGE 49
aged 44 at diagnosis

The nurses in the hospital where you had your mastectomy will most likely have given you information about where to get a prosthesis. As you can tell from the quotes women have mixed feelings about a prosthesis.

Each woman will need to decide whether she prefers to use a prosthesis or whether she wants to have a reconstruction. These are individual choices and, again, there's no one right thing to do.

The women who fit you for a prosthesis are trained and are generally very kind and considerate. It's important that you are not rushed with your choice. You might like to take a good friend with you when you have the fitting or you may prefer to do it alone.

There are prostheses now which actually adhere to the skin via velcro strips. Many women find that this gives them more of a sense of the prosthesis being part of their body because its weight is actually carried by the body rather than just the bra.

Your state Cancer Council will have information also on where a prosthesis can be fitted and bought.

Radiotherapy

I'm a very independent person. One of the first things Petrea said to me was that I could let those who were offering me help to do so. I've never been one to do that and I started doing it, and I found it was marvellous. I went to radiotherapy for six weeks and the whole time I had people cooking me meals, driving me, and a whole group of people, thirty or forty people were just constantly around me. And as Petrea said to me, it's good for them because they're wanting to help me. I wouldn't have allowed that previously, I would have got in the car and driven myself. I didn't drive once and I sat back and . . . I think it was good for me, to find out other people could help too.

SUE, AGE 54
aged 50 at diagnosis

The weeks of radiotherapy were fairly easy—I felt OK, felt positive and had no bad side-effects. I had been to see Petrea before I started this and her suggestions on diet and how to cope made a tremendous difference. I did get tired but as my treatments were after school each afternoon, I could rest when I got home. At school, everyone was giving me extra support, doing playground duties, etc. They were great.

LYNNE, AGE 55
aged 52 at diagnosis

When I was lying there I thought—this is awful, I've got to have this horrible treatment and also the thought that maybe they hadn't got it all out of your breast because they had to radiate the rest of it. And I felt really terrible. I had led such a protected life, when I was little my father wouldn't let me have a watch with luminous paint on it because of the radiation that might come off the luminous paint and I remember thinking, here am I, the girl who's not allowed to have luminous paint on her watch, lying under a linear accelerator, and then I thought on the other hand, fat lot of good not having luminous paint on a watch, I've still got bloody cancer.

RUTH, AGE 42
aged 40 at diagnosis

I was loathe to have radiotherapy. I was more scared of it than I was of chemotherapy. However, the pain in my bones was becoming increasingly debilitating and I finally agreed to have it. I couldn't believe the difference it made. I'm now completely pain free and have gone back, after a three month absence, to playing golf every week.

JOANNA, AGE 68
aged 56 at diagnosis

The side-effects of radiotherapy will depend very much on the amount of radiation administered and the area of the body to which it's given. People are often told that there are no side-effects from radiotherapy. However, this claim is inaccurate unless it's palliative radiotherapy which usually involves only a small amount of radiation given to a fairly limited area.

I've touched upon the effects of radiotherapy when it's given to the abdominal area (see Diarrhoea and Nausea earlier this chapter). Here, I want to talk about radiotherapy which is given to other parts of the body and its effects.

A course of radiotherapy which runs over a number of weeks nearly always makes us feel somewhere between tired and completely exhausted. Some women find they can continue working during their course of radiotherapy whilst others find it very taxing and they need to rest for many more hours in the day. Some women find they become despondent, depressed and/or tearful during radiotherapy or they experience unusual mood swings. *These symptoms are associated with the treatment.*

Many doctors don't explain that radiotherapy continues to be active for a while after the last treatment. For instance, if you've been prescribed a course of five weeks' radiotherapy five days a week, the treatment will continue to work *as strongly for the first couple of weeks as if you were still going to the hospital daily, and will continue to work at a lesser level for as long as you* had *the treatment.*

This means that the side-effects of the treatment will last for that period of time also, and you won't begin to recover your energies and emotional equilibrium until several weeks after you've finished your treatment. For example, where radiotherapy is prescribed for five weeks, it will be ten weeks from commencement of treatment before you begin to recover your full energy and emotional equilibrium.

If your support person knows this, they can reassure you that you *will* pass through this time and what you're experiencing is an effect of the treatment. You won't *always* feel that way.

It can be very difficult to keep your spirits up when you're feeling exhausted and depressed as a result of treatment. It's easy to forget you're not your usual self. The support person's role is very important because they can reassure and comfort you with the knowledge that it will pass.

I often see women who say, 'I can't understand what's wrong with me. I finished my radiotherapy three weeks ago and I still feel exhausted and emotional. Am I ever going to feel better than this?' If they'd been properly informed, they'd understand they're *still* 'having' therapy even though they're not going to the hospital for treatment; it's continuing to work in their bodies.

I believe the vitamins mentioned in the section on Nausea are valuable for all people who have cancer or any other disease which affects the immune system. People who are having radiotherapy will benefit from the addition of vitamins and minerals which are particularly in demand for tissue repair work. These are vitamins A, C, E and the B complex plus selenium, magnesium, methionine, histidine, copper salicylate and zinc. Seek guidance from a doctor trained in nutritional medicine or a naturopath (or health food store).

Scarring after radiation

Many people benefit from the application of aloe vera gel alternated with a vitamin E cream after radiation treatment has ceased. Your radiotherapist will have instructed you about the care of your skin whilst you're having treatment. Once you're allowed to apply creams and so on to the skin, you may find they assist the healing process and minimise any permanent scarring in the area. Many radiotherapists will allow aloe vera gel or a non-metal based cream to be applied during therapy. Ask your radiotherapist. Aloe vera gel is the juice from the aloe vera plant and is widely available from health food and department stores. Many women have applied aloe vera gel every two hours throughout their radiotherapy treatment program and have experienced no burning at all to the tissue and their skin has stayed in excellent condition. Vitamin E cream is also readily available. Some people add vitamin A oil as well.

Others claim they've benefited by drinking one to two cups of aloe vera juice per day both during and after their treatment.

Reconstruction

I went to the doctor and said I wanted a reconstruction done and he said, "What do you want that done for"? Three years later I had a reconstruction done, it looked so fantastic I cried when the bandages came off, it was great to have a breast back again. I find that with swimmers, I have to get them made, even though I've had the reconstruction done, because I can never get them high enough to cover the scar under my arm. It's sort of quite puckery. I hate looking in mirrors. If I can get a costume that

210

*covers it all up, I'm fine. I don't wear sleeveless things. I've got
everything with a sleeve. It doesn't matter how hot the day is.*

GERALDINE, AGE 42
aged 32 at diagnosis

*I forgot my prosthesis and had to take a seminar and I'm stuff-
ing tissues down my bra and I thought no, this is it. You've got to
find a plastic surgeon. This isn't good. I had my doctor send me
to three plastic surgeons. One of them asked me, "Oh you're
divorced, is a man forcing you into having this done"? I thought
he insulted my integrity. So he was gone. The second one who
I thought had no bedside manner, my doctor had said women
say he could leave his slippers under their bed any time but he
couldn't leave them outside my gate. He got a lump of silicone,
said it'll look like this with skin over it and I really couldn't
believe that that was his bedside manner and I thought, "If this
was your penis"—he'd be a lot more tender I'm sure.*

JOYE, AGE 50
aged 42 at diagnosis

The decision for a reconstruction is a personal one. Some women
have felt that they're able to really put breast cancer behind them
once they have a breast back, whilst others can't imagine why
anyone would bother or they wouldn't choose to have further
surgery. You'll need to think about whether you want to have a
reconstruction and why. You might find it helpful to talk to
other women who have had one done. Most surgeons are more
than happy to connect you up to one or two of their patients who
are happy with their reconstruction and who will talk to you
about it (and invariably show you what theirs looks like).

Some women have cursed their reconstruction for having
concealed a secondary growth from early detection, although
sophisticated methods for detecting a recurrence should prevent
this from happening. Most of my clients who've had a reconstruction done are delighted with the results.

Many surgeons prefer to know at the time of your mastectomy

whether you want a reconstruction as it alters their surgical technique. They can often do the reconstruction at the time of the mastectomy. Some women may prefer to have the reconstruction done by a specially trained plastic surgeon. They should consult such a surgeon, with the consent of the cancer surgeon, if possible, before the mastectomy takes place.

A reconstruction can be done months or years later. Nowadays, some surgeons are using the fatty tissue of your belly or buttock for the reconstruction and they can even fashion a nipple out of tissue taken from the groin (or elsewhere). This means that you don't have any foreign tissue in your body.

Shingles

To be treated effectively, shingles needs to be diagnosed as early as possible. It's often a very painful and debilitating condition that can develop when the immune system is not functioning very effectively. If your immune system isn't functioning well then it's essential you avoid children who might have the chicken-pox virus (which also causes shingles).

Your doctor will prescribe appropriate treatment for you. If you have any residual nerve pain after shingles, or simply want to hurry up the healing process, you might find the following homeopathics helpful.

Shingles Drops

Croton tiglium	6x
Mezerum	3x
Natrum chloratum	6x
Rhus toxicodendron	4x

For shingles: Take 10–15 drops in a couple of teaspoons of water every quarter to half an hour. Hold the liquid in your mouth for a few seconds before swallowing. Gradually reduce the frequency as improvement becomes evident. Take once an hour, then every two hours, and so on. If pain returns, increase frequency.

These drops are also very effective for those who suffer with post-shingles neuralgia. Sometimes the pain or sensitivity can continue for months in the previously blistered area. The Shingles Drops are effective in alleviating this sensitivity. They're taken in the same dosage and manner; however, they only need to be taken four times daily, gradually reducing the frequency as improvement is evident.

Tamoxifen

When I first started Tamoxifen I was always hot and dripping wet and had to shower two to three times in the night. Each day I had sheets to wash and the bed seemed to get bigger each day as I got weaker.

PATRICIA, AGE 56
aged 52 at diagnosis

Tamoxifen is often recommended to women with breast cancer. It does have some side-effects and these can be more or less pronounced depending on the individual. Side-effects from Tamoxifen can include:

- Post-menopausal bleeding.
- Hot flushes.
- Raised blood pressure.
- Nausea.
- Weight gain.
- Excessive perspiration.

Many of the remedies mentioned throughout this chapter will help to alleviate these side-effects.

Ticks

There have been two documented cases of tick bites to the affected arm of women who've had mastectomies. Ticks can be particularly dangerous to women who have had their lymph glands removed from the armpit. In both cases the women were very

213

sick, experienced paralysis in their affected arm and needed anti-venene. It's worth being aware that, if you live on the east coast of Australia or in any other tick affected area, you should be particularly careful about checking your arm for ticks if you've been outdoors.

Vitamins

Vitamins are invaluable for the woman with breast cancer, especially if she's undergoing any treatment. The dosage of these vitamins/supplements will depend upon your individual state of health, weight, and so on. It's essential therefore to have them tailored to your individual needs by seeing a naturopath or doctor who specialises in vitamin therapy. Ask other women with breast cancer, your doctor, clinic, Cancer Council or friends to recommend such a person. Then ask them if they've had experience with people with breast cancer and if they're happy to work alongside your conventional therapy.

Please inform your oncologist/doctor before taking vitamins/supplements. Don't expect any enthusiastic encouragement, as most doctors are fairly uninformed about the benefits of this approach. It's important that the doctor be made aware of your intention to take vitamins, as very occasionally, there are contra-indications for them. Let them know if you feel you've benefited from this approach, as it's only when many people return to their oncologist/doctor with encouraging reports that all this information will be offered within the hospital system.

The following may be suitable vitamin supplements to take:

- Vitamin C—use a formula which combines sodium ascorbate, calcium ascorbate, ascorbic acid and the bio-flavinoids. The powdered form is easy to take, can be added to juice or water and is certainly the most economical way to take Vitamin C. Dosage is usually between 3–10grams per day.
- Vitamin B complex formula.
- Vitamin E.

- Selenium.
- A mineral formula containing zinc.
- A herbal formula which benefits the immune system.

Watery Eyes

Occasionally, women undergoing chemotherapy will experience a constant overproduction of tears. It's a side-effect which is experienced by very few people. The medical team may assure you the tears have nothing to do with the treatment. This leaves you feeling uncertain about an annoying and unexplained symptom. I've seen enough people with this symptom to assure them that it *is* a side-effect of the treatment and that it *will* settle down when they finish their chemotherapy.

Weight Gain

The oncology nurses said that it was normal to gain a kilo per month which I did do. But at the end of six months, you can imagine: I was overweight, so I was having to contend with the loss of a breast, and this big person. I felt huge and I lost my confidence in myself too and these were interrelated.

JEANNIE, AGE 54
aged 50 at diagnosis

I've put on a terrific lot of weight but I don't care.

ROS, AGE 49
aged 47 at diagnosis

Four years after I was diagnosed I became so depressed because of my weight. I almost felt like life wasn't worth living if I had to be this big person. I tried diets and exercise and nothing seemed to work. It is only since using the homeopathics and keeping up the exercise and lowering still further my intake of calories that I've had any success.

LYNETTE, AGE 44
aged 39 at diagnosis

Increased weight can be a very depressing side-effect of breast cancer and its treatment. Many a woman has worked hard at her recovery only to feel overwhelmed by the added weight she's left with. Adjusting calories and increasing physical activity doesn't always seem to be effective and, if there are any metastases in the bones or lungs, exercise might need to be greatly restricted. For some women, this weight gain feels a bit like the last straw. You've worked hard at adjusting to so many changes in your body image and capabilities that it can all feel too much to bear. If you have secondaries which restrict your breathing or movement then, of course, the added weight won't help your mobility, circulation or comfort.

Sadly, there is no easy answer to this problem. The best results have come from a combination of reducing caloric intake, increasing suitable exercise and taking a homeopathic drop formula which contains:

Calcarea carbonica	12x
Fucus vesiculosus	2x
Graphites	12x
Natrum sulphuricum	2x
Oleum crotonis	4x
Spongia tosta	3x

For excessive weight gain: Take 10–15 drops in a couple of teaspoons of water four times daily, before meals and before bed. Hold the liquid in your mouth for a few seconds before swallowing. Continue with these drops for several months after weight has stabilised.

Wound Healing

Women find the application of either a vitamin E based cream or chickweed ointment often speeds up the healing process of the wound once the stitches have been removed and it has completely sealed. I would suggest you alternate between these two products

(available through health food stores) applying one in the morning and one in the evening (or more frequently). Massage them
into the tissue very gently. Taking vitamins A, C and E plus zinc
pre-operatively will also provide your body with the nutrients for
proper healing of the skin. The vegetable juice mentioned in
Chapter 5 also provides an excellent preparation for surgery.

7
Dealing with Recurrence

I mean, the surgeon said to me, "I expect you to live your normal life-span". A recurrence didn't occur to me. I thought I'd been caught early, and so on. So, when I was diagnosed with this the second time, that's when it really was shattering. It was shattering for my husband and myself. I think we only slept about an hour that night.

MARGARET, AGE 61
aged 59 at diagnosis

One thing I still find surprising is the reaction of some people, even now three years on, of, "But you look so well"! Initially my response was a knee-jerk one that I hadn't been ill. Nowadays the remark sometimes comes across as a morbid expectation that, having had breast cancer, I'm due for a recurrence any day.

Some assume that because I had breast cancer, I now live every *day with the fear of a recurrence. Sure, there have been the times when I've been sent for a chest X-ray or an ultrasound or liver function test because of various symptoms I've had and my wonderful GP says, "I don't expect to find anything sinister but I can't afford to take the risk". At times like that a recurrence is in my mind and one hopes all will be well. But to live every day in fear is not really living. If I lived in fear each day, I wouldn't have the energy to celebrate each day and that (celebrating), to me, is a much more preferable way to live—and die.*

PAT, AGE 60
aged 57 at diagnosis

Once I got over the initial trauma of having the mastectomy, because I felt so well, I just left it behind me and sailed on with my life and I didn't give it another thought—until it came back again.

I then got brain tumours which were treated. That was the most terrifying thing for me because it was back and it was really much more real than it has ever been in the other parts of my body. Because it became life-threatening and they actually gave me two months to live if I didn't have them treated.

But then, five weeks ago, I found out it's in my bones, liver, kidney and lungs as well as the brain. I'm going through a transition of "Am I dying yet"? "Am I dying now"? That's how it felt when I first was given the news of the recurrence. And I suppose this has been the worst time. The first time it's a great shock and the second time, then you think you're over it. Every time I have a new recurrence it is worse than the one before and so it is more shocking than just knowing I had cancer right at the beginning. I've thought that "I'm going to get better", all the time and I think, "Well, if all that treatment didn't work when I had one tumour, why should it work now when I am riddled with it"?

So it's hard not to be realistic about the fact that it's probable my life will be considerably shortened. And then, not dwelling on that, not thinking am I getting caught up with being a person who

220

is dying of cancer. I went through a few weeks of that, feeling very grief-stricken but then I just woke up one morning and thought "Well, here we go". I'm working and getting on with it. So I haven't got any really big issues, it's just holding on to life a day at a time. It has brought my husband and me very close. He has been wonderfully supportive and caring and it's a fascinating spiritual journey, for me, and I feel fairly accepting that I probably will die. Nobody can put a time on it.

SHARNE, AGE 45
aged 37 at diagnosis

I've had secondaries in my liver for three and a half years but I'm still expecting to see seventy. And that's being modest!

SUE, AGE 59
aged 53 at diagnosis

There's always a worry it will come back—that will never go. Sometimes when I get pains or something, I go, "Oh! I hope I don't get it somewhere else", but it doesn't last too long, you think, "Come off it, I'm getting paranoid about this".

SUE, AGE 54
aged 50 at diagnosis

I fell very heavily right on to my chest area. The outcome of that was, I had several cracked ribs on the left-hand side and I had the incredible pain you get with that, for a month or so, and that really shook me up. I didn't take time off work. I sort of put on the stiff upper lip, even though I looked quite ill, and so on. But I think that maybe that set the secondaries off. I mean, it's hard to know in these situations, I really feel some physical or psychological trauma can often contribute to the cancer being re-activated.

MARGARET, AGE 61
aged 59 at diagnosis

Another thing that was a real grief was I went along to the Cancer Council and started doing the training to be a member of the Breast Cancer Support Service. I was really pleased with that,

I thought this was something that I can give back. Then I got the recurrence and was told I could no longer be in it and that I had to be two years clear of the disease. I was really hurt by that but at the time I didn't think I was allowed to feel hurt. I felt so strongly that I was shut out and that's one of the reasons we started our support group, because I wasn't allowed to have any contact with women who had had breast cancer, because of the recurrence. As I have had a recurrence every two years since, obviously I was never going to be one of the Breast Cancer Support Service women.

HELEN, AGE 42
aged 34 at diagnosis

I mean, when one of us gets an unexplained illness or an unexplained pain we immediately think—it's cancer! But in some ways, the more false alarms you have, the more you learn to ignore them, and I've had a few false alarms. So has my husband. Whenever somebody has a headache we go round the house saying— "It's gone to the brain. It's gone to the brain!" We've got a very black sense of humour and that still exists here.

CATHERINE, AGE 47
aged 41 at diagnosis

I was told that after five years I didn't have to see the surgeon again. He said, "If you get cancer again it will have nothing to do with this cancer". In fact, eleven years later, when I had pain in my hip, had he not said those words, I'd have suspected something, but I didn't even think about secondaries. By the time it was diagnosed, the cancer was so extensive I had to have a total hip replacement.

CAROL, AGE 53
aged 42 at diagnosis

I never thought for a minute that I was going to die, and I still don't. I'm going to go and get that telegram from the Queen!

SALLY, AGE 58
aged 50 at diagnosis

Look, I have a great belief in miracles and I have believed in miracles, but I suppose my faith in miracles is running out. I know there's a real fighting spirit in some people but I'm not a fighting person. I'm much more of an accepting, watching person. So I watch it with great interest and I feel a greater acceptance.

SHARNE, AGE 45
aged 37 at diagnosis

I made a good recovery, but two and a half years later, acting on gut feelings again and some minor physical symptoms, I decided to consult my doctor ahead of time. The discovery of some cancer cells in the other breast was at first deflating and discouraging. I had recently begun a new job which incorporated the previous one and greatly added to it. Had I made a mistake? Should I resign now, in fairness to the job, my colleagues, and the team I'd been pulling together? Again, I came to the conclusion that while alive I should live, and continue what I'd started.

The second round of chemo, with different drugs, isn't as harsh, and isn't yet completed. It's impossible to know what the outcome will be, but I'm well, busy, content and at peace.

JOAN, AGE 67
aged 63 at diagnosis

When I first got it, I followed the Bristol diet and hated every minute of it. I really resented and hated it. I stuck on it religiously for the six months that I had radiotherapy and I did the juices. I had no side-effects at all during the radiotherapy. Then, gradually, my diet went back to what it had been before. It had never been a particularly bad diet. I ate a lot of grains and pulses, wholemeal bread, a lot of fruit and vegetables. We do eat meat and we do drink wine. And then, when I got the disease back in 1990, I was really stunned and I thought I've got to do something. I love cooking and serving food and it's a real interest of mine and I just felt stultified by what I was supposed to eat. I'm careful about what I eat, I don't eat a lot of fat. I try to eat a healthy diet but I do enjoy a drink or two and I don't think I got the cancer because of what I ate and drank. And I don't think I'm going to be cured or not cured because of what I eat and drink. I'm not saying that diet doesn't work for some people, it does, but I think there are people who've recovered and they didn't do anything with their diet.

HELEN, AGE 42
aged 34 at diagnosis

The X-rays looked good, my attitude was good. I got a clean bill of health—until the next morning. My surgeon's office rang to say I was booked into hospital the next day for another operation. This time it took my local doctor to find out just why. My hard won acceptance and my delight at yesterday's result fled.

Again, cancer was the enemy. I faced another biopsy, another adjustment. And so, finally, came another mastectomy, different this time. I knew what to expect but still the fear gnawed at me and was in turn chased away by the thought that having no breasts was probably better than one large breast and the prosthesis heavily keeping up the other side of my bra. I would be free and perhaps even have a reconstruction and be the envy of all my friends. Still, the thought of another cancer was lurking but I overruled this by the certainty that I could never have breast cancer again. My mind was running around in circles.

Three months later I was no longer living my life as I had before. I gave up the heady, frantic corporate life I'd fought so hard to achieve. I had time for my family and friends who had supported me through this marathon experience. I changed my way of dressing to suit the new shape I'd become and had fun experimenting with the large leap from corporate dressing.

JOAN, AGE 54
aged 51 at diagnosis

I acquired a dog as part of my recovery program, and Jack and I go walking every day up in the mountains behind Canberra and chase kangaroos. I'm writing a book. All those things are *wonderful but they're predicated on the fact that I've got cancer. And how do I keep that wonderful stuff and also say I can give the cancer up. That's the problem for me. That somehow, inside me, not my intelligence, but somewhere inside me says to have all these great things, to learn these spiritual things you have to have the disease, but can you give the disease up and still keep the spiritual things you've learnt.*

Many women with breast cancer aren't sick, unlike with other cancers, and until you get extensive secondaries many people don't have much pain and discomfort and yet you're told your life expectancy is really low. It doesn't seem to make sense.

HELEN, AGE 42
aged 34 at diagnosis

There's still a part of me which would like to embrace fully the belief that I could fully recover.

HELEN, AGE 42
aged 34 at diagnosis

There are days when I still feel like crying, and times when I'm frightened that if I start, I'll never stop. The last time I had "one of those days" I felt grief-stricken, but strong. And I felt good about that. One of the most important lessons I've learnt is that it's OK to have a negative thought. Just because your imagination runs wild and you start seeing your own funeral, and hear the eulogies at the service, it doesn't mean it's going to happen! And it's OK to let go.

FIONA, AGE 34
aged 33 at diagnosis

Coping with Recurrence

Most women find that it is much more challenging to deal with a recurrence than it was to deal with their initial diagnosis. Many women feel that they have 'done breast cancer' and they never expected to have to 'do' it again. Many women also find it more threatening the second time.

As Michelle expressed it:

When I was first diagnosed I was shocked to think I could be a woman who'd get breast cancer. It shattered some of the beliefs I had about myself and it certainly undermined my confidence. Gradually, I regained my equilibrium as I underwent the treatments and did many things to help myself.

When I was diagnosed with a recurrence I felt completely devastated. I felt, there's nothing I can do that I haven't done already. Some days, it feels like it's out to get me and I've lost faith in my body's ability to respond positively.

MICHELLE, AGE 38
aged 35 at diagnosis

Some women feel let down by their treatments or the many things they've been doing to help themselves in addition to their medical treatment. For some of these women there could also be anger and frustration. If we believe that we were doing everything we could to prevent a recurrence, then it can be easy to either blame ourselves for not staying with some program we had adopted 100 per cent, or blame the therapies for letting us down.

Many women find it much more difficult to get through the initial shock of a recurrence than when they were first diagnosed with breast cancer. You may find that, not only your reaction, but your response will differ this second time. You might well experience another change in priorities and decide, perhaps, to adopt different treatment programs, different complementary therapies, and so on. Give yourself time to assimilate this new information.

Talking to understanding friends, a partner or support group is often the first step in putting this recurrence into a perspective which seems more manageable.

For women who are also mothers, there's the added strain of having to confront their children with more bad news. For some women, who hadn't told their children about their initial diagnosis, there may now be the necessity to include them in what has happened to you. The joy we have in loving each other is counter-balanced by the pain of any threat to our being together.

Occasionally, people who we thought of as friends can attrib-ute blame to us, believing that if we'd done everything perfectly then we wouldn't be in this situation. This comes from fearful thinking that says, 'I can control what happens to me if I try hard enough'.

Some women blame their recurrence on a particularly stressful time they've been through, and they may be angry at the person or situation which upset them. Many women have had a bad fall which seems to have immediately preceded a recurrence. Regard-less of how we feel about a recurrence, we find ourselves back on the treadmill of doctors, hospitals, treatments and the tedium of losing hair, feeling unwell, dealing with pain or the myriad other reminders of our illness.

> *We can't always change what happens to us but we can change the way we respond to what happens to us.*

For many women, a recurrence of breast cancer is another oppor-tunity to let go even more deeply into living each day, one at a time. In fact, most women find that is the only way to live well!

> *When I had my first recurrence two years after my mastec-tomy I thought, "This is the beginning of the end"! However, I went into remission. The second recurrence, I felt pretty much the same way. But again I went into remission. Now, I've had many flare-ups of my breast cancer and I hardly get upset at all any more. I feel I'm managing breast cancer and that it's not managing me.*

> STELLA, AGE 54
> *aged 41 at diagnosis*

> *I realised I was always thinking, "I'll start living again once I'm over my treatment" or "I'll start living again once I'm over breast cancer". What I came to realise is that this is my life. Living with the ups and downs that cancer brings me. Working*

with the process of living on a day by day basis. Letting it be the way it is and not railing against the disease has brought me a lot more peace.

It's hard to let go the cherished dreams of how I thought my life was meant to be. But I have to say that I'm really very content. I'm enjoying the simple things in life far more than ever before. I feel truly and deeply alive. This has only come about because of a willingness to find peace, which meant I had to let go of how I thought it should be and just let it be the way it is.

ANNIE, AGE 48
aged 40 at diagnosis

Many women struggle with the lack of certainty in the future, particularly if they've been very goal-oriented or had never contemplated the precariousness of life. For some, the realisation that we all live with vast amounts of uncertainty most of the time is a new and frightening one.

Strangely enough, when I deeply contemplated my own uncertain future and realised that I only had day by day to experience life, it was a relief in some ways; to not have to decide upon the future, to let each day be sufficient and not lacking. The more I've been able to live in the present, the less there is to worry about. Each moment, each day, becomes a gift in simply being present to whatever *is* happening. Then, every day becomes a bonus, every moment a gift. This is, of course, easier to experience if we're not feeling really ill or are in pain.

Bilateral Mastectomy

Some women may face the difficult choice of having a bilateral mastectomy, even though there is no cancer activity present in their breasts. This may be because of a very strong likelihood of developing breast cancer due to their family history. For instance, where there are several women within the family who have had breast cancer.

Other women will choose to have their second breast removed because of the possibility of developing breast cancer in the future. This is sometimes recommended when the tissue has been described as pre-cancerous. This choice, though very difficult, often gives a woman confidence in believing she can no longer develop breast cancer because all breast tissue is removed.

This decision can only be made after consultation with your doctor. You may need to have a second or third opinion in order to feel confidence in your decision.

Types of Pain

Even when we're free of it, pain is the symptom we probably worry about most. We mightn't be talking about physical pain only. There are many different pains from which we can suffer. At its simplest level, we experience pain as something that hurts. It might have many different causes, depending on what kind of pain is being experienced. The important thing with pain, as with all symptoms, is to find and understand the *cause*.

The pain which concerns us most is the physical pain we believe our illness will produce. It's important to realise that breast cancer is *not* always painful, not even if it leads to death. In most cases where people *do* experience pain, it can be controlled and in many cases eliminated.

Most of us have heard stories about the pain of cancer and it's understandable that anxiety and fear are experienced. You could even be feeling, right now, pain which isn't being adequately controlled. Very often oncologists, immunologists, general practitioners and nurses aren't knowledgeable about appropriate pain management. When you've looked to them for your guidance in the past they've probably had suitable answers or solutions to your medical problems. However, to treat pain adequately is a specialised field and *you* must become educated about your *own* pain and its relief.

Perhaps we feel the pain of deprivation. It can be some kind of obvious deprivation as in the loss of your breast or physical disfigurement. Or it can be more subtle, as in the loss of your ability to work, your self-confidence or esteem. Many women say they can come to terms with having breast cancer but are deeply affected by the loss of their hair, brought about through treatment. It could be the loss of weight which preys upon the mind or the loss of energy.

We might not be feeling the pain of a physical loss and yet our pain can be intense. We might have suffered the loss of those we love, either through death or divorce or simply having moved away from our loved ones. The pain felt by these separations can be deep and unacknowledged—our private pain. This pain is often more intense and makes us feel dispirited because no one quite understands our personal loss.

Emotional pain is something to which we can all relate. Unfulfilled dreams, loss of face, disappointing relationships, lack of success in our chosen career, shattered expectations, and so on. We deal with these pains according to our past experiences. For one woman, divorce will be a shattering conclusion to all potential happiness in relationships, whilst to another, it will be another educational step along the way. Likewise, a childhood where there's been little to build self-esteem or where there's been sexual, physical or psychological abuse could leave scars which take a lifetime to heal. They could be scars which *never* heal and which influence the way a person makes all future choices.

There's the pain of separation: a child leaving home, ready to start life on his or her own; friends or family who move to another town or country; a child going to boarding school; leaving childhood and entering adolescence.

One pain often overlooked is the pain of clinging to life. For some, their ultimate pain will be the final separation by death— the leaving of everything familiar, the leaving of our loved ones. The pain of not seeing our children grow to maturity and beyond. Letting go and trusting all is well. Leaving a body which has

230

completed its task. Leaving a body when we believe we *haven't* completed our task.

However, in retrospect, it's plain to me that many of the greatest traumas and pains in my life were fertile soil for growth and understanding. These pains included months in hospital with extensive reconstructive surgery to my legs as a teenager, rape, the death of my much-loved brother, a divorce and leukaemia—to name just a few of the more potent ones! The understanding and growth these experiences allowed was probably unavailable in any other way.

It's difficult for people to witness a loved-one's pain. We can empathise but beyond that, we might feel helpless in our inability to give relief. The pain of our helplessness can be most acute. There are many misunderstandings about pain and its relief.

It's true we can learn much about ourselves through the experience of pain. However, we also need to temper our pursuit of understanding with gentleness and compassion. Unrelenting pain is both exhausting and dispiriting. Even the most positive attitude or resolve weakens when pain is persistent.

Pain is only a symptom of some distress which the body or mind is experiencing, and is a cry for help. And help is needed. Pain shouldn't be ignored. It's essential to investigate thoroughly and deal with its cause. This applies regardless of whether the pain is a physical or emotional one.

Unless emotional pain is dealt with, it will erode our peace of mind and ultimately cause more stress to the body. Suppressed resentments, angers, jealousies and hurts prevent us from living happy and fulfilled lives and inevitably damage our health. It has become apparent that many people have suffered some major pain or loss in the six months to two years before the onset of their cancer. This observation is not a new revelation. For centuries both doctors and lay people knew that after major stress, people were much more prone to disease. In the eighteen months previous to my diagnosis my brother had died, I'd moved to a new country to undertake further studies, and had separated from my husband!

In Chapter 3, 'A Place of Peace Within' we discussed many ways of dealing with these stressors and you can refer to that chapter for further practical assistance. The techniques for forgiveness are particularly useful for past situations which still cause us stress. This implies a willingness to let go the pain of the past and an openness to seeing the situation differently. Why hang onto the pain of unforgivingness?

As has been said before, physical pain requires investigation so we can learn what its cause actually is. It's a common trap, once we've been diagnosed with a serious disease, to believe every ache and pain is associated with the disease. We forget we could be suffering from muscular tension, arthritis, indigestion or a tension headache. Immediately we think we might have tumours in the brain, bones or stomach! Rather than worry unnecessarily, it's better to find out what the cause of the pain is, and find an appropriate treatment.

The mind will conjure up all kinds of frightening answers to our pain and it can be far more worrying than knowing exactly what we're dealing with. When we know what's causing the pain, we can marshal our resources to work within that situation. The unknown is always more intimidating than the known. It's good to remember also that everything seems much worse at 3 a.m. What's quite tolerable in the clear light of day is sometimes overwhelming in the still watches of the night. The feeling of isolation in the middle of the night can be very acute. Sometimes I used to feel everyone was sleeping contentedly in their beds while I was quietly dying in my room. I was fortunate to have a very understanding mother to whom I could express my fears. Often just being able to talk to a sympathetic friend is sufficient to alleviate the stress associated with our fears and anxieties.

Likewise with past resentments, hurts, jealousies, and so on. Once aired with an understanding person, they diminish in their intensity. If we don't have such a person in our lives then we might need to enlist the aid of a support group or trained counsellor who can help us to resolve our difficulties. Often the emotional or psychological pain we hold in directly contributes to the physical pain we experience in our body.

Some avenues worth exploring for the relief of pain are listed here. It's a matter of trying out different suggestions and finding which ones are most appropriate for you. They're only suggestions which have proven useful for others and require no prescription. You might wish to discuss any of the following techniques with your physician before embarking upon them. It's expected that you'll be under appropriate pain-management supervision from either your doctor or a palliative care team. However, here are some additional thoughts that might prove useful to you.

If I'm doing something I'm interested in, if I'm in a comfortable position, or if I'm meditating, I don't feel it. These are times when I am pain free.

MARGARET, AGE 61
aged 59 at diagnosis

The Pain Scale

Using a scale to talk about your pain can be a very useful tool. This means you measure your pain on a scale of 0 to 10. A zero means you're pain free, a ten means something really needs to be done about your pain *right now*. To scale pain in this way seems somehow to objectify it. It puts it 'out there' for discussion with your loved-ones or carer. After a time you'll also learn which number on the scale corresponds with the technique most useful in alleviating it. For instance, a rating of '3' could mean some diversional activity will take care of it. Perhaps a walk in the garden or a game of Scrabble or cards. A '5' could mean it's necessary to practise a particular relaxation technique for its relief, whilst a '7' might mean you need to look for assistance in the form of appropriate analgesics. It will be a very individual scale and it will take a little time in order to become familiar with exactly what will help most. Our pain tolerance can vary enormously. Some people have a very high pain threshold, whilst others will experience fear immediately and that will almost lock in their pain and make it all-consuming. Sometimes, if a disease progresses, our tolerance to pain becomes diminished and we require more effective techniques for its control. Factors such as the weather, weariness, boredom, fear or the anticipation of some unpleasant procedure, can influence how we will experience our pain.

Pain often restricts our activities, both mental and physical, and when boredom is added to pain it becomes much worse. If boredom is a facet of pain, it's helpful to have recourse to activities which stimulate the mind. These could include everything from a walk in the garden, to doing a crossword, to playing Scrabble or listening to a talking book. These books are usually available from your local library. Other activities such as cross-stitch, tapestry, painting, drawing and other crafts can also be beneficial in this way.

Massage

Often, gentle massage will relieve the symptoms of discomfort and immediately increase ease and mobility. No one with a serious disease is free of muscular tension. Massage is a wonderful means by which we can release tension and the vast majority of people find it extremely relaxing and helpful. Often, when we experience pain, we hold that area in an unnatural position to protect it from being bumped. For instance, if you have a pain in your shoulder blade, it's very likely you'll tense the surrounding muscles in order to protect the painful area. This might well lead to tension in neck and other muscles which will then cause more pain. Massage can relieve all the surrounding tension. *Then* you can deal effectively with the residual (and original) pain.

It can be useful to immobilise a painful part of the body. This can be done through the use of a splint, a sling or creating support through the use of pillows or cushions. If an area of the body is immobilised, it might also be beneficial to use gentle massage to the surrounding areas in order to minimise tension held there. Elevating a limb on pillows might also be advisable if there's any swelling. Massage can be used to reduce swelling in arms (see the section on Lymphoedema in Chapter 6).

If you're seeking professional massage, find a therapist who's had experience with people with cancer or serious illness and who's familiar with some of the particular problems associated with breast cancer. You might wish to check out the advisability of massage with your doctor. In some cases where there are metastases or 'hot spots' in the bones, massage *could* be contra-indicated. However, any therapist who's had experience working with such people would provide very gentle massage to those areas and would pose no problem at all. The benefits are so valuable I'd encourage anyone to give it a try. The principal benefits of massage are:

- It induces deep relaxation.
- It provides nurturing.
- It improves the overall circulation.
- It relieves muscular spasms which could be causing pain, discomfort or limited mobility.
- It's fun!

If you choose to have a professional massage don't be afraid to tell the therapist exactly what it is you want. Many therapists also visit the home and this might prove to be more convenient for you. In this latter case, the therapist usually brings a portable massage table to your home. If they don't bring a table, you can remain in your bed. If you're particularly weak or bed-bound, then explain to the therapist over the telephone that you'll need to remain in bed.

Massage increases the blood flow to the immediate and surrounding areas. With a restored and adequate blood flow, the area then receives both the nutrients and oxygen which the tissues require. It also means toxins from muscular activity or spasm can be effectively eliminated. Parts of the body which are cold and lifeless can be restored to warmth and mobility. As relaxation becomes deeper, the overall blood flow in the body is increased.

Hospital beds were never designed for physical relaxation! They're designed almost entirely for the ease of the nurses. Modern technology is gradually improving the situation for both nurse and patient. Of course it's not just a matter of the bed. If we're hospitalised there are all the added tensions of diagnostic tests, disrupted routines, endless people, noise, hustle and bustle, and frequently unfamiliar (and, perhaps, unpalatable) food. It's no wonder our muscles are all of a-twitter.

Most people will say, after a massage in the hospital, that it's the best thing that's happened to them since they were admitted. Some massage therapists will visit people in hospital or in their home. If you wish to have a therapist visit you in hospital, it's essential you receive permission from your doctor first. To check with the doctor is a simple matter of courtesy. And don't forget massage for the support person or carer! Everyone needs nurturing and support, and massage is a great way of having it.

Acupressure and Acupuncture

These therapies work by stimulating the circulation and the energy flow to an area. They can be very helpful in alleviating pain. A trained therapist is usually needed, certainly for acupuncture. However, a therapist could be willing to show the support person the appropriate points to massage so they can bring relief to the patient. Some acupuncturists will leave small needles in place between visits. These needles will continue to stimulate the nerve endings in the area leading to pain relief.

Warmth

Don't forget the value of simple warmth. A hot-water bottle can be very comforting for many pains. For safety's sake, regular checks on the integrity of the rubber and a cover for the hot-water bottle are recommended. Breville also make electrical heating pads, like mini-electric blankets, which can be placed over areas of pain.

Exercise

A pleasant distraction involving exercise can be helpful in dealing with pain. This could involve a favourite sport or a gentle stroll in the garden. Sometimes all that can be managed is a slow shuffle up and down the hallway. Even quiet exercises done whilst in bed can relieve stiffness and poor circulation. Ankle rotation, and the tensing and releasing of muscles throughout the body, are helpful for those confined to bed. The support person or carer can assist the patient by gently moving the various parts of the body.

For other people, quite vigorous exercise will bring pain relief. One of the effects of vigorous exercise is that the body secretes endorphins into the blood stream. These endorphins are the body's own natural pain relievers. They're also released into the blood stream when we laugh heartily or when we weep. You might well have experienced the deep relaxation throughout your body after a really good cry or laugh.

Many people have adequately controlled their pain through their sporting activities. They generally find that it *increases* their pain initially; then find they receive very valuable pain relief which lasts for a considerable period of time after their exercise.

In his book, *Anatomy of an Illness*, Norman Cousins gives a really excellent account of dealing with his painful and crippling disease by the conscious use of laughter. He found ten minutes of good belly laughter gave him two hours of pain relief. We don't even need to leave our bed. Funny friends, videos or books can be a godsend. Laughter makes everything much more tolerable and helps us to keep our perspective. It's one form of exercise in which everyone can participate. Learn to escalate a smile into a chuckle, a chuckle into a laugh, a laugh into a real belly laugh. Our own laughter is a very reassuring sound to our ears!

Poetry

Some people find release from their pain by listening to poetry. Its beauty and imagery can provide a very special oasis for the mind, taking the concentration away from the difficulties of the present. Having someone read to us when we're unwell can be very comforting. Recordings of poetry or novels are becoming more widely available and can bring another world into our home. Don't overlook the possibility of writing poetry yourself either. This can be a useful means of expression for those whose activities are curtailed or who simply revel in the use of words to describe their world.

Music

Like poetry, music can soothe, comfort and uplift us. We can go beyond our pain to a space of calm and peace. Listening to music which is bright, cheerful or inspiring can certainly lift our spirits. Sometimes, it takes an effort even to reach out for the things which we know will bring us comfort. It's almost as if we'd rather stay in a depressed or painful space than make the effort to shift our perception of things. *Feel* the pain, *feel* the inertia, then make the effort anyway.

Music has a tremendous capacity to lift us out of depression or pain. Experiment with the various kinds of music and be flexible in your choice. Music can also be used to put us in touch with our anger or frustration. By allowing it to flow over us we, like the music, find the resolution of these feelings. Some music is full of passion and torment and yet, having given full reign to these feelings, finds its rest and peace once more.

Touch

Like massage, the simple loving touch of someone can bring great comfort. A hand held, a brow softly stroked, a foot gently massaged. These small gestures sometimes convey all that's necessary. To be in pain is stressful in itself. To be in pain and to feel isolated from love is much worse. A gentle hug or caress is one of love's most natural means of expression.

By our response to the care and love shown to us we can bring comfort to our carers. It's important for the carers to feel appreciated and that their 'loving' of us is acknowledged. A simple smile or returned gesture often speaks more eloquently than words.

Prayer and Affirmations

The repetition of a positive statement or the offering up of our pain to a Higher Source can bring comfort and a changed perception of our situation. When we're in pain, at least we know with certainty that we *are* alive. To practise a technique of relaxation at this time can be challenging. It helps if we've been practising on the little pains before we tackle the more intrusive ones. Once we're in a deeply relaxed state it can be very helpful to quietly repeat a word or phrase which we find comforting. To work with the inward and outward breath adds power to our practice. Some affirmations which have been found useful are:

Let go and let God, All is Well, Healing Peace, Peace and Calm, Healing into Light, and *Peace and Joy*.

These words, repeated silently and slowly in the mind, can be rhythmically attached to the breath. For instance, on the inward breath, we can repeat silently 'Let go and . . .', and on the outward breath, 'let God'.

These techniques become powerful with practice and perseverance. With a strong faith all things are possible. It even becomes achievable to transmute pain into warmth and joy. It's often resistance to pain which makes it unbearable, not the pain itself. It is its limiting character which we resist. Some have the determination and faith to go beyond their pain, to find a way of living at peace with their pain.

Breathing Patterns

There are times when we need to will our way through pain. It can be a real effort sometimes to go for a walk, or have a swim, or finish that job when we're in pain. There are other times when we need to stop what we're doing and consciously practise some technique to help alleviate it. Sometimes one approach is just right, other times a different one is needed.

Technique 1

A technique which is enormously valuable is simply breathing! Often when we're in pain it's reflected in the manner in which we breathe. Our breathing can become restricted or laboured. Sometimes we develop the habit of breathing in, holding the breath and taking an age to let it out again. Once we detect this pattern we're in a position to establish a healthier rhythm. More often than not, with this sort of breathing, there are some emotional factors at play, emotions such as fear or uncertainty. To establish a better rhythm helps to calm those emotions. It can be helpful to adopt a counting method with the breathing. For instance, we can breathe in to the count of four, hold for four, and breathe out to the count of four. We can gradually lengthen the breath so we breathe in to the count of say, ten or even twelve, hold for that long—or a shorter period—and breathe out for the same count. Experiment until you find what works best for you. There's no right or optimum way to do it. The right or optimum way is the one which works for you.

Technique 2

Another very restful technique is to breathe in and then focus on the little pause at the end of the inward breath. Then breathe out, and again focus on the little pause at the end of the outward breath—each inward and outward breath leading to that comfortable pause. As the mind quietens, the pause naturally lengthens. No effort is required to lengthen it. Some people like to hold in the mind the image of a crescent moon. One point of the moon 10 centimetres (4 inches) in front of the nostrils, the other point of the crescent at the space between the eyebrows.

Technique 3

Some may find the practice of 'breathing in love, breathing out fear' helpful. With each inward breath, focus on love as you breathe in, and let all fear drain out of the body with the outward breath. Some might wish to give 'love' and 'fear' different colours, perhaps breathing in a soft pink, breathing out brown or grey.

The Role of Analgesics

It's a common yet erroneous belief that taking medical analgesics will somehow interfere with the process of healing. I've often seen people who haven't slept for days, who are dispirited and depressed through continuous pain because they refuse to take any prescribed medication. This is a sad and short-sighted view. Whilst the body is in pain, very little healing can take place, as all one's energy goes into dealing with it. Constant pain is very debilitating and it's difficult to keep one's spirits up when it's relentless. Often, all that's needed is forty-eight hours of good pain relief in which the patient gets some sound sleep. After this time the medication can often cease or be lessened. Once we're rested and our spirits are restored, everything becomes easier. This pain relief program needs to be administered by someone who's entirely qualified and competent to do so.

Some people are concerned that if they go onto strong analgesics like morphine they'll become addicted. Some fear if they're taking morphine then their end must be close. Often these fears are held more by the surrounding family than by the person with the pain. They're all understandable anxieties. With proper explanation from your prescribing physician these anxieties are easily eliminated. The technique described above, whereby strong analgesics are given for a short period of time, does *not* result in addiction. On the contrary, it results in a contented person who's gained some valuable rest and whose spirits are restored. Morphine, appropriately prescribed, never becomes addictive.

It's a good idea to make arrangements in advance for after-hours medical care. You might never need to call on it but it will comfort you to know that help *is* at hand should you require it. If it isn't your local doctor who will come after-hours, make sure you have a summary of your medical history available in your home for the visiting doctor. This will save time and concern on your part.

If you are taking prescribed oral analgesics, it's essential that you keep a chart which clearly outlines the times when your medication is due. This is particularly important if you live alone and are the sole supervisor of your medication schedule. If you don't live alone, this chart should be kept by someone who resides there. Rule up a sheet of paper with these headings at the tops of the columns so it looks like this:

Date	Time	Amount given	Pain scale? 1–10	Drowsiness?	Other remarks

Radiotherapy given to a specific area can often be of tremendous benefit in relieving localised pain. It's often used when a tumour is in the bone; you'll only know if it will help you when you discuss the possibility with your doctor.

If pain is chronic and is being managed routinely by analgesics then again, they must be competently prescribed and administered. There are often pain clinics attached to hospitals. These clinics specialise in appropriate pain management. Often the analgesics prescribed are correct but the administration technique is at fault, and these clinics can assist with relevant information.

Many of the more powerful analgesics are given on a routine basis rather than on the basis of 'pain demand'. If they're given every four hours, for instance, the patient might well not experience *any* strong pain. If you wait for the pain to come before administration of analgesics, it takes *much* longer for them to be effective, by which time you're probably experiencing very strong pain. Morphine is now available in slow-release tablets which means you only need to take them twice a day.

In my experience, there are three places to get expert advice on pain management. They are:

- Pain clinics, that is, clinics with doctors who specialise in nothing but pain management. Some of these clinics include many of the techniques mentioned in this chapter whilst others rely solely on drug analgesia.
- Local palliative care/hospice units whose doctors and staff are all trained and well-experienced in pain control.
- Your palliative care nurse who's part of the community nursing team. You can ask to be referred to your community nursing service by your oncologist or general practitioner. They will come to your home to ascertain your pain management or any other practical need.

It's your right to have the best pain management skills available. It's your right to be pain free or as close to it as is possible. Don't be fobbed off with anything less than a great reduction in, and possibly complete alleviation of, pain. Keep asking until you get the assistance you need.

Constipation

Most of the medically prescribed, or even over the counter variety of analgesics will cause constipation. See also Constipation in Chapter 6.

Pets

Don't underestimate the value a pet can be in helping us deal with the stress of pain. Many a pet has known exactly what's going on with their owner and has been able to bring about some magic by its presence. Some people have deeper relationships with their pets than they do with people! Most of us have had times when it's easier to understand the cat or dog than it is to understand our teenagers (or partner).

One of the loveliest things about the companionship of a cat or dog is that they accept us just the way we are. Even when we're so confused and bewildered that we don't know what to think, ol' Fido or Puss will be there to nuzzle, cuddle or sit on us to reassure us of their love. These pets can be great company when we're feeling out of sorts and they can help us to relax and calm ourselves.

If animals, pets or nature are important to you then remember to have contact with them. So often we let slip by the little things that bring us so much contentment.

There's every reason to have your pets around you when you're unwell. The animals will probably love it as you'll be *their* captive audience, providing pats, strokes and conversation whenever *they* desire. Cats and dogs particularly seem to know when you're feeling unwell and will often deliberately 'gentle' themselves to your level of activity. A warm, furry friend can soothe and comfort without words or side-effects.

Vitamin C

There are many people who claim to have had pain relief through the frequent administration of high dosages of vitamin C. These dosages can be taken orally or intravenously. Obviously, the administration of vitamin C directly into the blood stream can only be performed by a willing doctor. There are many such doctors in the community today who believe in and advocate the use of intravenous vitamin C. Oral dosages of vitamin C need to be administered on a very individual basis as everyone's demand for it varies. It's essential you work with an experienced doctor or naturopath to establish the best dosage for you. When vitamin C is given this way, orally, it must be composed of sodium ascorbate, calcium ascorbate, ascorbic acid and the bio-flavinoids in order to give a balanced formula. Ascorbic acid on its own in high doses, is very irritating to the stomach.

Relaxation Techniques for Pain Relief

Techniques of relaxation are extremely valuable in relation to pain relief. Whilst ever we're feeling uptight and anxious it will compound our pain and make even the smallest twinge a cause for fear. It's important to communicate with someone about *your* pain so you address any of the emotional or psychological components involved. Having done that, the regular practice of techniques which help to minimise or eliminate stress are invaluable.

Any of the techniques mentioned in this book will be helpful. There are two particularly which are most commonly used for pain management and I've put both these techniques on CD which is available from the address at the back of this book.

8
Body Image and Sexuality

Being single, as I am, I find it a bit distressing going out there to meet a man . . .

Lucy, age 43
aged 38 at diagnosis

I was told by one of the nurses, to make my husband stroke the scar. She said, "It's OK to have a sexual relationship even though you only have one breast. Just make love in a T-shirt". And I thought, "Oh, God".

Suzie, age 51
aged 49 at diagnosis

Breast cancer is a very confronting disease. Whether a woman loves or hates her breasts, to me they represent the very essence of womanhood, of being a woman, are an important part of

247

sexuality, mothering, self-image and to have that tampered with is devastating.

JUDY, AGE 38
aged 36 at diagnosis

I didn't realise how much my husband loved me until I got cancer . . .

NANCY, AGE 49
aged 48 at diagnosis

Since all this started I have not had a man in my life. No more romantic dinners, hugs and kisses and when could I tell a man how I am? After all I have been through I could not face rejection. Not every man you meet loves you for what you are.

PATRICIA, AGE 56
aged 52 at diagnosis

I thought that I was really ugly. Terribly ugly. I felt really lumpish and fat. I'd never been overweight. I'd always been slim and it was so frustrating for me. I looked in the mirror and I thought—this isn't me. This isn't me at all. I had no hair, hardly any eyebrows or any eye lashes, and the kind of face that disappeared into itself. And then I was much fatter. And one breast was missing. And I thought—you really do look dreadful. And I thought—how can anybody possibly want to have a relationship with you? The first thing I'm going to have to say, if anyone is interested in me, is "Oh look, excuse me, I've got no breast on the left side. Is that going to make a difference"?

JEANNIE, AGE 54
aged 50 at diagnosis

I've had a 30 kilogram weight gain as well. I put the weight on during chemotherapy. So for me it was a big issue. I remember my first sexual encounter following my mastectomy, which would have probably been about six weeks or so after. I'm divorced, so it was my lover, and I can still remember, we were in a motel and I was just sitting on the bed and weeping and weeping. And he came out of the shower and said to me, "After all

Lynne, some people don't have any nice breasts and you've still got one really nice one". He was just so loving and caring and I was able to move through that then. But it's still an issue for me. Up to now, which is five years since I've had my mastectomy, I wouldn't be comfortable with somebody new; it's OK with somebody who's known me for a long time, but it's still an issue with me now. I don't know what the feelings were at that time, if they were humiliation or embarrassment, or just a real sadness, probably all those things. All those losses I think.

LYNNE, AGE 49
aged 44 at diagnosis

An issue which crosses my mind several times a day is about the use of Tamoxifen and the effects on the vagina and, in my case, I was probably about to be menopausal anyway, but the chemotherapy brought on menopause with the associated vaginal problems and I feel it might affect my sexuality and there's a grief attached to that.

LOUISE, AGE 52
51 at diagnosis

I felt a great amount of grief going through menopause. It was worse in a way than losing a breast. I coped with the physical side but what was happening inside, the hormonal changes, were very difficult. I lost my libido totally. Just became totally disinterested in sex and my husband is the reverse. I feel so guilty because I'm just so unresponsive and he's still very loving. We have just had to come to terms with that, that our needs are very different, and find a compromise somewhere in the middle.

SHARNE, AGE 45
aged 37 at diagnosis

I was devastated when my husband told me he found the scars from my double mastectomies were repulsive to him and that he could no longer bear to touch me or even look at me naked.

LIZ, AGE 39
aged 39 at diagnosis

I found going through menopause for me was worse than having the breast removed. I felt robbed of part of my life. I was only forty-two.

CAROL, AGE 53
aged 42 at diagnosis

They don't tell you about menopause and it starts happening and when you tell them "This is happening", they say "Oh yes, by the way it does happen".

SHARNE, AGE 45
aged 37 at diagnosis

We decided we were going to try and have a family and I had a miscarriage about August and I had the lump diagnosed in November. Part of this whole thing has been first of all accepting that I was never going to have a family. That it was not going to be possible for me to do that. Then, having to go through menopause.

HELEN, AGE 42
aged 34 at diagnosis

My grief was also about not being able to have a baby. Although I had left it that long and had really decided I didn't want to have a child, when it became actual that I couldn't, then my grief was enormous.

SHARNE, AGE 45
aged 37 at diagnosis

Sometimes people have said to me, "Aren't you lucky you haven't got children". I don't think I'm lucky.

HELEN, AGE 42
aged 34 at diagnosis

Breast cancer has not altered our sexual relationship in any way. I suppose that's because we treat it fairly lightly. Not sex very lightly. We treat the operation, the scarring, the lack of a breast, his lack of half a neck. We used to lie in bed together and laugh, saying that between the two of us we'd make one reasonable body. At no stage was my sexuality tied up with my breast.

I'm pleased I've got the other one but if I should lose it, it would-
n't be the end of my sexuality. There's much more to sexuality
than breasts. It was funny. I lost a breast just when I decided that
I quite liked them. They'd always been rather too small for my
liking and I'd suddenly decided that I quite liked them. And now
I lost one. But at least I got to like them first. I breast-fed both
my kids for twelve months. You know, they were a bit big and
heavy and I decided that I didn't really want big breasts. Then
they went back to being normal size again. And I thought, yes,
they're actually quite nice. And next thing I know I lose one.
I thought—that's what you get for liking them!

CATHERINE, AGE 47
aged 41 at diagnosis

My breasts were my main turn on. I don't know what I am
going to do now.

PATRICIA, AGE 56
aged 52 at diagnosis

I was in a bookstore and I picked up this book written by a
cancer specialist. The book said that some husbands have diffi-
culty in accepting how the woman looks when she has had her
breast removed and so he, the male doctor writing the book, sug-
gests that the woman wears her bra and prosthesis in bed when
having sex and her partner mounts her from behind, so that his
feelings are dealt with. I was so angry, that I threw the book on
the floor and stomped out. I couldn't believe that his solution was
geared to how you overcome the problem for the moron you're
married to.

HELEN, AGE 42
aged 34 at diagnosis

The world places a lot of sexual importance on the female breast.
Breasts have been painted, written about and sung about for as
long as recorded history. Many of us have worried over our
cleavage or wished our breasts were bigger, smaller, less saggy or
whatever. However, they were *our* breasts and though we mightn't

always have felt fondly towards them, to find that we now have a life-threatening illness *because* of them can be shattering.

Some women feel that, if they've lost a breast, it signals the end of sexual attractiveness to their partner or spouse or it destroys the potential of ever having a sexual relationship with someone new in the future.

If you *have* had surgery the change in your body image will take time to get used to. Most women do come to terms with it remarkably well and quickly. If you're in a relationship, there'll undoubtedly be many issues to be worked through and it will become essential that open communication be established. For some people this is difficult because it was an area of their relationship which perhaps they didn't communicate well about before breast cancer. It's good to recognise that this *has* always been the case and that it's not *because* you have/had breast cancer that communication has broken down. It just may be an area in which you're now more sensitive.

Effects on the Relationship

Occasionally, a relationship which wasn't strong before breast cancer, will become unviable after the diagnosis. This is usually not so much to do with the changes in your body but the fact that your partner has been confronted with *their* mortality through *your* diagnosis.

Sadly, it sometimes happens that a partner simply cannot cope with the change in your body. This rarely happens unless the relationship is already struggling in other aspects. The daily reminder of their own mortality and/or the pressures they see the future might hold for them become insurmountable. This can be devastating and, knowing that you're better off without the company of someone who is unable to give meaningful support, is very little comfort. Some people simply cannot get past their own fear of illness, disfigurement or death. It can be a crushing blow to realise that your body was more important to your partner than *you* who lives *inside* it. You're probably better off without the person who's unable to give you any real emotional support. That sounds easier than it is. Sometimes women cling to a relationship no matter how poor it is simply because they're afraid to face cancer alone. Take courage and reach out for support outside your relationship if you find you aren't getting it within.

Some women find that their relationship becomes stronger than it ever was before cancer and that a deep bond of having suffered through a crisis together has strengthened them as individuals as well as a unit. Kevin writes, 'My relationship with Lynne is closer now than ever before. Just as our son's death has drawn us more closely together, so too has this. Perhaps crises drive the close, closer and the not-so-close, further apart'?

Often a relationship has been going along 'all right' until the advent of cancer. Many relationships slip into a habitual routine where there's not a great deal of honest and open communication. It's usually a fairly good relationship based on love and companionship but perhaps in the hurdy-gurdy of life it has become a little mundane.

Suddenly, cancer turns the household upside down and the poor habits of communication are no longer satisfying the very real needs of the partners. In such a situation it is definitely worth making the effort to improve things or perhaps find a counsellor who can help to establish meaningful communication. Sometimes that might involve several members of the family.

Many people think that counselling is only for people whose relationships have seriously broken down. This is not the case at all. Family members will only benefit by increased communication. I have often referred couples, both heterosexual and homosexual, to colleagues who are marriage guidance counsellors. They can be excellent at helping people to re-establish meaningful communication.

The advent of breast cancer may well take the lid off an emotionally unsatisfying relationship and sometimes considerable efforts will need to be exerted to bring back its value and spark. Occasionally, this task becomes insurmountable and separation appears to be the only course of action. Again, counselling can assist in bringing a relationship to as satisfactory a close as possible.

One woman, Kitty, found that when confronted by breast cancer, she could no longer tolerate her relationship with her husband, Tony. She didn't feel that leaving the relationship was the solution. She had children still living at home and her prognosis wasn't good. Her husband was now very loving and supportive yet she found she harboured enormous resentment towards him for his behaviour in the earlier part of their marriage. She decided, for her own peace of mind, that she would have to find some resolution to her pent-up anger and long-held resentment. She realised she would have to express her thoughts and feelings and work on forgiving Tony for the way he had treated her. In time, she accomplished this, though it wasn't easy. There were plenty of times when she would slip back into righteous indignation. However, she recognised that it was *she* who was suffering by maintaining her resentment and that *she* would be the beneficiary of finding her own peace.

Some partners are able to give wonderful support and understanding when their loved-one is first diagnosed with breast cancer but then cannot cope at all when she experiences a recurrence. This is a common occurrence but, nonetheless, a bewildering one for the woman. Some men feel that a recurrence of breast cancer is an affront to the power of their love for their partner.

One woman, Patsy, found this to be true of her husband Peter. Patsy could not have received more love, support and compassion from Peter when she was initially diagnosed with breast cancer. He accompanied her to all her appointments. They researched together the best treatment plan and adopted a healthier lifestyle which included meditation, juices and dietary changes. He took on the responsibility for preparing her juices and drove her to her meditation classes. Patsy enjoyed meditation and endeavoured to release herself from many of the stresses which she had lived with up until then. Several years passed happily. When Patsy began to experience pain in her ribs, Peter didn't want to know about it. When she finally went to her doctor and had her fears confirmed that her cancer had re-appeared in her bones, Peter was angry with her. He believed she hadn't been doing all the things which would keep her well. After all, he had done *his* part by supporting her. He loved her and believed that the power of his love would keep her well. When she confronted him with her recurrence Peter felt it made a mockery of his love for her; that she hadn't been fulfilling her end of the deal. It may seem an unlikely story, however, it is *very* common.

For many months Peter treated Patsy with disdain and anger. This was at a time when more than ever she needed his love and support. There were angry screaming matches in which accusations were used like swords. Peter had withdrawn all affection and they had begun to live separate lives. Finally, Patsy could tolerate it no longer and came to see me to discuss her situation and her thoughts about leaving Peter. She felt that there was still a bond of love between them but that too many hurtful words had been spoken and that she needed to martial all her inner resources in order to deal with her health and treatment.

Patsy was much comforted by the knowledge that she was not alone in her experience with Peter. She began to understand how frightened and helpless he felt; that he was being confronted, perhaps for the first time, with the fact that he couldn't control what happened to his loved-ones no matter how much he loved them. Patsy began to see his angry outbursts as a call for help rather than an attack. It was difficult for her to extend this understanding to Peter when she so desperately wanted his love and support. She finally took some time away from him where she could meditate, reflect upon her life and recover from her radiotherapy treatments. After initially refusing, Peter also came for counselling and they have begun to repair their damaged relationship.

Relationships and Sexuality

Relationships and sexuality are intrinsically entwined. It's difficult to have good sex unless there's an atmosphere of loving communication. Sometimes all a woman wants, *especially* when she's still recovering from surgery, is loving and supportive embraces or to cuddle up to her partner without any need to have sex.

If cuddling has *always* been the beginning of love-making in the past, she may resist the urge to cuddle for fear of it being misinterpreted as a desire for sex. If this happens it's really important that you tell your partner how you feel and what your needs *are*. Mary told her partner this, 'Right now, I'm not interested in sex because I'm feeling fragile and brittle but I really need to be cuddled and held and know that you still want me'.

Roma came to me one day because she was worried about a recurrence she'd had in her bones and that her libido had disappeared. The sexual relationship she shared with her partner George was very precious to her and she felt it was yet another loss she (and he) had to endure. When I explored with her the concerns she had, it transpired that it wasn't so much that her libido had gone but that she had a secondary in the pelvic bone and was afraid that if she became sexually aroused, the blood flow to that area would feed the cancer. We finally decided, together, that the joy and love she experienced with her husband in their sexual encounters could be nothing but healing and that she could visualise that whole area ablaze with golden light when aroused. She finally laughed about how, if sexual arousal caused intense golden light to flood that area, what would a good orgasm do!

Women have often been surprised and relieved by the reaction of their partners. One husband gently reminded his wife that there were many sexually attractive things about her that he liked and that they didn't all reside in one breast.

So often women withdraw sexually because they're unaccustomed to articulating their sexual needs. This may well compound the difficulties they're experiencing. It's difficult for many people to articulate their sexual feelings, however, the rewards of open and honest communication are plentiful.

Many women view their breasts as the outward sign of their femininity and to lose one or both breasts is to lose their attractiveness. Indeed, some women feel that they have somehow failed as a woman when they've lost a breast. You're not alone in your fears and uncertainties. Many women have been proud of their cleavage and find that when they've lost a breast they experience a change in their identity as a woman.

Chemotherapy, radiotherapy and/or hormone therapy will also change a woman's sexual feelings. Physical closeness and the support that that brings may become all the more important whilst further sexual activity may be the farthest thing from your mind. Again, the key to receiving the loving support you desire is open and honest communication. Some women find it easier to write than speak. Writing a letter to your partner saying how you feel and what you need in simple language is often the start to a more honest relationship.

On the other hand, many women are more than ready to resume a full sexual relationship whilst their partners are still feeling reticent about placing sexual demands upon them. One woman, Freda, laughingly told me, 'Some mornings I wake up and I'm itching to get my hands on his erection! He leaps out of bed and into the shower before I have a chance. It's such a waste for both of us'! There was a sadness and aloneness behind her humour and I encouraged her to discuss this issue with him. When she tentatively broached the subject with him she was surprised to learn that he felt embarrassed and ashamed. He felt it wasn't right to want her sexually when she was still coming to terms with her breast cancer. She told him she felt no longer sexually attractive to him. He was able to reassure and comfort her. He thought she probably wanted him to nurture, protect and support her without placing his sexual needs upon her.

Often people wrongly anticipate their partner's thoughts and feelings. No harm can be done by clarifying your partner's view point and your own. Open discussion might be difficult to begin but the benefits are definitely worth the awkwardness you might initially feel.

Many women feel they need physical space for fear of having their recent wound inadvertently touched or bumped while they sleep. Some women prefer to swap sides of the bed or place a pillow between themselves and their partner until the tenderness has subsided.

Instant menopause nearly always changes how a woman feels about sex. Many women find that a dry vagina fills them with apprehension about having sex and diminishes their enjoyment. Knowing that there are lubricants which work well still doesn't lessen the grief for a part of the sexuality which they formerly took for granted. Some feel that much of their sexual spontaneity has been lost.

Some women find that when they think about sex it only acts as a reminder of their breast cancer and it becomes yet another area of their life which they must grieve for.

To suddenly lose one's libido can be devastating. This can happen through serious illness, various treatments or stress. It's not something we necessarily expect when living with breast cancer. People enjoy sex for many different reasons. Here are some:

- Sex is a release and an enjoyment of one's self.
- Sex is life-affirming.
- Sex is a deep communion between partners.
- Sex is reassuring.
- Sex is comforting.
- Sex is fun.
- Sexual enjoyment means I must be OK.
- Sex means someone wants me.

Many women not in a relationship at the time of their breast cancer find the prospect of ever finding a partner completely daunting. You can become bogged down in only contemplating the hurdles between you and a relationship. Some of these hurdles might be:

- When is the right time to tell a potential partner.
- What will I actually say.
- How will I deal with rejection.
- Even if he/she says it's not a problem, how will I know if he/she's telling me the truth.
- How would I cope with the first time.
- Will he/she see me as 'damaged goods' or disfigured.

Be gentle with yourself and give yourself time to come to terms with the changes in your body. The best way to approach a potential new relationship is when you feel good about yourself. This applies whether you have breast cancer or not. Going into a relationship feeling really needy is never healthy. Talk to other women in your situation and, at least then, you'll know that your fears are shared by others. Many women find a sense of humour helps in dealing with the initial awkwardness.

A friend of mine with a great (and sick) sense of humour told me about an intimate moment with a potential new partner where she said, 'I think there's something about me you should know. I'm a mono-tit'!

Each of us will deal with the changes in our bodies in our own particular style and manner. Trust that you *will* find your way to acceptance of your body and that someone else will too. Don't assume that the person you're contemplating having a sexual relationship with is incapable of tenderness, understanding and acceptance. It does take courage to continue the process of growing and blossoming when you have/had breast cancer. That choice is ours, to let our spirit grow and flourish or to let it be defeated and become withered.

Many women only consider having sex with someone with whom they have a committed relationship that has grown out of deep friendship. If that's your situation, then at some point during that friendship, it would seem appropriate to inform your potential partner of various aspects of your history, including the fact of your breast cancer. It takes time to develop a deep friendship and you'll no doubt know when the time's right for such a conversation. A deep friendship might begin with sexual attraction but certainly goes far beyond it. Don't undermine your own efforts by thinking the whole of your sexuality resides in one breast.

There are no easy answers to the fears and dilemmas a woman might have around her body image and how that affects her sexuality. Give yourself time to become accustomed to your body after surgery. In time, once you have a level of acceptance, you'll be able to invite into the intimate world of your sexuality, someone you feel will honour and respect the person that *you* are.

9
Women Who Love Women

*B*REAST CANCER IS A BLOW TO ANY WOMAN. IF YOU ADD TO that the fear of discrimination or judgement, then it greatly increases the sense of vulnerability a woman experiences. Over the past eleven years, many of my clients have been lesbians. Most of their issues are the same as for any woman with breast cancer. However, there are some differences and they're mostly centred around prejudice. Rather than write about the issues of lesbians, I think they need to tell their own stories. So many women are hungry for each other's experiences. In this chapter, Wendie Batho details her own and others' experiences with breast cancer. She begins with her own story.

Wendie and Kay's Story

When Petrea wrote the second edition of Quest for Life, *one of the stories in the back of her book was written by Kay. Three words acknowledged our twenty-year relationship: "Thank you Wendie". At the time we agonised over whether or not Kay should talk about our relationship. I remember Petrea saying that it was really a sad state of affairs that Kay didn't tell our story, as it would be really helpful to other women. A little later, Sydney University produced a video on people with cancer and Kay was invited to participate. Again we had to choose. We decided again not to talk about our life and to present Kay as a single mother.*

At one level I really resented not being included but at another I was part of the decision to mask our life together; our life which involved working, studying, raising her three children, having two dogs and a mortgage. Like most families really except ours was different, we were two women; two women who loved each other. I remember the film crew at the time of the video, sometimes in tears, laughing with us, eating and walking with us. "We'd love to tell this story", they said.

Well, why didn't we tell our story as it was? After all Kay had a life-threatening illness and what was more important than coming to terms with her breast cancer; dealing with all the issues in her life and finding a place of peace so she could face what was becoming more and more evident; that cancer was a big part of our lives and it would most probably be what she'd die from. The answer was fear. *Fear of what other people would think about us. Fear of being discriminated against; all those fears that gay and lesbian people face in their daily lives. Kay was an administrator and I was principal of a primary school and we were both terrified of what the implications would be for our respective positions. There's an unwritten rule in the Catholic system that it's OK to be gay or lesbian providing you don't actually "come out", and then they don't have to do anything about it. We had three young adults still living at home. We needed our jobs and both of us felt deeply committed to Catholic education.*

Kay said to me over and over, "Whatever you do, don't say anything about our relationship publicly at my funeral. It's not going to affect me, but it may affect you".

Kay's funeral was a beautiful celebration of her life which she organised herself. Our dear friends made our relationship very clear to all present and I remember wondering why did she have to die before our love and life together could be spoken of so lovingly and openly. I want to tell this part of our story now because I loved her so much and I miss every aspect of our wonderful life together. It wasn't a fairy tale story but a real story of two very real and alive people.

Kay hated ironing, in fact she never did any if she could possibly avoid it. It was a continual source of angst with us because she'd go through periods of buying clothes that needed much ironing, not just a bit of a touch up like most of mine. Anyway, I did most of our ironing. One morning, and I can't remember why, Kay decided to iron and when she was collapsing the ironing board it clamped closed on her left breast. I remember her yelling out in her usual sardonic manner, "I think I've performed a bloody self-mastectomy of my left breast." We both checked it out and she'd definitely inflicted damage as it was very red and started to bruise straight away. Over the next few days we kept an eye on it and after about a week it was very badly bruised and didn't seem to be getting any better. Kay made an appointment with our local GP, who was also a very dear friend, to check it out. She prescribed some cream to get rid of the bruising and when it didn't go away she suggested we go to the Breast Clinic to have a mammogram "just to be sure".

A mammogram and fine needle biopsy later confirmed our worst fears. Kay had a 5 centimetre malignant tumour in her left breast against the chest wall. Her breasts were large and normal breast examination hadn't detected the tumour. Within three days

Kay was in hospital having a radical mastectomy. We hardly had time to absorb the news and its implications before we were thrown into making decisions based on very little knowledge. Our doctors assured us there was no connection between the ironing incident and breast cancer but we were never really convinced. The cause is not really the issue I guess. What is important is what you do about it.

The evening of Kay's mastectomy her mother and I wanted to talk to the doctor on duty. I remember he was very young and not at all approachable. Here we were, two women, Kay's mum and partner wanting to know about how she was and when we could find out about the pathology results. This chump was asking Mum what our relationship was to Kay and saying that he'd only talk to immediate family. This is all of three days after we found out and we were both in a state of shock. Mum's really hard of hearing and we both knew she wouldn't hear him properly anyway. I thought, "If I'm not here, Mum won't hear or understand and she, like most people, defers to doctors". God love Mum, she said, "Just say you're Kay's sister, we're not going to have to put up with all this nonsense with them are we"? Even after telling him he still said, "Oh well, I'd prefer to speak to Kay's mother alone".

By this time we were both beside ourselves. I finally said, "Look, Mum's deaf, aren't you Mum?" Mum played it to the hilt and replied, "Yes love, what"? and pulled a "I can't hear you face".

Can you imagine what it was like? Probably not if you aren't gay or lesbian.

We went through this whole farce and then he still didn't want to talk to me. Imagine if I'd said, "She's my partner, we love each other. We're terrified of what's happening and what might happen in the future. Please tell us what is going on". Perhaps he would have said, 'fine'. I'll never know because I'm used to getting off-hand treatment from some people when I make my sexuality clear.

Getting information out of this man was extremely difficult. I learned then that you have to be assertive and persistent with some people in the medical profession if you want to get any information otherwise they're simply not forthcoming. Why is it such a big deal to give patients or their partners medical information? Now I think it's important to give feedback to doctors and everyone you have to work with, whether it's positive or negative; tell them how what they *say makes you* feel.

There's always that nagging fear in the back (or in the forefront) of your mind of exposing your sexuality because of the fear of what others may think. The irony is, of course, that unless you're brave enough to 'come out', people will always think in stereotypes because they've no real examples of lesbians to show them it's different. Most gay women I know are assertive because they've had to be just to survive a lifetime of oppression.

Years later, when Kay had secondaries and was in and out of the hospital as either a day patient or an in-patient, we made it our business to tell people that we wanted to be together and if they baulked we would tell them we were partners. Nurses were on the whole very supportive.

Nothing that ever happened before in our lives prepared us for dealing with the years of medical treatments and the people involved in hospitals and clinics. We're all wiser in retrospect. Kay and I used to say, "If I'd only known that then, things would've been so different". At that time the biggest issue was the mastectomy. In her last year Kay said if she'd known in the beginning what she knew then she'd have never had the mastectomy. You just have to say, that's where you're at and don't give yourself a hard time over it. That's one of the reasons why it's important to talk to other people in the same situation and go to support groups and listen to other people's experiences. The medical profession as a whole are a hard group to crack for the average lay person. It takes years to become basically proficient in negotiating a public hospital system. Everyone seems to be in awe of the medical fraternity. I used to be at first, but not now. They're just people doing a job; some are wonderful and some aren't. They're all just human beings like the rest of us. We all deserve respect and care, especially when we're feeling vulnerable.

Kay's file had, on the front of it, in big red letters, 'this is a difficult woman'. We didn't see that until years down the track. Regardless of why that was there, it does raise the issue of what effect those words on your file have on those who don't know you. It sets up an expectation in that person's mind. I believe that no one should write subjective opinions on medical files and that those files should be freely available to the patient and anyone else the patient nominates. I remember Kay and I getting her file from a co-operative member of staff (after much reluctance at first) and sneaking off into the women's toilet to read it. Imagine that. Two grown women hiding in the toilet or feeling they had to, to read something they should have been encouraged to read in the first place. You don't forget those things. Today, I still hear women say they didn't know it's OK to ask to see your file.

Another important issue during radiotherapy was the rule that you had to wear the surgical gown provided by the hospital. While we understood that the wearing of the gown made it easier for the staff, it did make Kay feel that she'd lost her identity. Whilst this may not be an issue for others, it was for her. People's feelings need to be taken into account. We spoke to a lot of women waiting for treatment and they felt the same. They didn't want to say anything as it might be interpreted as them being difficult and they feared what might happen to them. Women undergoing radiotherapy are already feeling powerless enough. Even if their fears and concerns are misplaced they're still real to them and need to be acknowledged.

I remember also that the surgeon didn't really explain what Kay's chest was going to be like after the mastectomy. We thought there was going to be a big round wound which would look horrible and take months to heal physically. It wasn't like that at all *and when it healed it looked good really. It was just her skin across her chest. There was no flesh or muscle left at all, just this beautiful . . . it was a beautiful scar. She was beautiful, with or without her breast.*

I don't know whether I'm just prejudiced in this way, but I think that the relationship between two women, because we are women, is much closer and more intimate. We can identify more closely because we have the same bodies. I don't think you can ever know how another person is feeling but I believe that women can identify more closely. You just have to ask yourself how you would feel in this situation. I believe women are better able to empathise with other women.

There's always that feeling of, "what can I do"? I used to feel so frustrated by being almost paralysed as to what I could do to help. Kay would say, "You do everything you can. I don't want you to do anything more". I'd say, "But what am I doing, for God's sake". It was like I wanted to fix it, I wanted to change it, I wanted to make it right, I wanted to swap places. I'd say, "If only we could swap". And she'd say, "Don't be ridiculous, that's the last thing you need to feel". And then I'd feel guilty. "I don't have it, why didn't I get it?"

You have to sort all through that stuff. I think it's important to cry. At one time I was crying all the time. I'd be thinking, should I cry in front of her? I want her to know how I feel. Yet if I keep crying it's going to make her depressed, she's going to get sicker. I actually said, "Does my crying like this get on your works, is it annoying you"? And she'd say, "No, I need to know that that's how you feel, because you're not always good at telling me". I still found it hard to make a balance of not crying too much as it must be really depressing to have someone bursting into tears at, often, the most inopportune times.

I always worried about Kay, she didn't seem to cry enough, but she wasn't really the crying sort, not that I thought I was either at the time. Now I just let it go! I worried that not crying was part of her problem and if she'd let her emotions out and not bottle them up, it might be a lot easier for her. We always seem to know what's best for the other person!

I was really the one who used to fall to pieces and say to myself, "I'm not coping, I'm not coping". Petrea used to say to us, "Well, you are coping, because that's what you're doing to cope. You're crying, you're talking to people, you're having friends around, you've made a decision not to see people who depress you, you are coping, and that's what you're doing to cope". So simple when you think of it. I took time off work, my long service leave, and that was a way of coping.

Kay still lives deeply in my heart and she always will. I'm not afraid any more.

In learning to be women in our own society, we have accepted, and even internalised, what is often a derogatory and constraining image of ourselves. Women are becoming increasingly aware of sexual inequities in economic, social, and political institutions and are looking to redress them.

Like the gay male identity, the lesbian identity has a political as well as a social and personal implication. There's no necessary relationship between sexual practice and sexual identity.

Women who identify themselves as lesbians generally do not view lesbianism as a sexual phenomenon first and foremost. It is more a relationship in which two women's strongest emotions and affection are directed towards one another.

Jo's Story (age 42, aged 41 at Diagnosis)

One of the biggest issues for me in having cancer is that I realise nobody's "managing" me. There are so many specialists involved who each have a piece of the puzzle, or think they do. They have pieces of each other's puzzle which conflict, but you actually have to manage yourself and that was enormously difficult for me to come to grips with. I'm not normally a person who does give over to the other person. I have this real need to know as much as I possibly can and to make the decision myself. Even being that sort of person, I found it difficult to know who was managing me. And nobody is; I am.

After my mastectomy, I asked my surgeon who was going to manage me. He said he and an oncologist would jointly do it, but it's not like that at all. One of the best things for me is that I have a wonderful GP. She is just extraordinary. Most of her patients have HIV or AIDS and she's totally unconventional in that sense. She's one of those GP's I can ask anything and I can tell her anything about how I'm feeling. In fact, she encourages me. When she doesn't know something, she'll say it, and she tries to find out for me. She also helps by explaining how the medical profession works, which I found very helpful and also quite depressing. I wanted my breast surgeon to be just like my GP. He wasn't. He'll answer questions if I push him and if I ask them precisely and clearly. He gives very brief and monosyllabic answers. He doesn't help me work anything out. My decision whether to have a lumpectomy or a mastectomy was made after consulting other people. Finally, I opted for a full mastectomy and no radiotherapy.

My partner was so helpful. She was just wonderful, truly wonderful. I have my partner to thank for the success of most of our encounters with medical people because, even though I think I'm rather pushy myself, I was often so shocked and reeling at what I was hearing that I didn't know what to say. She was always there with me, helping and asking questions and making notes.

I started to keep a notebook because you do forget, especially when you're feeling anxious. So if I write things down it can actually help the relationship, providing, of course, that it doesn't aggravate the doctor. We had one situation where I could tell by his reaction that he was getting quite annoyed at being asked a lot of questions.

After the operation and since, I've worried a lot over the fact that I haven't grieved over the loss of my breast. And I don't *know why that is. I think it's different because I'm a lesbian and there are some lesbians who are just as body image conscious as a heterosexual woman might be. But I think for a lot of lesbians, and maybe particularly those my age, you simply aren't your breasts; your femininity, your womanhood, who you are, and your sexuality isn't your breasts. And I think that's much more so than for heterosexual women. Because of men's attitudes, breasts are really important, they define a woman to some extent. The vagina, I think, is very threatening and it's hidden. It's not only physically hidden in women, but in our society it's not on display, whereas breasts are frequently on display for men and it's what identifies women as women. So I think it's a lot harder for heterosexual women. I think they would be much more concerned about that sense of loss. They've had a vital part of their womanhood cut off. So I don't really know whether my lack of grieving yet is tied up with that or whether it's just not that important to me. Maybe I'm not facing something that's going to hit me like a sledge-hammer in six months' time.*

The main thing is that you want to know that your feelings are normal, and that it's OK to be feeling whatever you're feeling. I got so worried that I was doing something dangerous to myself by not grieving at the right time, or that I'm not feeling sorrow or expressing it properly.

I've had some pretty rough treatment in the past when I made my sexuality clear. Although I think that in some circles it's very trendy to have gay friends or even to be gay. So it was really terrifying when my surgeon asked me who the person was who was waiting for me. I hesitated and said she was a very good friend. That's always the way isn't it? I mean that's what you always tell people. Your own honesty versus some sort of euphemism that kind of tells people that they're very important but it doesn't expose you.

When I asked my GP what she thought she said, "Ask them. It's really important to ask up front and then see what their reaction is. You'll know then whether or not they're comfortable with dealing with your sexuality or not". So the next time we went to see my surgeon it was my partner who actually told him. He said, "That's fine, I thought that was the case and I don't have a problem with that".

When I was in hospital I didn't get out of theatre until late at night and my partner had been ringing up constantly and had insisted on coming over to the hospital really late to see me. It was very clear to the nursing staff that we were more than just girlfriends and my partner talked quite openly and said a couple of them were really wonderful, really helpful. One particular nurse, an older woman, spent the next day, every minute she got, sitting on my bed talking about cancer. She was just wonderful, she truly was. She told me how lucky I was to have such a wonderful partner. A couple of the others barely concealed their distaste. They'd been fine when I was admitted but were not so fine afterwards.

When I went for chemotherapy my partner put the issue of our sexuality to the doctor straight up. She said, "We're partners, we're lesbians, do you have a problem with that"? She was a bit embarrassed at first, but she said in the end, "No, no, not at all, it doesn't worry me". In fact, she told us about a woman, a lesbian she'd treated the year before who'd since died. She said she knew we had special problems and went on to tell us that the lesbian couple had been treated so badly in this hospital, they had requested a transfer to another hospital where more gay people were treated. However, because it was mid-treatment they weren't allowed to transfer to another hospital. The whole thing was very distressing to them.

Deb's Story (age 40, aged 38 at Diagnosis)

I'd had the lump there for quite a while. I was aware of it before I left my husband. I was sort of ambivalent about it. I almost thought of it as my little friend. Somewhere in the back of my mind I must have thought it's possible that this is cancer and I don't know if I want to do anything about it. For as long as I can remember, since I was a child, I'd wanted to die. Part of my affection for this little lump was that it was better than a whole big bottle of sleeping pills. This could be a socially acceptable form of suicide. That was well and truly at the back of my awareness though mostly I was in crisis.

I had fallen in love with Tina and I was in my second marriage and I just didn't want to deal with the lump. Then my relationship with my husband ended. I was in so much turmoil having come out as a lesbian and having left my marriage and fallen in love with Tina. I moved to the mountains and put my son in a school there. I was struggling for my life in terms of just keeping my head above water. I was really working very hard to establish myself as a sculptor in the mountains so that I could be financially more secure. Tina is very kind and gentle and respectful of what I want. When she got mad at me and said, "You go and have that mammogram. I don't ask much of you", it was a big emotional plea on her part. So I went and had it checked out. I did it for her. (And for me too, as I wanted to get her off my back!) I had the mammogram.

It was obvious straight away that it was cancerous. It's hard to describe what it's like when you're told you have cancer, it's almost like an out of body experience. On the one hand I was elated. Now I have this thing I can die and nobody will blame me for dying, for bailing out. You're allowed to die if you have cancer and it doesn't look cowardly, it almost looks heroic, so this is the way to go. On the other hand I was as terrified as anyone would be, discovering they had a potentially fatal disease.

I thought to myself, I'm not a great parent but who's going to do a better job of raising my son? How can I tell him that I didn't care enough about him to try and live? How can I tell Tina, whom I've just turned my whole life inside out for and who's the woman of my dreams? How can I tell her I don't love her enough to try and stick around? I just couldn't think of anything to say to them. I suppose I kept living by default really. I said to myself "I'll go for it, give it my best shot for them". However, my writing is something I do for myself.

When I was up in the Blue Mountains I had to do this radio interview about myself and my poetry. I was reading the manuscript late one night, by way of preparation. I hadn't looked at it for a very long time. I suddenly realised what I'd been writing about for twenty years. I'd been trying to remember through my writing; trying to remember my abuse. There are references to it all the way through my poetry. I'd been writing about it for twenty years and I didn't even know.

Creative work comes from somewhere very deep inside you and obviously this stuff was buried very deep. I sat up that night and it was like finding out I had cancer all over again. It really blew me away. Since then I've said to myself, "Well, now I know what I've been writing for and writing about all this time, will I write any more? Maybe the purpose of the writing is gone". But it hasn't. Now, in my writing, there are other things I'm trying to understand as well. Deeply spiritual things. Most of my poems are about people. Why people do what they do.

Since I recovered from cancer I've read a lot of books about childhood sexual abuse. I've been in therapy since then working on those issues. What I've found is that when you suffer something like the death of your mother, a severe car accident or a horrendous divorce, it can take so much of your energy in terms of getting through it. All your energy goes into getting through whatever it is, dealing with the grief and the pain, and the demands on your emotions. So that energy is no longer available to keep all the walls up in your memory, to keep those areas of your brain blocked off, to protect yourself. You've stored them since childhood or since the abuse occurred. They're so overwhelming that you can't deal with them; they'd have destroyed you or sent you mad. It takes quite a lot of energy to maintain that, and you're not aware of how much energy it takes until you see the damage it causes in your life.

So when this other tremendous demand on that energy comes up, you channel it in to this new demand, cancer in my case, and there's no energy left to keep those walls up anymore.

Remembering was great and dreadful for me at the same time. All my life I'd felt like there was something wrong with me that I didn't understand. When I remembered, I was able to understand why my life had been so painful and so difficult and why I hadn't been able to do anything about it despite having tried very hard. Once I found out what the problem was, it was tremendously liberating because I was then able to say, "Ah, that's what it was. Now I can begin to do something about it". It has taken a long time. I do want to live now, but I still have days when I feel like it's all too hard.

When I first started remembering the abuse I had all the symptoms associated with post-traumatic stress. I remembered what he'd done to me and the horror of it all and gradually I saw how every part of my being and my life and my experience had been affected by it. Lots of acts of utter bestiality and hatred. The desire to want to die became very acute throughout that.

You either get better or you die. What actually doesn't kill you makes you stronger. So it almost killed me but it didn't. I think I'm past the point where it can kill me. I don't want to die any more and I have, in fact, survived it all.

We're living in a patriarchy, and it's essentially hostile, by its very nature, to women. It's not easy for women to express their grief, anger and outrage or to act against the oppression of individual men and the patriarchy in general. Women are effectively punished for expressing their frustration and rage about what's done to them. So where does it go? If it doesn't have an outlet it stays inside you and it makes you sick. Anything you feel that doesn't find legitimate expression will find another form of *expression. The connection between cancer and stress is well known. There are various personality profiles of the kind of people who get cancer. Those people who are very nice, who are in control of their feelings, who put other people first. Who in our society is most likely to have that kind of profile? Women!*

It doesn't seem surprising to me that breast cancer is increasingly common among women. The whole institutionalisation of the oppression of men against women is against woman and 'womanness'. So, naturally, all that rage and grief about this oppression and the assault against your womanness every day in the patriarchy or if you have oppressive men in your life really close up, where is the rage against that oppression going to show up? It's going to show up in the outward symbol of your womanness which is your breast.

There's also the biochemical effects that occur in your body when you're under stress. Women are tremendously stressed. This stress is increasing because of the added demands on women to do more and more and to be more and more. Women are probably more stressed than ever.

If women had more control over their lives and their bodies fewer would feel this tremendous rage and frustration and perhaps the high incidence of breast cancer would abate. The environmental and hereditary factors that contribute to cancer are generally acknowledged. I have no desire to dismiss or diminish the relevance of these. However, the time is long overdue for society to acknowledge that violence against women and children is an urgent public health issue. In the meantime, the least we can hope for is that women can find a safe way to express their rage and grief as they're growing up in this society.

My outlet, my poetry, probably saved my life. Amongst other things it gave expression to what I was feeling. When I was a child I found ways to tell the whole world what he was doing to me. I was making paintings and drawings and I played the piano obsessively. When I was nineteen I started writing poetry. I was

275

still playing the piano and still making art. That was my voice, my way to speak as it were. I obviously couldn't speak of the abuse, because I'd blocked off the memory of it.

I'm very fortunate that I'm gifted in these ways and am able to express myself. That's one of the reasons I'm so committed to teaching creative writing in the community to groups of women. I love it. I can see how it enables women to claim themselves and claim their lives and find a voice.

Now that I've decided to live I'm not so much worried about dying, it's not an issue any more. I just want to heal my heart. I want to feel whole; to know joy and peace before I die.

I think our being lesbians has affected Tina more than me in many ways. Her family don't acknowledge our relationship. In a heterosexual relationship if the woman gets cancer, probably the family would cluster around, people would try to support the man.

In the eyes of some families and in the general public, lesbian relationships are not legitimate and that support simply doesn't happen. So Tina got none of that support. She was working full time and looking after me and no one offered her any support. That limited the amount of support she was able to give me because eventually she was exhausted. I know I'll never find the words to express my gratitude to her; she gave me her all.

Judith's Story (age 53, aged 52 at Diagnosis)

I've been married for thirty-two years. I share the same home as my husband, but have lived as a lesbian for the past twenty-two years. I've been involved with the same partner for twenty of those years, in a very loving and fulfilling relationship. She also lives with her husband, but we spend a great deal of time together. Both husbands have been aware of this strong bond for all those years. It's complicated, but it works.

I discovered the lump when we were making love. I became

aware of a soreness under my arm. I felt a lump tucked deep down on the muscle at the tail end of the breast up under the armpit. I immediately felt the other breast in the same position for comparison, and was aware there was definitely a problem. Because of the position of the lump the mammogram had not picked it up twelve months previously, however, my surgeon felt it must have been there. I never did feel angry, or have a "why me" attitude. I just saw the lump in terms of a battle which had to be fought. I was a warrior. This use of my imagination and visualisation helped me through everything that happened over the following months.

I took the diagnosis in my stride. By the time the tests were done, the X-rays, ultrasounds, and fine needle biopsy, I knew we were dealing with something big, so I just concentrated on being strong in mind and body to meet the foe.

I was anxious, however, about telling my lover. I could imagine how she'd feel. I knew she'd support me the whole way however, and was content in that feeling. Her strength was my greatest asset. I don't remember crying at this stage. I wasn't shocked, I wasn't angry, upset, fearful or sorry for myself. I didn't get depressed.

My daughter, who was twenty-two at the time, was living at home with her boyfriend, so I told her and held her when she cried. I rang my two married sons, and they reacted in a concerned manner, and wished me luck and I reassured them all would be well. They believed me. Hadn't Mum always coped with everything? It would be OK. My husband was extremely happy that Marge, my lover, was in my life for he silently handed over any responsibility for emotional support to her. It was out of his realm of experience. Women's business. His wife had her lover, what else would she need? At no time did he have to be an emotional support. This suited him admirably. He's not a sensitive man, and neither knows nor cares about feelings.

Marge rang most of our friends for me, and broke the news

over the telephone. This created different responses. One friend flew up from Canberra, another drove from Nimbin. While in hospital my room was constantly filled with flowers and friends. One friend read me stories and brought the puppets she used for her students. I loved that. Another friend sneaked in her pup for me to nurse.

I went back to work after five months, so I wasn't at home alone to dwell on what happened. I'm fortunate to have family, although they're leading their own lives. But my real strength lay in my lover Marge, and my friends both gay and straight. I don't lead an isolated existence. I do appreciate the loneliness which must be experienced by women who have no support, who come from the hospital and have no one who cares, no one to hold them, and no one to talk with. My advice would be to join a support group, even if you're gay and it's a heterosexual group. You'll find that within the group there'll be support. You'll be able to laugh and cry and discuss different problems related to breast surgery and recovery. If there isn't a group, start one. *It works wonders, and you'll be surprised at how many women out there are travelling the same road.*

My message to other women is to speak up and take charge, as you have the power to call the shots if you're well informed. Annoy hell out of the doctors if you aren't happy with what's being said or done. Of course, the private patient can probably score here easier than women who have to go through a very over-worked and under-staffed public health system. There's a big need for patients to be treated as people, not for just the mechanics of the disease. Where possible we need counselling provided before treatment, as well as after. How can women know what to ask, when they're not aware of their options?

Some women don't want to know anything about it at all, and they choose to ignore their problem. These women know they have a lump in their breast and refuse to do anything about it. I personally know of this; fear is a big factor.

My experiences were all positive. I have heard from our support group that not everyone has been so fortunate. That makes me angry and frustrated. I see my oncologist annually now, but I know I could talk to her at any time if I had a problem. She always makes time to explain procedures. I trust her with my care. I see my surgeon every three months. We have many conversations. I continually ask him questions, and he does his best to answer them. He is a reserved man, but is very caring. I found that I had to initiate many of the subjects, but once broached, he always makes the effort. My medical team has always been optimistic and positive, without promising me anything over which they have no control.

Breast cancer has been a positive experience for me. I've grown in leaps and bounds, tapped into new strengths, and started new projects. I've taken charge of many areas of my life. I'm more content and life seems such a wonderful adventure and a continuing challenge. Yes, I have changed. I look at myself on many levels now, and try do something positive in each of them.

I've changed my beliefs based on Native American and women's ritual and philosophy. I've joined a writing course which is something I've always wanted to do and I've taken to walking daily and eating more healthily. I keep active by going to work, reading, bird watching, bushwalking and, of course, the support group. I continue to work on developing my relationship with Marge to its fullest potential.

*Breast cancer is a challenge to be met and overcome and it's a chance to make life an adventure, to start on a new path. I've found it a strengthening experience. Many women have travelled this road before me, have survived their cancer and have been enriched by their experience. I want to be one of those women, and I'd like it to be said of me by my friends and loved ones—*Judy really celebrated her life!

10

My Children, My Life

"*Do you think I'm back to my old self?*" *And as one of my children replied,* "*You're never going to be back to your old self. You are your new self, which in some ways is actually better than your old self*".

RUTH, AGE 42
aged 40 at diagnosis

The youngest one, whom I would have thought would have been too young to be aware of what was happening (he was two), really regressed. He started wetting the bed and became very clingy and dependent. My second daughter's behaviour (she's the quiet worrying type), she never said anything about it but would have these terribly angry, aggressive outbursts, not about me but just about anything. My oldest daughter was very upset when I first told her that I had it. I remember going into her room one *night and she was lying in bed crying and I asked her what's wrong, and she said, "Oh Mum, I've just read a book and the mother died of breast cancer. Are you going to die?" And I said no, no, I'm not going to die, well, not for a long time anyway. Since then she's mentioned the fact that she thinks about being the daughter of a woman with breast cancer knowing that she has an increased risk of getting it.*

RUTH, AGE 42
aged 40 at diagnosis

By far the hardest thing was the day-to-day coping with two children (three years and a six-month-old baby) and a new job while feeling sick and tired most of the time from treatment. Most helpful were not people saying ring us if there's anything we can do, but the people who said, "I'll take the children to childcare", "Would your daughter like to come and play for a couple of hours"? or "Can we come over and bring dinner next week?"

The sheer logistics of getting to the hospital and coping with the children was an incredible strain. Trying to juggle their sleep, mealtimes, the drive to the hospital and parking and then to keep them amused in an extremely ugly waiting room.

Sometimes, I'd lie down for five minutes and get up five hours later. This is very hard to explain to a three-year-old. It was hard to tell how much of my daughter's behaviour was normal three-year-old and how much it related to a worried, sick and tired mother. She resented the live-in housekeeper and the various helpers we had and her behaviour certainly improved as soon as she had a Mummy who wasn't lying down all the time.

BARBARA, AGE 35
aged 33 at diagnosis

My children, eleven, nine, seven and six years, all thought I was going to die and all asked me the question, which broke my heart. Their reactions have ranged between anger, denial, sickness and acceptance, each child taking on an aspect of the experience and relating to me through the particular role they had adopted.

Particularly disturbing is my seven-year-old's behaviour. He really believes that he himself is very ill and wakes during the night unable to breathe thinking he's going to die.

JUDY, AGE 38
aged 36 at diagnosis

The oldest one was at primary school at the time and had always been a very high achiever. He dropped to about the middle of the class in the next set of exams, but that wasn't a great disturbance to him. I think that was his way of showing his distress. But he subsequently picked up again. They're quite used to the word cancer. It's around them all the time.

They were quite young at the time. We thought we were doing very well. And I think we probably have.

CATHERINE, AGE 47
aged 41 at diagnosis

My oldest son said to me—"will you die, from cancer?" And I said— "I don't believe that I will. I think I will survive because it was caught in a very early stage. And, you know, we all believe it's going to be fine". I didn't say, I'm definitely not going to die of cancer. You can't make that statement. But I think that the reassurance was sufficient that it never really worried him again.

There are visual reminders for us all the time; my husband's operation, which removed a large piece of his neck, and my operation, which removed a breast. It's just—that's Mum and that's Dad. They've grown up with it. I don't think it disturbed them enormously. I mean, they were safe at the times of the operations. They were either with me, when my husband was in hospital, or with him, or with their grandparents who they'd often been to stay with. So nothing really different happened for them. They came to hospital plenty of times.

We certainly didn't sit down and discuss on a one to one basis the problems of having two cancers in the family. We protected them to a degree from the "what if both of us die?" syndrome.

But we had to discuss those things because there always is that possibility.

I guess there were times when I thought it was inappropriate to break down in front of them. But there are times when it's inappropriate to discuss all sorts of things in front of your children. You just pick your time. They'd go to bed fairly early so there were always the evenings when we could talk and discuss. I don't think we really hid a lot of emotions from them. They knew there was a lot of stress going on in the family at the time. But I don't think it's damaged them at all. You could say that it has done the opposite.

We have a friend at the moment who's going through the experience of cancer. And his son and my son know each other. And his daughter and my other son are in the same class. And I think that in some way there's some connection between those children. They see their father going through some fairly debilitating medical treatment. And my children, although it's a long way back in their history, have seen that sort of thing as well. I don't think my children will ever see cancer and death as a natural progression.

We were frightened in the first place. But we're no longer frightened by the word cancer. Nor do we instantly think somebody's going to die because they've got it or had it. That's not to say that somebody with a very serious case of cancer, isn't going to die. But there are so many that are caught early now.

I mean, we don't consider ourselves out of the woods. Because that's the nature of the disease. But if you keep that in the back of your mind then you just get on with the rest of your life.

CATHERINE, AGE 47
aged 41 at diagnosis

In addition to all my thoughts about what's going to happen to the children if I die, there's concern for my daughter. I felt very strong guilt about the potential legacy I've given her.

ROBIN, AGE 44
aged 44 at diagnosis

How Much to Tell Children

Surely it's one of the most difficult tasks, to tell your children that you have a potentially life-threatening illness. All parents want to spare their children pain. However, part of being a member of a loving family is also to experience the joys and sorrows that loving each other brings. Your children will need simple explanations about your diagnosis, treatment and any other factors which affect them. This information needs to be tailored to their individual age and ability to understand. Obviously, a child under the age of five will require a different explanation from the details you might give to a teenager.

Many parents have been amazed at the support and comfort their child was able to give to them once they were informed. To withhold your diagnosis and what it means to you, is to withhold a great deal of yourself from your child. Nothing is more painful for a child than to feel excluded from those they love. The experience of breast cancer isn't a totally negative one. It's also an opportunity for the human spirit to gather its resources and marshal its strengths. Your children will learn much from you in this and will grow in understanding and strength.

To have a member of one's family diagnosed with a life-threatening disease is a bewildering experience for a child. Obviously, the response of the child will depend very much on their age and maturity. A three-year-old's response to her mother's absence due to hospitalisation will be very different from an eight-year-old's, as will a teenager's.

The ideas within this chapter will need to be adjusted to your children's age and maturity. You know your child better than anybody and it's important that you do what you believe to be best in your particular situation. It's important to remember that:

Children are great at overhearing conversations but are very poor interpreters of the information they hear.

Many children sense the truth, even though no one has directly told them. Conversations whispered behind doors can prove much more frightening to children than simply being told the truth. Likewise, conversations which are stopped when a child enters a room can be very distressing. Meaningful looks amongst adults when a child is present also cause unnecessary fear and anxiety in children. If you keep your children informed of what's happening to you then they'll feel acknowledged as valuable members of the family who are entitled to know important details.

Many adults have told stories of their own families when they were children where the knowledge that a family member had cancer was withheld. These children felt hurt and confused by being left out. They knew something terrible was going on but didn't have explained to them what it was. Often they also feel an enormous lack of attention to their needs and some have felt scarred for life. This is quite unnecessary if clear, honest and open communication is encouraged amongst family members.

The amount of information you give to your children will depend on their age and maturity and also on the extent of your cancer and its treatment. Many women who have required only a lumpectomy with minimal follow-up treatment have decided not to let their young children know what has happened. Listen to the voice within your own heart to know how much to tell your children.

Some mothers prefer not to disclose to their children (of any age) that anything is wrong because they hope that it's a concern which will never be a problem in the future. If, however, their routine is changed in some significant way or you're going to continue to have problems which will require their understanding or co-operation then you'll certainly want to include them in the knowledge of your situation.

Often children think things are far worse than if you simply tell them the truth. If you tell them the truth in a manner which is easy for them to understand they will feel reassured that, though there is a problem, something can be done about it and that you are united as a family.

Children have an amazing capacity to deal with the truth and will come to terms with your diagnosis and what it means to them, in their own time and in their own way. This might mean the child retreats into their own world to adjust, or that they "act out" their feelings in some way. Even very sad truths will relieve the anxiety of too much uncertainty. You'll see from observing your child's behaviour how they're coping.

If you exclude your children from the truth, they could very well interpret this to mean they're not important enough to be included in a family matter. If the child hears the truth from somebody else they could be ill-informed and might believe that something too terrible to be talked about is happening. It's not healthy for children to grow up with an abnormal fear of illness.

How to Tell Children

You'll know if you're the best person to tell your children of your diagnosis. If you think you can explain simply to them what has happened whilst maintaining fairly good emotional control, then you're probably the best person to tell them. Emotional control doesn't mean without a tear. If you shed tears it gives your children the permission and opportunity to cry too. However, you won't want to be unnecessarily upsetting to them. You might prefer to tell your children in the company of their other parent or a close relative or friend.

If you feel you're not the best person to tell your children, then perhaps their father or this relative or friend could speak to them. Make sure the close friend is considered close by the children also.

Another possibility is to have the children told by your doctor or a member of the professional staff of the hospital. Who should tell your child will also depend very much upon their age.

If your children are aware you're unwell and are having tests, then they might need or wish to know what the problem is just as soon as you do. If this diagnosis has come without warning, as is often the case with breast cancer, then you might prefer to take a little time to adjust to the situation yourself before including your children. This might mean several hours to a few days depending on your initial reaction.

Firstly, you'll need to explain what's wrong. Then, once they understand what's wrong, you can explain to them how the doctor wants to treat you and what you intend to do in addition to your medical treatment. They'll want to know if this means you're going into hospital for treatment or will be remaining at home. Are there likely to be any changes at home or will things stay the same? If your treatment is on an out-patient basis, you could explain to them the likely side-effects of chemotherapy or radiotherapy. Tell them you'll let them know if there are any changes to the treatment and how you're feeling as you go along.

After you've told the children any new information, give them time to assimilate it so they can formulate questions of their own. Their questions and responses will let you know how much information they can handle. Answer their questions simply. If they wish to have further, or more in-depth, information they'll ask if you give them the opportunity. You can ask them what they think breast cancer is. In this way you can ascertain how much they've actually taken in and correct any misinformation they might have. It's OK to say to children, 'I don't know'. It's *much* better to say 'I don't know', than to make up something which could prove to be inaccurate. There are some *dont's* worth listing:

- Don't lie.
- Don't frighten them with all the unnecessary medical details or financial worries (unless they'll be affected by them).
- Don't trouble them with things which haven't happened yet, for example, operations or treatments which mightn't be needed, etc.
- Don't make promises you mightn't be able to keep. Keep your options open by saying things like, 'I'd love to watch you play cricket and I think I'll be up to it by Saturday' or 'I'll be doing my best to . . .'.
- Don't push children to talk. They will in their own time.

Here are some ways of explaining things to children which will give them information they can grasp. Obviously you'll need to gear whatever you say to their age and understanding.

1 'You might have noticed that sometimes I feel sick and don't have enough energy to play with you as before. I have an illness which is called (breast) cancer. The doctor's giving me medicine to help me get well. Some days I'll feel tired or sick and other days I'll feel fine. Daddy (or Aunty Jane or other) will help me take care of you until I feel better.'

2 'Sometimes our bodies don't behave as we would like. I had something growing in my body (breast) that didn't belong inside me, so the doctor did an operation to take it out (remove it). I'll have treatment now so it won't come back. Sometimes people say scary things about cancer, so if you want to know anything about it, ask me.'

3 'Because I have this sickness, sometimes I'm sad and angry. You might feel like that too when you see me feeling sick. It's OK to be angry; it's OK to be sad. Some feelings will change but the love we have together won't ever change. Having you around, your hugs, drawings and rainbows are helping me.'

4 'I have to have another operation because the cancer in my body has started to grow again. The doctor thinks this will get rid of it. After the operation he'll give me more treatment to see it doesn't come back again. We believe this will work. I feel angry and sad this has happened. We all hoped I was finished with treatment.'

5 'Because I have this sickness, I've decided to make some changes so that I can help myself get well. I'm going to eat foods which will give my body what it needs to fight this disease, and I'm going to spend time each day just being quiet and still so my body can help itself to get well. You can help me by doing activities which aren't noisy during my quiet time. You might like to come and sit with me so we can share some quiet time together.'

Wrapping Children in Rainbows

When I was diagnosed with leukaemia my children were aged four and seven. Kate, the eldest, understood something was wrong but Simon, at just four, was only aware that I wasn't my usual energetic self. He wasn't worried because he was at an age where he could easily adjust to a more sedentary Mum. His father and I had recently separated and so, for much of the time, he and Kate were living away from me. When they came to visit at the weekends, it was my mother who took care of their (and my!) practical needs. I found it very depressing not to be able to do all the things which I had formerly taken for granted. I wasn't only depressed, I was angry. I almost preferred them *not* to come than to see me as I was. The energy level of little children is very high and they are extremely difficult to be with for any long period of time when one is feeling so debilitated. I'm sure other unwell mothers of young children will be nodding in agreement. My children had difficulty in understanding why I was depressed and angry, and this in turn made them more distant. They gradually preferred to run to my mother with their woes, achievements and for their peanut butter sandwich. On the one hand I was very grateful for the assistance I had, but resentful that I couldn't do all those little things a mother usually does.

For the first two months I refused to say the word leukaemia. I was afraid if everyone thought I had leukaemia they'd start relating to me as a 'dying person'. I wasn't ready for anyone to put me in a coffin, not even in their imaginations! However, this made it difficult to talk about my situation with both my parents and my children. Kate was surprisingly supportive for her young years. She used to tell me if meditation was going to help me then I *must* meditate. Support is a word or a gesture that lets us know we're loved. Kate would bring me a flower, or a drawing, some small token of her love, and it often changed my day. Even Simon was able to convey his concern and love with a gentle pat, a wet kiss or a mini bear-hug. They were difficult times. One of the gifts of that time was the discovery of wrapping the children in rainbows. What child doesn't love a rainbow, its beauty and magic?

Once Simon was tucked up in bed, I'd ask him to close his eyes and imagine I was wrapping him up in a cloud of red. As I talked quietly to him about this beautiful soft cloud of red light, I'd pass my hand very slowly and lightly over the whole of his body several times. Talking quietly about this beautiful, soft light, like a cocoon, I would be gently and slowly stroking him all the while. Then we would visualise the lovely clear colour of orange: the colour of nasturtiums in the sunshine (one of his favourite flowers). Wrapped in a cloud of clear colour . . . still moving my hand gently and softly over his body . . . and so on through all the colours of the rainbow.

The yellow of early morning sunshine, or whatever is appropriate to your child's understanding or preference. The green of lush grass. Blue, like the sky. Indigo, the colour of the heavens at night. And violet, the colour of the flower, violet. This ritual can take as long a time as seems appropriate to the age of your child. At the end, I would place my hand over Simon's heart and together we would visualise a strong rainbow beginning in his heart, then stretching out through the air to my heart. In this way we'd stay connected to each other all through the night. I'd also repeat a little poem which we made up, that went like this:

I wrap you in a rainbow of light
To care for you all through the night.
Your guardian angel watches from above
And showers you with her great love.

For a copy of this ritual, please see my website, www.petreaking.com.

It isn't just the child who benefits, we parents enjoy it too. During my illness I was separated from my children for weeks at a time and every night I'd send them a rainbow, as they did to me. Some of this time I was in Europe and America whilst the children were in Australia with their father, and yet we knew these rainbows were always sent and delivered. Even after my recovery, sending rainbows was a regular feature of our going-to-bed ritual. Love can bridge all distances.

I've shared this technique with many dozens of parents and children since, and I know many children to whom sending rainbows continues to be very important. These children became accustomed to sending them to a parent when their parent had a life-threatening illness. It was the child's way of sending love and healing. Even after the parent died, the ritual continued, the child knowing their rainbow was being received wherever their loved one is now. For the child it's a sacred time of joining with someone they love who's no longer with them.

This technique allows us comfort and a tangible way of expressing our emotions. With a protracted illness, often it's not solutions we're needing. Sometimes it's just the strength to continue, day after day with seemingly no end in sight, and still the uncertainty of what the future will bring . . .

Some people mistakenly believe that to be positive is to look only on the outcome which they'd like to see. So, to be positive is to have things 100 per cent the way we'd like them to be. This presupposes we know precisely what *is* the best outcome. One of my great realisations when I was sick was, not only did I *not* know what was best for everyone else in the world (!) but I didn't have a clue what was best for me either. I genuinely believed if things weren't the way *I* thought they were meant to be, then they had to be wrong. Such was my attitude at that time. This attitude precluded any self-acceptance. At this stage I'd never heard of the concept of self-love or self-acceptance.

Talking About Death and Dying

Many people regard thoughts or conversations about death and dying as being thoughts of 'negativity', 'failure' or 'being morbid'. If you're feeling concerned about discussing death with your children, you're not alone! Most of us hesitate to talk of death to children, however, it is an inescapable part of life. We must find ways of dealing with death and so must our children. One of the ways to help them (and reassure ourselves at the same time!) is to let them know that it's all right to talk about it. When we talk to them about the thoughts and feelings they have we can discover what they know or don't know. They might have fears, misconceptions or concerns which we can help allay through information, understanding and reassurance. Talking through our feelings might not change the situation but it will certainly change the way we *feel* about the situation. It's important to show interest in and respect for what a child has to say. In this way we can better *hear* what their perceptions are rather than giving further information which might only confuse.

Your children are probably far more aware of death than you realise. Even very young children have seen dead lizards, birds or insects. If they're older and watch television they probably see at least one death a day on the screen and their games will often play out their fantasies about death and dying. However, a child can feel quite confused and frightened when the possibility of death and loss comes close through the advent of an illness in their mother.

What you will say to your child and *how* and *when* you will say it will depend very much upon their age and understanding. For instance, pre-school children often have the notion that death is completely reversible or temporary, whilst five- to nine-year-olds will realise that death is final and that all things which are alive, must die. In this age group though, the children often have the notion that it happens to other people, and that it couldn't happen to them or their loved-ones. They often feel they can control death through their own cleverness, bargaining or efforts. From about the age of nine children begin to fully comprehend that death is irreversible, that all living things die and that they too will some day die. The precise age at which children will comprehend death and its implications will vary according to a whole host of factors.

Death isn't the opposite of life. We live through the process of dying. Each and every one of us is going to pass through the experience of death, and *not* to talk about it can isolate us in our experience. Death is one of the most mysterious and awesome adventures upon which we're all obliged to embark, and to share openly with our loved-ones the concepts, uncertainties and apprehensions we hold can bring us to a much greater depth of intimacy and understanding.

Young children cannot fully comprehend death (can any of us?). Sometimes we can use symbols to help children understand the concept. A walk in the garden is full of possibilities for discussions on death and dying. Leaves that turn from green to yellow to brown; that let go the tree of life only when they're ready; to fly free through the air and land softly; to become mulch and soil to give new life to the tree. The seasons constantly demonstrate the ebb and flow of life. One mother, Susan, explained about life and spirit and bodies in a tangible way to her three small children whose father was very ill. She blew up a balloon and explained to the children that the balloon was only made beautiful and special by the air which was inside it. The balloon was like the body; a shell in which they each lived. When she let the air out of the balloon, she explained how the life, the spirit when it leaves the body becomes part of everything.

Communication Needs—Verbal and Non-Verbal

How much you include your children in your thoughts and discussions will depend entirely upon their age and development. Trust in what you know of your children and listen to your own heart. You'll then know how much of yourself to share with them.

What makes living with breast cancer especially difficult are the many unknowns. Living with such an illness means living with uncertainty. There are some questions you won't be able to answer. We as adults need to accept that fact, and we need to assist our children to accept it also. It's fine to answer a child's query by answering, 'I don't know'. If it's the kind of issue to which someone (perhaps your doctor) knows the answer, reassure the child you'll find out and let them know.

You'll find you go through many stages in coming to terms with your illness. Perhaps disbelief, anger, depression, hope and acceptance. Like you, your child is endeavouring to understand this in their own way and behaviour might well reflect these inner struggles.

Very young children fear separation, being left alone, strange people and surroundings. If you're hospitalised, have a familiar person take care of them in their own home, if at all possible. Talk to them, and when you do, reassure them you're coming home soon and you're thinking of them (and sending them rainbows!). One of the most challenging aspects of talking to children is to get the timing right. When you're ready to have a deep and meaningful talk they disappear to a neighbour's house to play. Or they ask you the most profound questions just as their baby brother is screaming for his dinner. It isn't always easy to get the timing right and we need to hang on to our sense of humour. Maintaining a sense of humour when you're feeling frazzled or debilitated is a challenge in itself!

Hospitals aren't always geared for very young children so when they come to visit you, be sure they bring some activities with them or a favourite toy. Perhaps you could keep some things at the hospital which will amuse them and be different from their toys at home.

Young children often feel they can control what happens to them and that they have magical powers. They often believe what they wish for will come true. It's not uncommon for children to feel guilty about their 'bad' thoughts; they might feel guilty their mother is ill.

Reassure them from time to time, that nothing they've thought, wished, said or done has in any way caused your illness.

Some children become overly concerned about their mother's health. It's important not to overload the children with too much information so they become worried about details. Let your children's teacher know about your illness early on so they can support the child at school and can let you know of any unusual behaviour.

Disturbances in eating, sleeping, schoolwork and friendships are not unusual. This applies to children of all ages. Teenagers as well as younger children sometimes regress in behaviour.

Teenagers have an especially hard time because their own emotional balance is often still precarious. At a time when they're just exploring their emotional and social independence from family, they're thrust into a situation where their mother might need to depend upon *them*. Some react by rebelling and becoming difficult to deal with whilst others will want to take on responsibilities which are really beyond their years. Some will retreat into their own world and seem not to care whilst others will not seem to overreact in any way and will remain their usual selves. All these reactions fall within the normal range. However, if you find their behaviour becomes a real problem, seek assistance from your church (if you have one), your child's school counsellor, your hospital or the children's hospital in your area. Seeking professional help isn't a sign of failure on your part. Your hospital will be able to put you in touch with some books, videos or groups which could assist your teenager understand what they're experiencing.

In some families, communication wasn't particularly good *before* the diagnosis of an illness. Just because someone has a physical problem doesn't mean everyone's now able to be openly loving and supportive. There are often strained relationships within families and this won't automatically dissolve. There are professional counsellors who'll see a family together to help iron out the difficulties and to assist in re-establishing healthy communication. This can be a tremendously enriching experience for the family who is committed to improving relationships. Even if all the family members choose not to participate in this kind of counselling, it can still be valuable for those who do.

Helping Children Deal with Change

Many changes could take place in your home because of your illness. These might range from emotional upheavals to the fact that you have no hair and are drinking carrot juice instead of coffee. Children are very observant of all these changes and will require explanations to ease their concerns. Don't take for granted your child will understand why suddenly you have to rest every afternoon. Explain to them in a language they can understand why you're doing these things. Children love routine and habit and when you start breaking routines the children need to adjust. This becomes much easier if they know why. For instance, it's preferable to tell your children that one of the side-effects of chemotherapy is your hair will fall out when it first begins to rather than when you're almost bald.

Some mothers are happy to show their mastectomy scar to their children whilst others prefer not. Children are intensely curious and having had their curiosity assuaged are usually content— until their *next* question arises.

You'll need to explain you're not able to do all the things you did before; that rest is essential; that their aunt (or whoever) will pick them up from school today; that you can't make their chocolate brownies this week; and that your love for them is always there.

As much as is possible, endeavour to maintain a daily routine.

Make sure all the essential things are attended to. Perhaps one family member can take over much of your role. Perhaps your twelve-year-old can take over the lawns. They might not do them perfectly, but does it really matter? One of my favourite sayings is, 'Would you rather be right, or happy?' Sometimes we need to let go the way we've always done things and let others make their own contribution in their own way. That's how we learn.

If you can afford it, you could employ someone to help you at the times which are most stressful in your day. There might even be a teenager in your area who'd be willing to do a couple of hours work for you after school. If friends or relatives offer to help, accept it. Let one of them organise the efforts of the others so you don't have to supervise. Again, they won't do things the way *you* did them, but at least they'll get done. If you allow other people to support you, it enables you to spend time with those who are really important. If possible, make space each day to spend some quiet time with each of your children. If not daily, then weekly. Short amounts of quality time are far more beneficial than long periods of chaos. If you've very young children who are in need of consistent care, try to have the same person helping.

One of our young mums, Tessa, decided her two-year-old should go into Day Care. The toddler loved the company of the other children and it enabled Tessa to rest and do the things she needed to, and be relatively fresh for his return in the afternoon. She would've preferred to be a full-time mum to him, but that was impractical. He doesn't seem to have suffered any ill-effects from this experience. Remember many single parent/parents who are working require Day Care facilities. You're not being a failure to place your child somewhere where they'll get the consistent care they need.

Children are usually more accepting of physical changes and disabilities than adults. If you look or feel different from your usual self, give your child a brief explanation. Don't go into all the unnecessary details unless you're asked for more information. If you're not upset, it's very likely your child won't be and they'll accept the changes easily. You may find your children's friends discussing your illness and you can let your children know you or your partner are happy to talk with them if they've any questions. Sometimes children will go to extraordinary lengths to *not* let their friends know things have changed at home. Just continue to be reassuring and leave the door wide open for discussions or questions.

Discipline

A breakdown in discipline can be very distressing for a child and can convince them something has definitely gone wrong at home. It might be difficult to maintain law and order as the children themselves are under stress and are likely to act up more than usual to get attention. Remember *it wasn't always perfect before*. It's important to set firm limits and find suitable ways of enforcing them. If you let them know you especially appreciate their co-operation now, you can reward their good behaviour whilst enforcing the discipline necessary to halt their misbehaviour. You're doing this for your own sake and for theirs.

I've Never Felt This Way Before!

If you're the kind of person who never shows how you feel, it's very likely your child won't either. They might be experiencing all kinds of feelings which are quite new and unfamiliar. When you allow yourself expression of your feelings it will give your child the permission and opportunity to do the same. To suppress strong emotions is like sitting on a volcano. *You* might be used to living that way but it could be very scary for your child to feel so strongly and not be able to express their feelings. By expressing *your* feelings you help your child to feel OK about all the feelings they have.

It's natural for you to feel sad about what has happened. Have the courage to express your feelings. If you can let the sadness out and cry together, everyone will feel the tension ease. It's not a sign of weakness to cry with one's family. To feel powerful emotions and express them is part of being a member of a family.

Children might feel other things which can confuse and bewilder not only themselves, but you too! If these situations arise, remember they'll pass, and give reassurance to your child (and to yourself!). Here's a list of possibilities:

- Some children will disappear to the neighbours or their friends much more often to avoid being at home.
- Some will be afraid they'll get breast cancer too.
- Some children will behave badly to cover up their real feelings.
- Some will laugh at everything to cover up their real feelings.
- Some children will retreat into their own world and won't let you in.
- Some will withdraw, unconsciously trying to become more independent in case something happens to you.
- Some children will become angry and resentful of you now needing *their* care when previously the opposite was true.
- Some will pretend to be sick in order to get the attention they feel they're missing.
- Some children will pretend to be sick or play up a minor illness in order to spend more time with you.
- Some will become very possessive or clingy and won't let you out of their sight in case something happens to you.
- Some children will feel sorry for themselves when a parent is ill and then feel guilty about that. Others will wish their parent wasn't there and then feel guilty.
- Some will over-compensate for having had 'bad' thoughts about you and will be unnaturally good or set unrealistic standards for themselves.
- Some children will form strong attachments to the other parent and avoid being with you.

All these feelings and behaviour patterns are common reactions of children endeavouring to come to terms with a situation which is stressful to them. For the parent who's feeling tired, anxious or debilitated these reactions can be extremely difficult to deal with appropriately, and yet anger towards the child is rarely the appropriate response. It's important to realise this behaviour will pass and it's just the child's way of coping with the situation. You'll find by talking *your* feelings through you're able to maintain a larger perspective in which the behaviour of the child can be more easily tolerated.

It's not just young children who can behave in this way. Adult children who have cancer can be very difficult to live with also. Much of my time being sick was spent with my very loving and supportive parents. However, I'd often retreat into my room and close the door. They felt shut out and tended to tip-toe around me for fear of emotionally upsetting me further. I refused to talk about all the things I was feeling, mostly because I couldn't have articulated what was going on inside myself even if I'd wanted to.

Once, a very wise and wonderful little girl called Kate, aged ten, said to me, 'sometimes hearts have got to break before they heal'.

Quiet Times Together

One of the positives of having breast cancer might be you can spend more time with those you love. Often the bonds within a family strengthen as they become closer by sharing time, thoughts and feelings. Often you'll see your children grow in maturity and independence and you know this will help them to face other challenging experiences in life. They might develop more compassion and sensitivity towards people. Don't forget to acknowledge their achievements and express your gratitude and pride in them.

If you've chosen meditation techniques to help you, you might find it very enriching to include your child in practice sessions occasionally. There are many guided meditation practices available which appeal to young children (as well as adults) and, for teenagers and adults, there are practices on increasing self-esteem, meditation and visualisation techniques. Young children love 'Dolphin Magic'. A full list is given at the back of this book. Over the years I've had many children attend our meditation classes. Many of the teenagers have continued to use these techniques on a regular basis as they find them particularly useful in preparing for examinations and coping with the stresses of being a teenager. To meditate together is a very special experience. The silence shared by two or more people can touch the very depths of our being.

There are many ways you can involve your children so they feel they're actively supporting you at this time. Even the youngest children can have responsibilities—sending you a rainbow every night before they go to bed, bringing a fresh-picked flower or leaf from the garden, so many hugs or kisses a day, bringing a book or a meal. Keep it light and fun so the children don't resent having to do things for you *all* the time and make sure they've sufficient free time to do whatever pleases them.

Here are some additional suggestions for times when you're in need of quietness and still want to include your children.

You can:
- Read a book or watch television or a DVD together.
- Write your family history, including major events, pets, holidays, hobbies and idiosyncrasies of each member.
- Draw pictures of the family. Perhaps suggest the child draw pictures of what it's like to have their mother ill.
- Share stories, poems or songs that are meaningful to you.
- Use a guided meditation practice together which takes you on a journey using your imaginations.
- Give your children the opportunity to express what they feel through role playing. Use dolls to represent the various

members of the family and have the child direct the play. Listen to what is being said in the play and ask questions about how each doll is feeling—if appropriate: Don't push!
· Meet with other families who are affected by breast cancer.
· Learn about the body and show where your cancer is by reading a picture book about the body.
· Make up a family song or saying which encourages you all.

It can sometimes be a bit of a challenge to entertain children whilst you're in hospital. You mightn't have much energy to entertain with! However, as playing in the elevators or corridors is to be discouraged, here are some suggestions for hospital activities.

You can:
· Record a story.
· Ask your child to record a message at home to bring to you and you can have one ready for them when the child arrives.
· Have a computer game, colouring in supplies, or other toys which stay at the hospital so the novelty doesn't wear off.
· Make drawings for your children and have them do the same.
· Ask the children to make telephone calls for you.
· Practise a meditation together, perhaps using a tape.
· Explain how the hospital works. All the people in different uniforms and what their functions are. The bed, buzzer, meal service and how they each work. There could be intravenous drips or other equipment which your child would like explained. Don't overload, just give enough information so your child feels you're being well looked after.
· Perhaps have your visit in the lounge, lobby or in the garden if appropriate.

Never make a child do something they don't want to do. Rather, try to understand what's behind their refusal. Usually

303

there's anxiety or a fear of some sort. If they don't want to visit the hospital, it could be because they're frightened of the hospital, the illness, the apparatus surrounding you, or they simply don't know what to say. If you are receiving oxygen, you could organise a member of the family to bring home an oxygen mask for the young child to play with in order to be familiar with it before they visit. Talk to them to see if you can ascertain what the fear is and encourage them to tell you about things at school, their friends, pets, and so on. It's usually easy for children to talk about such things. You might want to encourage this fearful child to make things at home for you.

It's important too, for young children, to keep their visits to the hospital short. Try to organise their visits at a time when you feel fairly refreshed and/or pain free, perhaps after medication has been given. If you are barely conscious, or even unconscious, it is important that the child only spend a short time visiting and that they are reassured by a member of the family that you are no longer in discomfort or pain.

Whoever is looking after the children at home whilst you're in hospital might want to encourage them to make a 'Welcome Home' banner for you. This can be as simple or as elaborate as the child's imagination can create. They could help prepare your bedroom, pick some flowers, make some favourite food or drawings for you. Don't forget to notice and appreciate their gestures of love and support.

Seemingly strange behaviour isn't always related to your illness; children have fears we can't even guess at. As has been mentioned before, children are often very literal. I remember when I was about nine or ten I became a Christian. I believed the message I was given in a very literal way. If you were a Christian you went to heaven when you died, if you weren't, you went to a place where there was gnashing of teeth and you burned forever. So I was OK but what about my grandmother whom I adored and who was the spirit of love and generosity itself, but who certainly wasn't a Christian? (She even married a minister of the church in her latter years on condition he never mentioned religion in the house!) I beseeched her to mend her ways. I couldn't bear the thought of an eternity of separation from someone I loved so much, any more than I could bear the thought of her eternal suffering. She used to hug me and say, 'Never you mind, darling! I'll be with all my friends'. This was no comfort to me at all and I used to lie awake at nights praying for some miracle of conversion!

Some children are more literal in their interpretation of life than others. I believe all we can do as parents is establish an open and honest line of communication with our children and allow *any* question about *any* subject to be voiced. Just as we think after diagnosis that every ache and pain is related to our breast cancer, let us not assume every fear and anxiety our children show is related to our illness.

Breast cancer is a challenge for any family. To respond to such a challenge in a creative way requires inspiration and all the strength the human spirit can muster. It's important to acknowledge the creative solutions you've found to your many dilemmas and take pride in your children's ability to rise above adversity.

11

What if I Die?

What is it that we have to learn
Before passing on?
A few short years
Strutting and fretting our hour upon the stage
Before we are heard no more.
What are some keen words to hand on
To our offspring and theirs?
Courage, of course,
And compassion, for others and for ourselves.

JULIET, AGE 61
aged 46 at diagnosis

Now that I've decided to live I'm not so much worried about

307

dying, it's not an issue any more. I just want to heal my heart. I want to feel whole. And to know joy and peace before I die.

DEB, AGE 40
aged 38 at diagnosis

It's hard not to think about dying when you've been diagnosed with breast cancer. On the other hand, it is also hard to think about dying.

TRACEY, AGE 49
aged 44 at diagnosis

I found cancer as a subject boring, but the fact that my death was quite likely going to be sooner rather than later I found fascinating.

JULIET, AGE 61
aged 46 at diagnosis

I'm not afraid of dying, I just don't want to do it yet!

SUE, AGE 59
aged 53 at diagnosis

I suppose my spiritual journey is through Buddhism and meditation and that is far more accepting of just seeing things as they are and moving towards death with as much graciousness and curiosity as I can.

SHARNE, AGE 45
aged 37 at diagnosis

It certainly made me think about death and dying and I've done all the usual things, like I went and saw my solicitor. I thought I didn't have all that long and I was very teary-eyed and he was very sweet and I updated my will.

Through counselling and the support groups, I don't feel all that fearful about dying. I feel concerned about leaving my husband who'd be terribly alone because he hasn't any family here in Australia and I really have been his whole life, so I know that he'd be very lost without me. He's the one that I fear for. It would leave a gap in the lives of my brother and my father who's still alive, but it's my husband that I've more concern for. That's certainly been a real incentive for me, to take care and to do as much as I can to be around for as long as possible. If I don't really want to go somewhere or see someone or do something, then I just give myself some space.

MARGARET, AGE 61
aged 59 at diagnosis

Breast cancer has faced me with my fundamental belief system. It's involved confrontation, investigation, letting go, trusting that there is meaning in human suffering. I don't need the answers so much any more. I'm far more at peace living with the mystery of life.

SUSAN, AGE 48
aged 40 at diagnosis

Thinking about your own death can be scary.

SARAH, AGE 37
aged 34 at diagnosis

How could I let breast cancer get the better of me? I'm forty-nine years old with the most loving husband and children—how could I possibly leave them? How would they survive without me? I cried buckets for weeks. I don't know if my tears were for myself or for them . . .

ADRIANA, AGE 49
aged 45 at diagnosis

I found I could relax. I didn't have to hurry around doing lots of things thinking my time might be short, because I started to live in the hope, expectation and awe of the next hour or so, and to relish this bounty.

JULIET, AGE 61
aged 46 at diagnosis

Well, I decided I was really terrified of dying. Even though I'd sort of been around death for so many years in my nursing. My own death was really frightening. I had some counselling and that helped a lot. In fact the counselling helped enormously. I must say, I did overcome my fear of dying, which was something that was really good. And I learnt slowly through counselling and through coming to the support group that I deserved to have a really nice life for myself. And I hadn't probably ever thought that before. I thought I should be good at my job, and a good mother, and a good friend, but not really kind and good to myself. So I learnt these things and they were really valuable. I suppose my whole life has been changed around for good. It has been improved, since before the diagnosis.

I'm much happier than I used to be. And because I'm not afraid of dying it doesn't affect me like it did in the beginning when I was way back in hospital, faced with—maybe I was going to die, and being terrified. I'm not frightened any more. I certainly want to keep on living, because there are so many things I want to do.

JEANNIE, AGE 54
aged 50 at diagnosis

I'll be all alone and that terrible feeling of isolation and thinking about the reality of death—like everyone else, going on without you if you did die. How unfair is that going to be? My husband's going to see the kids grow up. Goodness, he's the one that's normally at work. I'm the one who's interested in the kids, how fair is that? And that is a terrible, terrible thought.

RUTH, AGE 42
aged 40 at diagnosis

That is something I've learnt—we're all going to die. And life's about living—none of us is terminally ill—there's no such thing as a dying person. I run a support group in Canberra and people from our group have died, and we have very sick people in our group and none of them are dying, they're living and learning to live and that's something breast cancer has given me—learning to live.

HELEN, AGE 42
aged 34 at diagnosis

I rang yesterday looking for travel insurance to America. And they said, "Pre-existing condition"? And they said, "Is it terminal"? I said, "We're all terminal—I'm not dying".

ROBIN, AGE 44
aged 44 at diagnosis

I'm so sick of everyone telling me how marvellous I look. I've said to them, "I'm going to have an open coffin so you can all pass by and say, 'My, doesn't she look well!'"

MARGERY, AGE 64
aged 56 at diagnosis

For some of us, maybe even for all of us, there can be a wonderful point in our lives when we say living is a fantastic option, dying is another one, and life—I don't know what life's going to offer me. Yes, I want to embrace life, I want to embrace many more years of it, but it's the pathway.

Many cancer institutions seem to focus on "winning the battle", and that means people recovering. But there are a hell of a lot of us who aren't going to recover. I feel tremendously alive and I'm not losing the battle because I feel my life is going to end because of cancer. Many women with breast cancer aren't going to recover from it, aren't going to be cured, are going to die from it. But to see their death as necessarily a failure is just not on.

HELEN, AGE 42
aged 34 at diagnosis

When my cousin was tragically killed in a car accident, I realised that breast cancer has amongst its blessings the fact that I can contemplate my life, its meaning and my death and its meaning. Sudden death robs us of the opportunity to explore who we are, to heal the past, to say goodbye.

LAURA, AGE 46
aged 39 at diagnosis

Over the years, many women have echoed Laura's words—that cancer gives us an opportunity to complete our lives in a more conscious way; to say things we hold precious in our hearts; to forgive and let go the past and to leave a legacy of love for those who cared deeply for us.

We all have a tendency to hold fast to the familiar and are fearful of the unknown. This certainly is so when we're speaking of our death. That is why I always encourage people to go all out for peace rather than for a cure. Peace is definitely attainable; peace creates the perfect environment for physical healing. If physical healing doesn't occur then we still have peace. We experience peace when we're affirming life in its fullness. We affirm life through our diet, exercise, treatment, positive and uplifting thoughts and attitudes, through meditation and relaxation techniques, through forgiveness of the past, through visualisation techniques, through relinquishing anger, guilt, blame, fear, and so on. This is not a laid-back, don't care attitude. That is not peace. Peace is a dynamic state achieved through conscious choice.

It is not resignation in the face of defeat, it is not a passive acceptance, but rather an attitude of maximising the possibilities for life in any given situation in a harmonious way. When we aim for this dynamic state of peace, we create the perfect environment for healing to take place. When we go all out for a cure, what we're really saying is that our healing has to be on our terms. With this thinking, if we don't succeed in curing our disease, we certainly won't experience peace either.

There's a certain frenetic quality about people who are determined to cure the illness at all costs. The cost, inevitably, is our peace of mind. This attitude rather misses the point of healing. Health is inner peace. Certainly, most of us would rather remain in our bodies, with our loved-ones, doing the things which are familiar and which we've always enjoyed. And yet, so many of us resist life—wanting it to be on our terms. To lose our clinging to life *isn't* giving up. It's more a *giving over* to life. It embodies a trust in the perfect unfolding of each moment—each moment full of potential, full of healing, full of peace.

Many people die having never discussed their impending

death. This *doesn't* mean they're necessarily in denial. Some people never discuss their innermost feelings with anyone, including close family members. For some there are no long discussions, no tears, no denial, just a simple acceptance and a willingness to let go.

For others, the ability to let go only comes through long discussion, deep contemplation, buckets of tears, intelligent exploration and conscious surrender. Just as in everything else, there's no right way to approach death, no right way to die.

I was assailed by the thought, 'How could I have children only to leave them'? It seemed ludicrous and unthinkable, especially in view of the fact that my brother had taken his own life just eighteen months before. To have found peace in the midst of this turmoil felt like the best miracle I could hope for.

Practicalities

If you desire it, it's possible to write a 'living will'. This will legally binds those in charge of your medical management to *not* do anything which will prolong your life. This means all the medical care is given to ensure comfort without any medical intervention which would prolong your life. Many people reach a point where they wish to concentrate all their energies on quality of life.

Sometimes this point isn't reached by all members of the family at the same time. It might be that you feel you've had enough of treatments, doctors and hospitals and that you'd prefer to be in your own home surrounded by the people and things you love. Your family might be keen for you to continue treatment. This situation needs to be talked out thoroughly so that the feelings *behind* the preferred options can be explored. It's likely that there'll be feelings which include impending loss, anger, frustration, powerlessness, resentment, isolation, fear, guilt, relief and perhaps a sense of being out of control. *These* are the issues which *need* to be addressed. *These* are the issues which are at the heart of the relationship.

There are many aspects surrounding dying which you might wish to discuss at some time with your family or loved ones. Some people prefer to do this right near the time of diagnosis. It isn't morbid to talk about your wishes and desires for the future. You'll want to tidy things up so that there's little unfinished business for your family to manage.

Part of this procedure would be the formalising of your will, if not already done. This isn't a negative action, nor does it mean you are affirming death. Any lawyer will suggest this be done at a young age. You might also wish to state certain preferences for the education of your children or even make tapes for them to play when they reach certain stages in their lives, or leave them something in writing.

When talking with your family, you might wish to give expression to any strongly held ideas you might have on how long life-support systems should be continued; how sedated you'd like to be; whether you'd prefer to be at home or in hospital, and who you'd like to have with you. These conversations can be difficult to get started and yet, once underway, they can be tremendously rewarding. Obviously, there will be many practical considerations which need to be addressed. These can be assessed and discussed with your family, doctor or visiting nurse.

The majority of people prefer to remain at home to die. This used to be the accepted practice. To die comfortably at home requires good support from your loved ones. They also need to feel supported. Your local palliative care nursing team will be able to provide practical and compassionate support for both you and your family. It's no longer surprising to me to hear the family left behind say they felt a kind of 'rightness' and joy, as well as sadness, at the passing of their loved one.

Be brave enough to face these practical questions so you know these details have been taken care of. In this way you'll be free to enjoy your family, enjoy your relaxation and flow into the peace of mind which your meditation brings and allow it to play its full part.

I know many people who've orchestrated their funeral well before the event. They've chosen the music, and, in some cases, have prepared the readings or other content they wish included in the service. In this way, their funeral becomes a celebration of their life rather than an occasion which focuses on the tragedy of their death.

Jeanette, who in her twenties and thirties struggled through both breast and then ovarian cancer, wrote a letter to those in attendance at her funeral. Part of it says:

On this beautiful sunny day, I'm wondering what to write for all of you present today. Firstly, I am so thankful for a life full of love and happiness. Secondly, for a life full of challenges—big events that really made me look at life and death and thus deeply feel my innermost emotions.

. . . I firmly believe that my diet, meditation, yoga, counselling and other natural therapies contributed greatly to both my quality and quantity of life. My death does not mean these therapies have failed for I believe that this was my time to die. However, it was these therapies that assisted my body to cope with the medical treatment and to help me find my inner peace.

I feel very much alive as I write this, although I am told I'm dying. What a horrible word—for I am surely alive, until the moment my body is dead; I am still enormously enjoying every day. I have no fear of death for I firmly believe that death is a transition to another life, whatever that may be. It is a new beginning and full of hope.

I also want to thank you for all your wonderful letters and conversations containing your deep, heartfelt emotions that you shared with me. These were such gifts of love and energy and I'm sure they gave me new strength every day.

Her husband Bernie was able to write of her:

Everyone saw the perpetual smile on Jeanette's face, but those who looked closely noticed that she was also struggling. And she was ultimately extremely successful. Not just because she lived much longer than medical experts predicted, or because she was able to maintain quality of life under adverse conditions, but more importantly, because she was able to find her place in the universe. She achieved inner peace.

Finding Peace

Know that as you prepare for the physical fact of death you'll also experience yet another wonderful and positive aspect of life. It's quite common for people fairly close to death to move through thoughts which seem at variance with each other. Some people describe a profound sense of being alive and, yet, are more frail and dependent than ever before in their life.

Monica lived alone in a tiny apartment in the inner city. The day before she died, I was visiting her and she was full of the sparkle of life even though her body seemed barely able to sustain another breath. She took my hand as I sat beside her and she said, 'Isn't it a glorious day? I can hear a cicada singing and earlier today the sunrise was so beautiful. What a precious place this earth is and how good it is to be alive'! Monica's living conditions were really what could only be described as appalling and she had had a very hard life with a lot of violence and fear. She had found her peace in the heart of her suffering and was able to let go life with dignity and grace. To find such peace is a miracle.

In addressing the fears and uncertainties of our own death, we also expose the fears and uncertainties present in our living. When we embrace life fully, we're more ably equipped to relinquish our hold on a body which has served its purpose well.

One of the greatest keys to living and to dying is the practice of meditation. Through this practice we begin to understand and experience our real and unlimited nature. With this experience comes a deep, unshakeable peace and the certain knowledge that we're indeed far more than just our bodies. When we are firmly rooted in this knowledge, derived from experience, our reality

316

becomes one of complete safety and trust, and we experience our true, indestructable nature.

Peace, of course, is not a place at which we arrive and never leave. Peace is a moment by moment opportunity. The willingness to be present and participate in each moment is our choice. To be at peace means to be anchored to a place that is beyond fear, beyond pain, beyond control.

No matter what attempts we might make to improve our health or reverse the process of our illness, for some, death will be the final outcome. However, to look upon death as a failure would be to miss the point in living. It's the *spirit* with which we live which is of importance rather than the length of life.

In my experience, most people aren't so much afraid of dying, as they are of the *process* of dying. People express concerns about whether they'll be in pain, alone or unable to breathe adequately. All these fears are natural and all of them can be allayed. Many people are afraid that if they begin with analgesics (pain-killers) early in their illness, there won't be drugs strong enough to deal with pain later on. This is totally inaccurate. There are stronger drugs or dosages which can be used for more severe pain. Often, it's simply a combination of drugs which will alleviate severe pain. Your doctor or palliative or community nurse will be able to assist you in managing your pain.

Some people are afraid they won't be able to breathe properly. This can be helped enormously by the use of oxygen, either in the home or hospital (see the section on Oxygen at Home in Chapter 6 'Reach for Recovery').

If you've been practising techniques of relaxation or meditation, you'll be familiar with 'light' breathing and will find that these techniques can be of tremendous assistance. As the breathing becomes lighter, the brain receives less oxygen and you become more sleepy, perhaps drifting into unconsciousness. All the people I've sat with, in their last hours, drift off very peacefully.

If you're tormented by fear about the manner in which you might die, talk to your doctor or the palliative care nurses and ask them for as much information as possible about the most likely way you'll die. This often alleviates unnecessary speculation.

Many people are loath to enter a hospice because they feel that that is the place you go to die. More often now, hospices are for the living. They are an oasis where you can find the easing of your physical, emotional and spiritual suffering. It's very common for people to go in and out of a hospice or to use it in accordance with what feels right for the individual. Many people go in for a few days to get their pain management under better control and then return to their home. Most hospices have an excellent outreach staff who visit you at home and help you manage whatever symptoms you might be experiencing. Use whatever supports are available in your community.

I believe that people die very much as they've lived. Those who've grasped at life, have always tried to control it, have squeezed the juice out of it and have bargained and manipulated, have a very hard time letting go lightly into the mystery of death. Those who have loved and been loved, who live with the joy of being here now and who have the faith to surrender into each unfolding moment, die with grace, peace, ease and dignity.

My grandmother, Phyllis, was such a one. She was such an enthusiastic participator in every aspect of life. Her heart knew no bounds, likewise her humour. She had never had a sick day in her life and the thought of slowing down was anathema to her. My mother tells her mother's story.

Phyllis's Story

My most unforgettable character was my mother. She exuded an aura of joy and zest for life. Blessed with a keen sense of humour and love of life, her compassion and balance made her a wonderful person to grow up with and her example always spoke much louder than her words.

As I grew older and my awareness began to blossom, I began to realise that there was much in her life about which it must have been very difficult to feel joy. A good marriage entered into when she was eighteen and her husband forty-one, became increasingly more restrictive and the companionship her spirit craved became more and more withdrawn. Increasingly, she lived her life with we three children as her friends and confidantes. I never remember a time when I did not feel loved and supported.

A month before my dear elder brother would have been twenty-one, he died in a most tragic drowning accident with three of his companions. The light dimmed for all of us, as he had had much of my mother's zest and wit and in our growing years, there was always much going on as in all families but never disharmony with each other. If the light dimmed for my brother and myself, it all but went out for my mother to have lost her dearly loved son.

For me, I felt bereft at the loss of my big brother but also at the change in my mother and I felt something in her had died also. She had just as much love and support for my brother and myself but the candle seemed to be burning very low.

But the candle did still burn and gradually over the years rekindled. I never remember a time when I did not have her love, her companionship and, increasingly as I got older, we shared many interests, music, art (she took up painting at sixty-seven and regularly attended art classes until she died). My husband and our family lived in Sydney, she in Brisbane and she always visited us twice a year, always spending Christmas with us. She loved her grandchildren and they adored her and brought her great joy. As the years passed, her energy seemed to increase and her interest in going to concerts, her garden club, her art classes all kept her busy and interested—and alive!

In the last year of her life (seventy-six) we all felt she could go on forever. She had accompanied us a few years before on a world trip and had been ten paces in front of us all the way and kept us amused at her unflagging interest in everything she saw. She had

had her usual lively Christmas visit to us and for some unknown reason I asked her to come again at Easter—a time she never usually came. When I met her at the airport I was shocked to see her pallor and to realise she had lost a vast amount of weight. She assured me she felt all right but reluctantly added that she had had a chest X-ray a few days earlier and that she was to go back for some tests. This was in the time when the mobile X-ray clinics visited the suburbs and a yearly chest X-ray was mandatory.

We had a fairly low-key few days and on the Tuesday after Easter I rang the Brisbane clinic to ask about the result of the X-ray and asked for all documents to be sent to our doctor in Sydney. I asked what was the problem and received the bald answer, "Oh, your mother has cancer. Didn't she tell you"?

A cherished part of my world fell about me at that moment. I wanted to go to her to comfort her and myself but I couldn't as she had set the ground rules by saying nothing and I felt she had to come to terms with this before she could talk about it. One of the hardest things was to appear natural with her when I said there was no problem—they would send down the records. Still no word from her when we visited our family doctor a couple of days later and having been warned by me that she obviously did not want to talk about it, he just said he'd like her to go into hospital the next day. Privately he told me that she had massive secondaries in both lungs. A few days later I spoke to the head of the thoracic unit and he confirmed that the situation was indeed quite hopeless and told me that he had explained exactly the situation to her. When I went to her room, she was sitting up surrounded by flowers and back to her old self again—cheerful, breezy, asking after everyone and saying she couldn't wait to come home. Playing by her rules, I said (I hope reasonably brightly), "Any results"? "Not really", was her reply, "Some sort of infection they think". When I left her I went straight back to the doctor to whom I had originally spoken and asked him was he sure she understood her condition. "Oh yes", he said. "I spent ages talking to her—she asked searching questions so she could fully understand and then we had a few laughs—a remarkable woman"!

We played cat and mouse for three days. I found it very painful not only because of the shock of the diagnosis but the fact that we had never had constraints in our relationship—we had always been up-front with each other.

On the fourth morning when I came in she gave me a rather sheepish grin and said, "It's a bit of a bugger isn't it"? The release of the tension of our being less than honest with each other was enormous and after some hugs and a few tears, we got down to talking about a few of the things that needed to be discussed. Important issues like, "I can't leave Jacqui (her beloved cat) for much longer; she'll be missing me". I said she must stay with us so we could take care of her and I would have her flown down right away.

Difficult days lay ahead for her with endless tests trying to locate the primary. Diagnostic skills were not then (1976) what they are today and it seemed to take forever to discover the tumour in her breast. It was quite large, but lying flat against her rib cage and it did not give up the secret of its whereabouts without a lot of discomfort and investigation for my mother and anxiety for us.

Doctors explained that there was no point in operating because, apart from the breast, the lungs were beyond any help. We must take her home, keep her as comfortable and happy as possible. Asked the inevitable "How long"? we were told six to twelve months. She had been in hospital five weeks. Enjoying superb health all her life, her only other visit to a hospital had been forty years previously when she had her appendix removed. On the way home, I asked her was there anything she particularly would like to do. "Yes", was the enthusiastic reply, "I'd like to have a party". The next few days were spent drawing up the guest list. She had many friends in Sydney and while she was in hospital they had all rallied about her. In fact, one of them visiting for the first time had asked the nursing sister which was her room and received the reply, "Go down the hall, turn the corner and she's in the room where all the laughter's coming from". That's how she was—that was my Mum.

We fixed the day, sent the invitations—it was to be a Sunday 11a.m.–1p.m. party, limiting the time so she would not be too fatigued. It was a riot of a party—she looked pretty as a picture, held court, told jokes and the last guest went home at six o'clock! She had a wonderful time.

She said she felt a bit tired and thought she would go to bed. Five days later she died—in the early morning—having sat up late to watch the tennis at Wimbledon.

My room was beside hers and I heard her breathing change to become rougher and more compelling and more difficult with each breath. I rang the doctor who told me to take my clothes into her room and get dressed in there so I didn't leave her unattended. He'd get an ambulance to come immediately and I'd, of course, go with her. She died before the doctor arrived, just five weeks after diagnosis.

Then, all the afterthoughts began. Should I have permitted or at least advised against her having chemotherapy? Her situation was hopeless so why put her through all the discomfort attendant on that procedure. Her appearance had always been important to her and yet she finished her life wearing a rather jaunty wig, her lovely honey coloured hair gone. If it was "hopeless" why the treatment?

Could I have done more if I had known more? What were these words being bandied about—"primaries", "secondaries", "biopsies"—they were all at that time foreign to me—I felt like a stranger in a land I could not understand. If I had known more, could I have been more reassuring for her—but reassuring for what if the die had been cast?

I pondered these and many other matters in my grief, trying to

*come to terms with the loss of such a dear friend. Gradually
I came to realise that one can only do the best one can. It is no
use thinking with hindsight "Could I have done this; could I have
done that"?*

*I did what I could and I did what I knew. At best we are only
able to perform in the light of our own knowledge and where we
come from at any one given time is the sum of our experience of
life, of love and our compassion. In the end it was Jacqui who
said it all, sitting patiently outside the bedroom door, not going in
any more. It was as if Jacqui was symbolically letting her go to
whatever lay ahead—with devotion but with the willingness to let
her go. Ultimately we have to release the person and it is better
sooner than later as one also frees oneself to go on. To remember
the joy of knowing and loving without the sadness of actual passing is to bring back the dignity and the blessing of life.*

Rae

Through the turbulent events in our lives, my mother and I
have come to share many perceptions about life and its extraordinary challenges. Our friendship and respect for one another
is constantly deepening. The tragedies and upsets we've faced
have forced us to both delve deeply within ourselves and reach
out to comfort and support one another.

It is for each of us to find our own answers to the many dilemmas with which we're confronted when we're diagnosed with a
life-threatening illness. When peace is our primary goal, we create
the ideal environment for healing—the healing of our hearts, our
minds, our spirits. If physical healing is not to be our lot, we still
have peace.

As Rae has so rightly said, "I did what I could and I did what
I knew". We can only perform in the light of our own knowledge,
understanding and experience. My hope and prayer for you, the
reader, is that the spirited women within this book have in some
way touched your heart and increased your belief in your own
ability to find true healing.

The Petrea King Quest for Life Centre

A T THE PETREA KING QUEST FOR LIFE CENTRE, WE GIVE people practical strategies for living well in challenging circumstances and for finding meaning in the midst of life's unexpected events. We recognise that we can't always change what happens to us in life but we can play an active role in how we're going to respond to what happens to us. We value peace of mind above all else.

There are many events in life that stop us in our tracks and cause us to consider how best to meet the challenge we face: an unexpected diagnosis, accident, loss or tragedy can be such an impetus.

Some people seek more meaningful ways of managing the challenging circumstances of chronic illness, multiple loss, anxiety, relationship breakdown, depression or the consequences of past abuse. Other people choose to take time-out to review their life with the intention of deepening their relationship with themselves and living a more satisfying and meaningful life in the future.

Since 1985 more than 50,000 people have attended residential programs or counselling with Petrea and her team of trained health professionals.

Since 1999 our residential programs and services have been

conducted at the Quest for Life Centre—an historic guesthouse set in 3.6 tranquil hectares of gardens at Bundanoon, in the beautiful Southern Highlands of New South Wales.

Our programs endeavour to support each participant to regain a sense of control over their lives and actively participate in their own healing. Each person leaves with a greater understanding of themselves and a deeper respect for their unique story. Content of the programs is tailored to the people attending each program and varies accordingly. Programs include the following five areas:

Techniques for living in the present
- Relaxation, visualisation and meditation techniques
- Living the life you came here to live
- Transforming adversity; learning to respond, not react

Mind–body connection
- The science of stress and illness
- Creating an environment for healing
- Harnessing the power of the mind
- The role of intuition

Managing thoughts and emotions
- Peace of mind: what it is and how to attain and maintain it
- Understanding the power of the mind to create and counter stress
- Forgiveness and getting 'up to date'
- What is a positive attitude; how to attain and maintain it

Complementary advice supporting medical treatment
- Natural therapies to help with pain, sleep, symptoms and side effects
- Practical advice on diet

Moving on from here
- Rearranging priorities
- Enhancing communication, resilience, relationship
- Getting back in the driver's seat of life
- Learning to live skillfully with stress and move beyond difficult emotions

If you feel we can assist you through one of our residential programs or other services, please call us with your particular needs. We look forward to our paths crossing with yours.

The Quest for Life Foundation
The Petrea King Quest for Life Centre is owned and operated by the Quest for Life Foundation, a registered charity established in 1990 by Petrea King.

The Quest for Life Foundation subsidises all programs as well as an additional subsidy with the support of the NSW Health Department for people on pensions and low incomes.

Donations assist us to support the provision and expansion of our services and are fully tax deductible.

Petrea King Quest for Life Centre
Ph: (61 2) 4883 6599
Fax: (61 2) 4883 6755
PO Box 390
Bundanoon NSW 2578
Australia
Email: info@questforlife.com.au
Web: www.questforlife.com.au

Petrea King Products

*M*UCH OF LIFE IS SPENT TAKING ON MORE INFORMATION, more identities and more learning. We then identify who we are by what we do. In meditation we unveil the treasure of our human 'being' beyond our human 'doing'.

As we quieten the chatter of our minds we discover an inner wellspring from which intuition, joy, inspiration, imagination, wisdom and contentment more effortlessly flow. Meditation becomes that sacred space in which we replenish and refresh ourselves.

Your life matters. You are not here by chance. You are here to make the journey of your life by taking responsibility for your physical, mental, emotional and spiritual wellbeing. My books and meditation practices detail practical ways in which you can reclaim your life and establish peace of mind. I trust they will assist you in creating health, happiness and harmony in your life.

Relaxation and Meditation Practices available on CD

Learning to Meditate (New Version 2004)

This title combines an excellent explanation of meditation with a guided progressive relaxation and meditation practice with Petrea.

You will learn what meditation is and how to practise

it. You will understand when and why to practise meditation, how the mind works and how to manage it more effectively.

Sleep (formerly Sleep Easy)
No one has ever heard the end of this practice! Designed to guide you into deep and restful sleep, it is ideal for the chronic insomniac or people having temporary difficulty with sleeping. You are guided through a progressive relaxation then into a beautiful garden of peace where sleep will overtake you. The CD comes with a bonus booklet of tips from Petrea for developing good sleep habits.

Relaxation
A guided relaxation to release stress and increase immune function. We imagine we're at the beach, where we put all our stresses in a rainbow hot air balloon and release it. We enter the water and, floating on our back, bathe in the golden light of the sun and feel its healing energy. After a brief meditation we return refreshed and energised. Plus the relaxing silver flute music of Gopal.

Golden Light Meditation
Petrea guides you through a progressive relaxation and uses golden light imagery through the body to create a powerful environment for physical, emotional and spiritual healing. After a brief meditation we return refreshed and energised. Plus the beautiful healing music of *Windsong* by Phil Colville.

Increasing Self Esteem
Petrea talks about what makes or damages self-esteem and how we can improve our self-confidence. We are guided deep into the rainforest where there's a waterfall

cascading into a peaceful pool of water and visualise ourselves living with all the qualities we want in our life. This practice is helpful in changing negative attitudes or for goal-setting and is a favourite with teenagers and adults.

Gift of Forgiveness

Through extending compassionate self-forgiveness we can enter a deeper relationship with ourselves and others built on self-understanding. In these two practices Petrea guides you through a progressive relaxation, then using imagery to connect with the qualities of our inner child we extend forgiveness to ourselves and others.

Rainbows to Heal

Petrea guides you through a progressive relaxation and self-healing practice that uses imagery to fill your energy centres with the colours of the rainbow. A second practice involves extending the colours of the rainbow to bring love or healing to another person or situation.

Healing Journey

Petrea guides you through a progressive relaxation and into a beautiful garden where water and light bring about peace and healing. After a brief meditation we return refreshed and energised. This is an ideal practice for those who want to create wellness, inner peace, strength and self-confidence. Plus the beautiful healing music of *Windsong* by Phil Colville.

Dolphin Magic

Journey deep beneath the sea with your own special dolphin to a crystal cavern full of the colours of the rainbow. Allow the colours to wash through your body to bring feelings of peace and renewal. After a healing meditation you return to the surface with your dolphin, refreshed and energised. Plus the beautiful healing music of *Earthsea* by Phil Colville.

Soar Like an Eagle
High on a mountaintop at sunset you relax and enjoy the peace and serenity before floating effortlessly as an eagle. Entering a meditation you absorb the qualities of self-confidence, strength, wisdom and clarity and return refreshed and energised. Plus the beautiful healing music of *Solis* by Phil Colville.

Zen Garden
A beautiful relaxation and meditation practice set in a garden full of cherry blossoms. We meet our wise inner being by a pool of water and ask for the gift of a quality we need or the answer to a question. We return refreshed and energised, bringing back with us what we need. Plus the beautiful silver flute music of Gopal.

Releasing Pain
Using progressive relaxation and imagery to release physical, mental and emotional pain, Petrea guides you through a relaxation and the practice of Yoga Nidra to effectively manage and release pain.

Books by Petrea

Sometimes Hearts Have to Break: 25 Inspirational Stories of Healing and Peace

Sometimes Hearts Have to Break details Petrea's story and those of 25 people whose lives she has enriched and been enriched by in return. These stories are full of hope—for the future, for healing, for finding peace, for reconciliation with the past. The people in this book are a tribute to the human spirit. The events of our lives, however tragic, can be a catalyst by which we shed all that stands in the way of feeling deeply alive and at peace.

Your Life Matters: The Power of Living Now

Your Life Matters is a guide to establishing peace of mind, and living an authentic and fulfilling life. In this wise, necessary and practical book, Petrea King teaches us how to live from the inside out rather than the outside in. By sharing her many principles and guidelines to developing our sense of self, treating our bodies right and adapting to life's challenges, Petrea shows us the way to peace and all-round health and wellbeing.

Quest for Life: Living Well with Cancer and Life-threatening Illnesses

This bestseller is an essential handbook for anyone with cancer and for those who love or care for them. It is the story of Petrea's recovery from leukaemia combined with the practical knowledge gained from working with tens of thousands of individuals with cancer and other life-challenging illnesses.

In *Quest for Life* Petrea provides accessible guidelines for combining the best of medical care with commonsense lifestyle practices and naturopathic advice—all based on Petrea's training in health, healing and meditation.

Further information or to order these products:

Petrea King Pty Ltd
PO Box 190
Bundanoon NSW 2578
Australia
Web: www.petreaking.com
Email: info@petreaking.com
Ph: (61 2) 4883 6805
Fax: (61 2) 4883 6632

Glossary

Adjuvant (or additional) treatment—adjuvant treatment means additional treatment after surgery. It may be radiotherapy, hormonal therapy or chemotherapy, or a combination of two or all three treatments.

Alopecia—baldness or lack of hair where you normally have hair. Some chemotherapy treatments will result (temporarily) in partial or complete hair loss.

Anaemia—condition in which there is a reduction in the number of circulating red blood cells (cells which carry oxygen to body tissues).

Anaesthetic—drug which is given before surgery to ensure that you feel no pain. A general anaesthetic renders you unconscious and unaware of what is happening to you. A local anaesthetic means you lose feeling in one part of your body.

Areola—the dark pigmented skin which surrounds the nipple.

Ascites—the accumulation of a fluid in the abdomen.

Aspiration biopsy—the removal of fluid and cells from a lump by means of a hypodermic needle.

Axillary nodes—axillary nodes are the lymph nodes situated in the armpit and in the chest and form part of the immune system.

Benign tumours—non-malignant, non-cancerous growths that will not spread to another part of the body.

Biopsy—biopsy is a surgical procedure that removes a small sample of tissue from the body so that it can be examined under a microscope by a pathologist. Once the tissue has been removed the pathologist will determine the identity and possible malignancy of the cells. It's good to remember that the vast majority of biopsies show non-malignant tissue.

335

Bone marrow—soft organic material filling the cavities of the bone.

Bone marrow transplant—procedure whereby either the patient's own marrow or a donor's marrow is given to the patient after treatment to eliminate as many of the cancerous cells as possible.

Bronchoscopy—examination of the bronchi (in the lungs) through a bronchoscope.

Calcifications—a process in which organic tissue becomes hardened by lime salt deposits.

Carcinoma or cancer—an abnormal and uncontrolled growth of cells.

CAT scan or CT scan—computerised axial tomography (CAT) uses radiation to create cross-sectional pictures. These pictures can give a very detailed image of the inside of the body. They show the density of tissue and are therefore useful as a diagnostic tool.

Cell—cells are the building blocks which make up the body. They are tiny and can only be seen under a microscope.

Chemotherapy—a treatment using cytotoxic drugs. The aim is to destroy any cells which may have been shed by the primary tumour and carried in the lymphatic system or blood stream to other sites in the body.

Cooper's ligaments—ligaments that hold the breast to the chest wall.

Corticosteroid—any of a number of hormonal steroid substances obtained from the cortex of the adrenal gland.

Cortisone—a hormone isolated from the cortex of the adrenal gland.

Cyst—a benign (non-cancerous) mass, filled with fluid.

Cytotoxic drugs—chemical compounds developed for use in cancer chemotherapy, which destroy fast-growing cancer cells and other tissue.

Diagnosis—the way in which doctors work out that you have a disease or problem. A diagnosis is arrived at usually by talking to you, examining you and perhaps doing some tests. Once they are sure what is wrong, then you are diagnosed as having a particular disease or problem.

Dissection—this usually refers to the removal of axillary nodes.

Diuretic—a substance which increases the amount of urine passed from the body. Water is a natural diuretic.

Duct—a narrow, tubular vessel or channel which conveys secretions.

Endoscopy—inspection of the oesophagus, stomach/and or small intestine by use of an endoscope.

Enzymes—an organic catalyst produced by living cells but capable of acting independently.

Fibroadenoma—solid, benign lumps made up of fibrous and glandular tissue. Fibroadenomas are not cancerous.

Fine needle aspiration—the removal (or aspiration) of fluid or cells from a lump using a very fine needle.

Haematologist—a medical specialist who studies and treats people with blood disorders.

Halsted mastectomy—a surgical procedure to remove the entire breast, chest muscles and lymph nodes.

Hickman device—another way of administering chemotherapy. As a surgical procedure, plastic tubing is inserted under the skin and connected to one of the larger veins leading to the heart. The device remains in place after it has been inserted for the duration of the treatment.

Hormonal therapy—breast tumours may carry receptors for the hormones oestrogen or progesterone. About 50 per cent of tumours are positive for oestrogen receptors. The anti-oestrogen compound Tamoxifen acts against the body's natural oestrogen to starve tumour cells of oestrogen and inhibit their growth. Many post-menopausal women are offered Tamoxifen as adjuvant (additional) therapy after surgery, regardless of whether they are positive or negative, so that the growth of secondary tumours may be inhibited.

Hormones—chemicals produced by special body cells which help to regulate and co-ordinate various body functions, including growth, metabolism and reproduction. For example, the female hormone oestrogen which is produced by the ovaries and adrenal glands.

'Hot spots'—these are markings on the skeleton which show malignancies in the bones.

Hysterectomy—the surgical removal of the uterus.

Impalpable—cannot be felt with the fingers.

Implant—breast form or prosthesis used in reconstructive surgery.

Infiltrating cancer—if the cancer cells have penetrated the membrane that surrounds the duct or lobule, they're said to be infiltrating or invasive and they eventually form a lump that can be felt on physical examination.

Infus-a-port—tubing is inserted under the skin via a flat, button-like port about the size of a 10 cent coin. The needle goes through the skin into this port each time an injection is given.

Iridium wires—radioactive wires which are implanted into the breast for two days to treat breast cancer.

Lobes—structures, radiating out from the nipples, which are made up of milk-producing cells.

Lobular carcinoma—cancer in the lobes of the breast.

Lobules—parts of the lobe which collect milk.

Lumpectomy—surgical removal of only the lump and surrounding tissue and occasionally the axillary nodes. Not all tumours are suited to lumpectomy, depending on the size, position and nature of the lump.

Lymph—lymph is a clear fluid which circulates throughout the body through the lymphatic system.

Lymph glands—small, bean-shaped structures which filter bacteria and other harmful agents out of the body. They are a component of the lymphatic system which is part of the body's natural defence against infection. There are lymph glands all over the body but they're more numerous in the neck, armpit and groin.

Lymph nodes—lymph nodes or glands are small sacs scattered throughout the lymphatic system. Their function is to get rid of bacteria and other harmful organisms in the body. There are lymph nodes in the neck, armpit, groin, abdomen and throughout the body.

Lymphoedema—swelling due to a collection of lymph in the tissues. Some women develop lymphodema in the arm after surgery in which some or all of the lymph glands in the armpit are removed.

Malignant tumour—cancerous growth which is likely to spread to another part of the body if it is not treated.

Mammogram/mammography—a mammogram is an X-ray of the breast. It pictures the lobes, blood vessels, fat, fibrous tissues, ducts and other tissues of the breast. The procedure is conducted by a mammographer. The results of the X-rays are determined by the radiologist. Mammograms are able to pick up microcalcifications and any other abnormality of the breast. It is the most accurate device for breast screening available at present.

Mastectomy—simple—the removal of the breast alone, leaving the pectoral muscles and axillary lymph nodes untouched.

Mastectomy—modified radical—the removal of the entire breast, some lymph nodes, and some of the pectoral muscles.

Mastectomy—radical—the removal of the entire breast, including the underlying pectoral muscles on the chest wall and axilla lymph nodes.

Mastitis—breast blockage and/or infection.

Medical oncologist—a doctor who specialises in the treatment of cancer using drug therapy.

Menopause—the permanent cessation of menstruation. Also commonly called the 'change of life'.

Metastases—cancer which has spread from the primary or first growth. This may occur either via the blood stream or the lymphatic system. One of the common methods of spread of breast cancer is through lymphatic drainage of the breast to the lymph glands of the axilla and chest. Some people refer to metastases as secondaries.

Milk ducts—channels connecting the lobes with the nipples.

Montgomery's tubercles—small lumps surrounding the areola.

MRI—magnetic resonance imaging (MRI) is a fairly recent diagnostic tool which relies on creating a magnetic field rather than using radiation to produce a picture of the breast.

Nolvadex—see Tamoxifen

Oedema—a swelling. Usually a collection of lymph in the tissues.

Oestrogen—see Hormones.

Oestrogen dependent—a cancer which grows better in the presence of oestrogen.

Oncologist—a doctor who specialises in studying and treating cancer.

Oncology—the study of cancers or tumours and malignant cells.

Oophorectomy—the surgical removal of the ovaries. Sometimes used as a type of hormone treatment for breast cancer.

Osteoporosis—increased porosity of the bones, mostly seen in the elderly.

Ovaries—twin glands at the ends of the Fallopian tubes which manufacture oestrogen and produce eggs.

Oxytocin—a hormone which plays a major part in lactation.

Palliative—treatment which is designed to control the symptoms rather than to cure the disease.

Palpable—able to be felt with the fingers.

Patey mastectomy—modified radical mastectomy.

Pathologist—a specialist in diagnosing changes in body tissue.

Pathology—the study of the nature and cause of disease which involves changes in structure and function.

Pituitary gland—a gland in the base of the brain which produces hormones and controls many physical functions.

Platelets—platelets play an important role in blood coagulation, and thrombus formation. When a small vessel is injured, platelets adhere to each other and the edges of the injury and form a plug which covers the area. The blood clot formed soon retracts and stops the loss of blood.

Postmenopausal women—this refers to women who have passed through menopause. Menopause can be either natural or induced through radiation to, or removal of, the ovaries, or through drug therapies which interfere with the production of oestrogen.

Progesterone—a female sex hormone produced mainly in the ovaries.

Prognosis—the likely outcome of a disease.

Prosthesis—an artificial body part or, in the case of the breast, an artificial breast form.

Quadrantectomy—surgical removal of a quarter of the breast.

Radiographer—a trained technician who works the radiotherapy machines.

Radiotherapist—a doctor who specialises in treating cancer with radiotherapy.

Radiotherapy or radiation treatment—external beam—this is the use of radiation which will destroy any remaining cancer cells in the breast. The treatment, which is quite painless, involves attendance as an outpatient at the hospital radiotherapy department for an hour or so every weekday for four to eight weeks. Side-effects can include tiredness or exhaustion, mood changes/depression and skin reddening (like sunburn).

Iridium implant—an alternative form of radiotherapy which necessitates four to five days in hospital, including a period in an isolation room (1 to 2 days). Under general anaesthetic, radioactive iridium wires are inserted into the breast at the site of the original lump. Combined with radiotherapy this has the effect of delivering radiation directly to the site of the tumour. The wires are removed under general anaesthetic.

Receptor assay—a test to see if a cancer is using oestrogen or progesterone for nourishment.

Recurrence—when a disease comes back again.

Relapse—the return of a disease after a time when there has been an improvement.

Remission—either a partial reduction in the cancer or when there is no evidence of any active disease. A remission does not necessarily mean that a cancer has been cured.

Secondary—the same as metastasis or spread of cancer.

Segmentectomy—the surgical removal of a small portion of the breast.

Side-effect—something which is a by-product of a treatment.

Stages of cancer—the determination of what stage a cancer is at. Tests are done to find out how big a cancer is and how far it has spread. In this way doctors can decide on the most appropriate form of treatment.

Staging—tests and examinations done prior to determining the eventual treatment, which will indicate if cancer has spread to other parts of the body. An essential requirement for an oncologist to determine the best treatment for an individual patient.

Symptoms—problems caused by an illness that you can experience or feel.

Tamoxifen—an anti-oestrogen, anti-cancer drug. The most common drug used in hormone therapy for breast cancer. Tamoxifen is the brand name for Nolvadex.

Tissue—a collection of similar cells that all do the same thing.

Tumour—abnormal cell growth; may or may not be malignant.

Ultrasound—an ultrasound is a procedure where high-frequency sound waves are used to examine the breast. These sound waves are picked up by a microphone device or transducer and are translated by computer into a picture. Many women are familiar with the use of ultrasounds when they're pregnant to monitor the growth changes in their unborn baby. The ultrasound relies on sound waves and not radiation. It is now used widely as a diagnostic tool to detect and monitor changes in other tissues within the body.

Ultrasound can not pick up very small tumours or microscopic calcifications in the breast and is not the best screening test for breast cancer. Its principal role is to determine the nature of a mass once it has been identified by a mammogram. If the mass is a cyst filled with fluid, the sound waves from the ultrasound will pass through it. If the tissue in the mass is fibrous or cancerous, the sound waves will bounce back.

X-rays—radiation which can, at low levels, detect cancer and, at high levels, destroy it.

$\mathcal{I}ndex$